DISCOVER YOURSELF

DISCOVER YOURSELF

(formerly *The Inner Reality*)

DR. PAUL BRUNTON

SAMUEL WEISER, INC.

York Beach, Maine

First American paper edition
Published in 1971 by
Samuel Weiser, Inc.
Box 612
York Beach, Maine 03910

Reprinted 1996

Library of Congress Catalog Card Number 83-60832

ISBN 0-87728-592-6
MV

Printed in the United States of America

The paper used in this publication meets the minimum requirements of the American National Standard for Permanence of
Paper for Printed Library Materials Z39.48-1984.

CONTENTS

A PERSONAL NOTE

Dr. Paul Brunton died July 27, 1981, in Vevey, Switzerland. Born in London in 1898, he authored thirteen books from "A Search in Secret India" published in 1935 to "The Spiritual Crisis of Man" in 1952. Dr. Brunton is generally recognized as having introduced yoga and meditation to the West, and for presenting their philosophical background in non-technical language.

His mode of writing was to jot down paragraphs as inspiration occurred. Often these were penned on the backs of envelopes or along margins of newspapers as he strolled amid the flower gardens bordering Lac Leman. They later were typed and classified by subject. He then would edit and meld these paragraphs into a coherent narrative.

Paul Brunton had lived in Switzerland for twenty years. He liked the mild climate and majestic mountain scenery. Visitors and correspondence came from all over the world. He played an important role in the lives of many.

"P.B.", as he is known to his followers, was a gentle man. An aura of kindliness emanated from him. His scholarly learning was forged in the crucible of life. His spirituality shone forth like a beacon. But he discouraged attempts to form a cult around him: "You must find your own P.B. within yourselves," he used to say.

KTH

CHAPTER I

HAD the gods so gifted me at birth, I would rather have played the laughing and satirical philosopher, like Democritus, than have acted my present part of the wise owl. How pleasant to have held the credo that in life it is not the matter that matters, but the manner, and that dullness is the essence of dignity! Anyway, it is a poor pen that never slips a leash and that can produce only a smileless progeny. It would have afforded me a greater pleasure to throw off a few pleasantries in prose than to exhibit the sad and saturnine face of the night bird. But my stars were dark ones and compelled me to brood over the mystery of life's spectacle when I should have liked to draw some fun from the show and to have contemplated its comedy rather than its tragedy.

When, on one unchronicled prehistoric night, thinking man raised his head for the first time and gazed at the boundless immensity of the star-filled sky overhead, his first thought could have been no other than the first thought which enters the mind of thinking man of our twentieth century when he gazes reflectively upon the mysterious canopy under which he lives and moves, frets and philanders.

"What is the meaning of it all?"

The profound difficulty of discovering a correct answer to this question is such that even today our greatest scientists must bow their heads in humble ignorance,

9

because all their victories of knowledge have still done little more than touch the fringe of this problem.

The depths of this problem would be unfathomable, were we to depend on human intellect alone. They cannot be plumbed without the help of higher revelation.

I made a wide research in consequence, and my studies embraced books which litter the shelves of little-known libraries; they included intimate conversations and long-drawn-out discussions with the masters of Occidental knowledge, and, finally, I studied with the best of all tutors, personal experiment and first-hand experience. In the end, fate put my feet on strange journeys to lands whose slender palm trees called to me with their outstretched leaves and bade me, as they bid all men, tie anew the earthless bonds which yoke the reluctant soul of man to God. Few Westerners have the time and the training, the will and the money, which these researches required; and so I tried to do for them what they could not do for themselves: I tried to recover from the obscurity of vanished epochs some secrets which the world needs today. Again and again as I stood under those star-panoplied Eastern skies, or as I walked in solitude in the mysterious silence of the menacing jungles, I was haunted by an overpowering sense of the strange paradox of human life. I followed a lone track in studying the ways and wisdom of the Orient, and still more so in trying to put the mysterious feats and doctrines of the yogis and fakirs upon a scientific basis.

My records of spiritual adventures under those fierce Oriental suns have been written down; I have tried to reveal to the man in the street what profound spiritual resources and what amazing psychological powers may be found within himself; even though I have been compelled to reserve the inscription of my divinest experiences and best thoughts for a later time. My reticence on this point is due to the limitations of the society which surrounds me, of the civilization into which I have been born. I wanted to address myself to the man of ordinary experience, even though my own has been so extraordinary. As I have seen him, during my wanderings around the world, I have found that he is painfully working out for himself an understanding of life's meaning which could be bought at far less cost. I wanted to tell him so, and to persuade him to put a living purpose into his life, to remove the appalling aimlessness which is the outstanding characteristic of our epoch. But alas! Each time I was put in mind of Grecian Socrates' question to Claucon, "Do you mean to say that you can persuade those who won't listen?"

The man of ordinary experience looks upon these abstract philosophies, these abstruse truths and austere practices, as matters which interest few and benefit none. Experience has explained to me, better than the warning speech of my Guides, why most seers keep their most recondite secrets for the few. Anyone who writes of such extraordinary subjects as I have chosen for my pen, writes under a great disadvantage. He dare not ignore the mysterious experiences which form their pith and kernel; he is not likely to be believed if he sets them all down exactly as they occurred; he finds the greatest difficulty in describing subtle psychological happenings which are unmeaning to merely materialistic intellects. And with reference to the supreme attainment, it seems at times a despairing enterprise for anyone to attempt this unveiling of an ineffable, intangible state of being in cold words and cool phrases, for half this high iridescent experience disappears in the telling, between brain and paper.

In the end, if he is wise, he will finish by writing for the few. Then, if others begin to understand and welcome him, he may be delighted, but if they do not, he need never be disappointed. But numbers do not matter. Inert people do not count. They are only humanity in bulk. Everything worth while is done or discovered, always and everywhere, by the few. "She believed in me when none else would believe," said Mahomet of his wife Kadijah. During three years he found but thirteen followers. Yet his doctrine spread later among millions. These ideas are new only to the modern West, for in the ancient Orient they were taught and understood thousands of years ago.

Destiny decided that the response to my books should be markedly encouraging. Properly comprehended, this is not a message for the few alone; its benefits are not for the yogis and saints alone; it is for all of us, for whoever is willing to *be* what God intended him to be. Whoever thinks that these pages present him with mere abstractions and ideas lacking practical value is greatly mistaken. In reply I can say only that they really deal in things which are vital to human beings because they are *the foundation things of life*. Properly understood, these "abstractions" will help men to more successful living. I have found that they put strength into my own will, guidance into my mind, peace into my heart, and truth into my soul. And if some things appear to be really subtle, I must defend myself by replying that in attempting to provide explanations of states of being that are ordinarily inarticulate, I have done the best I could. And whoever will endeavour to translate the ideas of this psychological technique into action will find the prize in equipoised existence, inner peace, and spiritual power.

So I have found myself forced, little by little, along a path which I had never intended to tread, the path of writing sequels to my own works and explaining my own explanations. In short, I have unconsciously become more and more a tutor, and less and less a seeker. And although I still hold strictly to my fixed attitude of complete independence, demanding absolute freedom from all who cross my path and gladly bestowing upon them the same freedom which I ask from them, refusing to accept either pedestal or following, organization or cult, nevertheless I could not forever resist the many calls for further en-

lightenment which have come to me. And so I have
yielded to the call which has induced me to put these
pages together in the midst of a busy life. I must make it
clear that I do not set myself up as a teacher, that I make
no personal claims whatever about my own spiritual
status, and that I am writing only to give what friendly
information and help I can, as any other traveller might
have done.

I do not desire to convince others, but simply to radiate
whatsoever of truth I have found; then others can pick it
up or not as they wish. They must approach me of their
own free will and not because I wish to act as a missionary to them. I do not seek to convert, much less compel, but to show others what they, too, can find within
themselves. Frankly, I have not become conscious of
possessing any mission to this world, but the only one I
would care to undertake, if the gods were to grant me
the ability, would be to make men aware of the value of
their own souls. Moreover, this personal freedom is not
without some peculiar value of its own. Because I am
independent of all allegiances and because I obey no other
authority than that of my own inward monitor, I can
freely afford to set down truths which have either been
selfishly hidden or foolishly distorted in the past. I want
my truths to sting. I want them to be bold—not for my
own sake alone, but also for that of my readers. I want
to feed my pen with fearless thoughts that will get under
the skin of the thoughtless. I am not concerned with
pleasing a particular class, a special sect, or any self-
admiring group. The approbation of these people means
nothing to me.

§

One of the names which count in the list of English
medieval religious mystics is that of Mother Julian of
Norwich. Her spiritual testament, the book called *Revelations*, which described some of her visions and gave

most of her teachings, bore some explanatory words, which the present writer might fitly put into his own book too.

She confessed that these visions and teachings were set down for the help of others because she saw it to be God's will. "But," she added, "God forbid that ye should say or take it so, that I am a teacher, for I mean not so. No, I never meant so! For I am a woman, unlearned, feeble and frail, but I know well that this that I say, I have it of the showing of Him that is Sovereign Teacher."

But in an edition published some years later these self-deprecatory phrases were left out. Mother Julian then spoke with quiet authority and definite self-confident assurance, for she no longer feared to be regarded as a teacher. Time had brought spiritual maturity.

In my own humbler way, I too have slowly moved slightly away from my former position and, whether I like it or not, find myself forced to accept the fact that hundreds of Spirit-hungry minds ardently desire to learn that which I have already learnt as a result of exceptional opportunities.

I have freely given my time and life and learning to the cause of Truth, because I profoundly believe it to be the best of causes today. I know that its message is worthy of my pen, and its expression brings peace to my heart. If, I repeat, in my heart I seek no disciples, desire no followers, and wish to inaugurate no new cult, nevertheless I have again temporarily donned the tutorial robe and put on the prophet's mantle, shivering though I did at their touch. I, who had become disheartened at being thought a prig and a superior person, and who wanted not a single disciple, who preferred a few loyal friends to many fickle followers, was compelled by a higher ethic to put aside my personal feelings and do what was plainly my duty in the matter. These pages were written because it was my duty to write them, not because I hope to attract the belief of an unbelieving world. I picked up my pen, not to contend in the war of opinions, but to establish truth. I have striven for many years in its research, only that my readers might strive for a few years. Utterly against my will and desire, I have been forced to become, for all intents and purposes, a kind of detached tutor to the distant tutorless. Thus I retain my independence and they theirs.

Both believers and sceptics may do what they wish with this work, for I have accepted my responsibility and done my duty. It was my melancholy fate to be born a writer who helps other people to an understanding of themselves but—painful paradox!—to a misunderstanding of himself, hence persecutions among the plaudits, but I have learnt to accept them. A very ancient Arab maxim comforts me with its promise: "Paradise is as much for him who has rightly used the pen as for him who has fallen by the sword."

A certain Oriental sage once observed to me that the ancient works were more valuable because they were pithy and condensed, and that this highly concentrated style tended to draw out the reader's intuition. There is something to be said for his remark. Few present-day books are fit to be evaluated by their bulk. Our modern manner has been much influenced by science; and being extended, particularized, and diffused, tends to unfold intellect rather than intuition. Certainly it demands width rather than depth, extension rather than condensation; in short, minutely-detailed explanation.

I should prefer to say all I have to say in a single page, or better still, compress it into the single line of the Biblical Psalmist: *Be still and know that I am God.* I should prefer to let others tap a larger sense out of those words. This whole business of particularizing that pregnant phrase and writing three hundred pages where I might have written less than one, is not delight but drudgery. Nevertheless, I know from the letters that reach me that such ink is surely not wasted, nor does the pen move in vain.

I envy the temerity with which so many would-be hierophants go forth and gather the gullible. Myself, I would flee five hundred miles rather than have any raise me to the stature of "Master." I am only a poor scribbler, only a free-lance among freethinkers. I make no pretense to despise the world, nor to assume a pseudo-indifference I do not possess, and one as worthless as the pseudo-chastity of those monks who used to put an apron upon the naked statues of Aphrodite!

But after stating this, I must in fairness state the other side of the matter. I do not forget to hold my pen to a larger cause. I do not forget that, if I seek no disciples, I should yet like my literary efforts to arouse their readers, to lead men really to know themselves, and to lure them into quest of the God who dwells within the depths of their own hearts. I would stir the apathetic to watch and wait for tidings from their starry selves and to be ready for its behests. This is my work as I conceive it. While there is breath in this body and ink in this pen, I pray God to forefend me from joining the ranks of those who exploit questing sincerity to satisfy an enlarged egotism or personal profit. Better let me remain the spiritual outlaw that I am, adherent to no religion and caught up in no cult; better let me move through this dingy world an exile from the comfortable societies of men, than that!

But because my own studies in the Orient have taught me to give a deeper meaning to the word "help" than that which it usually carries, and because I may modestly state the simple fact that I have indeed practiced meditation for many years and gone some distance within myself, I intend to make these writings of mine real communions of the higher mind between author and readers.

The thoughts which are presented in the following pages are *true* thoughts. Because millions of people in our

Western lands may be unable to believe them, the ideas do not lose one iota of their truth for all that. I have been taxed with assuming an air of cocksureness. I have assumed nothing. The truths which I am trying to explain have sunk through the red flesh of my body into the white bones. If I did not possess this fixed certainty and cast-iron conviction, how could I hope to confront an overwhelmingly sceptical modern world, materialistic to the tips of its fingers as it is, with such subtle and highly spiritual ideas? Why should I be ashamed or afraid to own that I am a transcendentalist?

Just as a slender ray of light creeping from the East betokens a broader dawn, so a man's interest in these ideas may betoken the dawn of a deeper understanding of them. I hope and believe that by the time sensitive readers have gone through part or all of my books, there will remain a legacy of definite and vital experience, not only through reading their pages, but through the quiet rumination which should follow. If they read not merely to play and juggle with ideas, then something will be communicated to them telepathically, as it were, to which, sooner or later, they may respond, and responding, they will begin to feel that they have entered into communication with a deeper reality than life has hitherto revealed. There must be receptivity so that thought and idea work like an inner force on the being. I hope and believe, too, that they will look back on these perusals as events which can be dated as constituting turning points in their spiritual quest. Yet that depends partly upon their own inner sensitivity, their own intuitive alertness. Not only should they read intently to understand the thoughts and ideas which the writer expresses, but they should try to catch the elusive atmosphere which hides behind the words. And not only should they read between the lines but sometimes along the blank margin also. It would not suffice to comprehend my utterances; they should also try to comprehend the spirit which hides behind them. Instead of presenting an avalanche of occult information, I put forward and reiterate a few profound truths badly needed by our generation.

We must forever feel the exquisite melancholy which pervades this quest of the self for the Overself, a melancholy which has been perfectly phrased by the Chinese poet, Yang Chi, in his lovely *Lines Written in Exile:*

> "I see,
> Far out upon the lake an island gleaming
> With a girdle of red nenuphar, and dreaming
> I fill my sail o' dreams in search of Thee."

So let my books stand as signposts for some discerning persons, for those who can find no quiet harbourage amid the maddening strain of twentieth century existence. Now I can say confidently to such persons: There *is* a way of escape, but that way lies neither to the East nor to the West; it lies entirely inwards. Yet if you follow this mysterious track, inevitably your outer life will begin to change its own face.

§

If in earlier books I was forced to accommodate the hidden doctrine of India to concrete intellect and popular experience, I now venture to pass upwards to a more exalted platform and make less of such accommodation. Indifferent as to whether or not it be palatable, I cast aside some reservations, some hesitations, and give the purer Truth as I know it. But the highest statement of this doctrine, scientifically covering the field of the universe itself, will appear only in my next book.

The following pages have been selected and expanded from addresses privately given before small audiences in four continents. Absolute clearness of exposition was sought, rather than elaborate treatment of theme. Although they dealt with important matters, I tried to make these talks as understandable to their hearers as was possible. Therefore I deliberately phrased the ideas in non-literary language.

The greatest truths are really the simplest, as the words of Jesus abundantly prove. But modern man has fallen into such confusion through one-sided development of the concrete intellect, that he has come to think the greatest truths must necessarily be difficult and complicated in the extreme.

I am too vividly aware of the confused condition of the contemporary world not to feel strongly that this is not the time to adopt the puzzling metaphors of medieval mystics or the unfamiliar jargon of Oriental philosophers, that much mystery is needlessly wrapped around ideas of the utmost value to human life, and that we must make truth plain, not only to the man in the street but also to the man in the back street. The original simplicity of style was so well appreciated that I have retained it during the revision for publication.

CHAPTER II

WHAT IS GOD?

"Without a spiritual belief in a Divine Being, in the knowledge of whom, and obedience to whom, mortal welfare alone consists, the human race must degenerate."—CARLYLE.

THROUGH the centuries millions of words have been uttered and written on the subject of God. But we do not seem to come any nearer to an understanding of this problem. Almost every people and race have had their own God, which means their own *idea* of God. These many varieties of deity are so surprising in their differences that a sceptic might well say, "All your gods are hallucinations, figures of your imagination." In fact, during the nineteenth century, when scientific minds made a study of comparative religions, they discovered hundreds of gods which have been worshipped by both primitive and civilized peoples. Therefore they came to the ironic conclusion that man creates God in his own image.

If you go to a primitive tribe in Central Africa, you will see God carved on a piece of wood, glaring at you with a frightful face from the local temple. The people who live there find in that barbaric countenance their conception of a higher or supernatural power. That is their idea of God.

On the other hand, if you come into a modern city, you will see churches dedicated to the worship of God

as Spirit, which means God without form, intangible—
a conception far removed from the God of Central
Africa. You will also find writers of today like Aldous
Huxley, who describes God as "a rich feeling in the pit
of the stomach."

Now it cannot be that each of these gods is the true
God. There can only be One, if by God we mean the
Supreme Creator, He Who created the universe, though
it may be that there are lesser beings which men take to
be God by mistake.

If you go to a country like India, you will find again
the same differences and the same multiplicity of deities.
But the more enlightened, thoughtful Indians have reduced the whole problem to a question of choosing between a personal and an impersonal God.

God means many things even to the same person at
different stages of his evolution. To the child, He is
almost invariably a personal deity, some individualized
Being Who is usually pictured with a human or angelic
figure, someone to whom he can pray and of whom he
can make requests. But if the child grows up and develops intellectually and spiritually, the old concept fades
away, and a new one replaces it. God is then seen as a
Power, not as a human image, but rather a Power which
permeates the universe.

The picture which the pious worship must be succeeded by the Presence which they feel. God must be
discovered within; it is not enough to know Him without. When seeker and the sought blend in eternal unity,
then knowledge becomes perfected and aspiration fulfilled. For the doom of spiritual ignorance is not to be
written for ever on the brow of man.

The most advanced scientists, representing man in his
higher development, are beginning to find that life exists
everywhere and is present in every atom of matter
throughout the universe. They picture God as this infinite power and life current.

If you look at orthodox religion, no matter in what country or what faith, you will find that the God there worshipped is usually pictured as a personal God, an individualized Being Who, they believe, rewards the adherents of that particular faith because they worship Him and praise Him. If, however, they begin to believe in the new concept of God as Power which science is bringing to the world through higher education, then faith in their original idea of a personal God tends to disappear. The two do not meet and mingle very well.

Much of the confusion in the religious world arises out of its dependence on feelings alone, unchecked by reason. There is no proper test for Truth in such dependence. We need not be naively uncritical of religion even when we accept its fourth-dimensional perspective of life's meaning. The doors are shut, the bolts have been pushed in, and our pious friends are no longer free to entertain a true thought. Every mystic can get up and say, "I have seen God," but how does he know that he has seen God? There is no label, and if there were, that would not necessarily prove its wearer to be God. It is a subject which has unquestionably been more misunderstood than perhaps any other. No, we must find a universal test for Truth which will always be applicable, and about which there could never be any difference of opinion.

The whole concept of God depends entirely upon where you stand, and the idea that suits you is the one which helps you most. And because people change their concepts, whether as child or adult, savage or scientist—for they will change their ideas at different times and under different circumstances—we are compelled to come to the conclusion that the concept of God is a relative one. In other words, there does not seem to be any absolute, ultimate, unchanging *idea*.

Man does not know God as He really is, but only as he imagines Him to be. "Not with this or that attribute," says the divine sage Krishna in the scripture of the yogis, "but in Essence." If, however, we admit that the concept of God is purely relative and not eternal, then we must also admit that we have not found reality in such a God. We have found what we *think* is real, but not Reality itself.

The worshipper in a temple or mosque or church holds within his mind a picture of what he believes God to be. That picture is purely a mental image and he is worshipping that image, not Reality. This image has come down to him by tradition through hundreds of years, perhaps, and backed by the force of the great organized religions though it may be, still it is only an idea passing through his consciousness, a picture which he has held because other people have suggested it to him.

Because he is worshipping an *idea*, something which by its very nature is not eternal, but comes and must eventually go, as all ideas must, he has not found Reality, and from the standpoint of deep inquiry he is even worshipping an illusion, if by the word "illusion" we mean "that which is not real," and if by "reality" we mean "that which is eternally true and abiding."

It may seem an appalling statement to say that millions of people have been worshipping their own idea, which they take to be God. Surely, you will point out, in religious buildings we often feel a holy presence. How is it that we are awed in such a place, and that these religions have, during their best days, exercised such a spell over the people?

It is because the power which man has found in religion, the power to help him and to lift him up, has come from *man himself*. He himself has given himself the guidance, help, exaltation, and spiritual consolation which he believed he found in his church or in his faith or in his idea of God. When man has learnt to build a quiet church inside his own heart and to be a ministering priest to his own self, religion will have done its true work.

Man has unconsciously deceived himself into thinking that an external power, something outside himself, has come to his help or guidance. This was only his belief, and an erroneous one. Man himself, through his concentration, called upon his own inner resources, and drew out from within himself, from his *own spirit*, that which he thought came to him from the God whom he believed to be outside himself.

It does not matter where the power comes from so long as he gets results. He must be practical, and if man believes in external deities, and thinks that they are helping him, it is all right for him. It does not matter so long as he is ready to let this idea go when he begins the quest of Truth—when he wants to understand the *inner* significance of life and of the universe.

Those who are content to accept their faith from the superstitions of a past age or from the suppositions of the present one, belong to a disappearing race. Every creed must now be able to prove its point, and that not by reference to faded bibles or yellowing parchments, but by the facts of the present day, by life, science, and knowledge. The anguishing horrors of the last war have caused religion to bow before realism; they have brought the scepticism of the scientist's laboratory into the popular life of the street.

When the time comes that man no longer wishes to remain a child, but wants to grow up and become an adult, then he must understand and neither deceive himself nor others. Then he will see that God is to be found not in any particular form, but in all forms, not in any particular place, but everywhere, not through any single vehicle, faith, cult, religion, building, or man, but in the Infinite.

You will never find God anywhere else but in those conditions; the rest is merely your *idea* of God, your mental picture. These are purely intellectual things, they are not God or Reality.

So if man wishes to awaken, if he wants to understand himself, he must face the fact that the real avenue to contact with God is not outside himself but within, directly *inside*. He must find his own way to God through and within himself. That is, if he seeks *God* there is no other way, but if he is looking for ideas, concepts, or mental images, then he can take what orthodox religions and cults offer him. And because most people have been content to let others do their thinking and their questing for them, they have been satisfied with those conditions.

During the past two or three centuries the mind and intelligence of man have begun to awaken at a most extraordinary rate, and he is no longer able to sit still within the mental prisons which have been built for him. He wants to know for himself. And the moment the mind begins such a quest, then there is no hope in finding other satisfaction; the ancient dogmas which convinced past generations are no longer sufficient. They no doubt suited the simpler mentality of earlier generations, but they will not suit ours. We want the truth—that which is scientifically true.

But first we must divest ourselves of the notion that truth is a creed, a set statement to be swallowed like a pill. Truth cannot be the prerogative of one age alone. The periods of Christ and of Buddha were sacred in the world's history, but unless there is a new revelation in our own time, there cannot be a new regeneration.

New wine cannot be put into old bottles without bursting them. Truth is not for existing organizations. The world is tired of dry intellectualism. It wants to hear fresh, living voices, the voices of men who have been privileged to come face to face with God, or who can report vital spiritual experiences in our own day and age.

The scientist is the man who commands this age, and what you see around you, from the electric light to almost everything else that you touch and use in your

daily life, is the result of applied science. If you will remember that the goal of the scientist is ultimately truth,
you will understand what is likely to be the fate of those
beliefs and dogmas upon which mankind has been fed
for thousands of years. However, the scientist has only
begun. At present he has reached a borderland on the
very edge of another world, and now that he is there he
will sooner or later have to cross over. And when he
finds truth, it will be the same truth that the seer and the
sage have also found, because there is only one *Ultimate
Truth.*

If that is so, what will the scientist discover about this
question of God? He has already begun to perceive that
there is no room for a personal God in the universe. The
source of the universe must be infinite, because the scientist knows that the universe itself cannot be measured,
and the part cannot be greater than the whole, nor the
creation greater than the creator. Therefore this infinite
universe must have an Infinite Creator, and no form, no
personalized being—which means a form—can be the
Creator. The Creator is something which is beyond form,
a *Force* if you wish. Hence God must be an Infinite
Force.

The scientist will see that. He sees it now, only he
will not call it God; he finds other names. Is there no
room in this creation for the Creator himself? Is man so
blind that because he watches the evolutionary stages
through which a boot is fashioned, he shall say there is
no bootmaker? Alas, it is because ignorant theologians
and unseeing priests have taught him to look for a God
who is but a glorified man; no such being exists and he
finds it not. God is life, intelligent life force, and all the
evolutionary cycles of this universe merely display the
outworkings of this power, not the arbitrary moves of
a man.

"I have swept the heavens with my telescope, and have
not found a God," announced Lalande. Alas! he had

but to put his telescope aside, still his mind, and there God would be found.

§

The materialist is not to be blamed because he is unaware of ultimate truths. He is to be blamed only if he will not investigate them. If he does not try to inquire, he can never find truth. He deceives himself and wants to deceive himself. Ignorance is often excusable, but not the will to remain ignorant.

If, as the scientist has already found, matter is ultimately a unity, then all the different kinds of matter, all the elements can be resolved into a *single element*, and all matter into a single Force. Eventually he will be compelled to say, as he has just begun to say today: "The source of the universe is a unity out of which the multiplicity of objects and forces which we see around us have sprung."

There is one root, a single root, and everything else has grown, developed, or evolved out of that root. The scientist will also have to admit that the Infinite Force which is God, is a single force—there is only one such Force, only one God and not two. And because it is an Infinite Force and not something which can be bottled up in a form or any shape whatsoever, he will have to look for God beyond the laboratory. I do not mean that he must fly out into space, but he will have to turn *inwards* to his own mind, because when he has exhausted all the instruments of his laboratory, *he will have to sit down and look at the man who has been using those instruments*, and find his way with that mind alone.

However, if we pursue this scientific quest of Truth and find the Ultimate Force which must exist as the root of everything, we shall then discover to our astonishment that we are verifying the oldest teachings in the world, teachings which were first given verbally, and later written down on parchment, tablets, or metal plates, declaring that God, the Sun, and Light are synonymous. The Bible says the first creation was light, and after that came all other forms. In other words, God could not create his universe until he had first made light.

And if you ask how God, then a single unit in existence, created light, how could He have created it except out of *Himself*, out of His own Being, as a spider spins a web out of its own body? The web is not different from the spider's body, it is really a part of it. And so God created light out of His own Being, which means that Light is none other than God, *the Being of God. Light is God.*

In the oldest Hindu scriptures, which are the *Vedas*, you will find the same statement, that in the beginning Brahma, which means "the Creator," made light, and out of light he made all other forms. The Babylonian tablets repeat the same statement.

The Egyptian and Druid priests, among many other ancient peoples, worshipped the sun, because they regarded it as the Father of all their life. To them it was the visible proxy on earth of the invisible Deity; not God, but the agent of God. Its splendour was a living thing and its rays full of divine life.

To the ancient Egyptians, light was the most spiritual of all material things. We call it "material" because it is present and visible in the universe, and therefore we may say with those ancient Egyptians that light is the element in the material universe which is nearest to divinity.

During the last two or three years scientific research has discovered increasing confirmation that all matter is ultimately the condensation of radiant energy, that is, of light. In fact, it is possible in the laboratory to convert light into matter, and to convert matter back again into light. In other words, this marvellous structure of the material universe which we see around us, and which the nineteenth-century scientists thought was nothing but matter—solid, hard substance—has dissolved away, does

not exist when you inquire into it and try to find its true
nature. It dissolves away and becomes that most intangible of all things, light.

Until recently, the monistic view of Nature had been
mostly a matter of speculation, belief, and opinion. Thirty
years ago, however, Professor J. Arthur Thomson, in his
Introduction to Science, ventured to state that "modern
work [on the atom] is suggesting that there may be a
common basis for matter of all kinds." The latest discoveries of the modern laboratory confirm this theory.
Consider the great advances made in our knowledge of
atomic structure. The solid atom, once considered the
building stone of the universe, was broken up into whirling electrons. When matter disappeared into electrical
energy, the first steps were taken.

Our solid material substance has dissolved into the mist
of electrons, protons, and deuterons. Matter has been
pursued until it vanished into energy. The results of
these developments are described by Dr. Karl K. Darrow, Research Physicist of the Bell Telephone Laboratories, in a lecture he gave at the Lowell Institute, and
reprinted in his book, *The Renaissance of Physics*[1]:

"Short of the contrast between life and death, no
contrast in Nature can ever have seemed greater than
that between matter on the one hand and light upon the
other. Unlike as are the photon which is the corpuscle
of light and the electron which is the smallest particle of
matter, either may vanish and be replaced by the other.
... Matter has been augmented out of light, but even in
that reaction there has not been complete creation of a
new piece of matter out of light. May we aspire to convert a corpuscle of light into a corpuscle of matter where
there was none before? This is so vast an ambition that
we must moderate it to the last possible degree. The
rest-energies of nuclei being as I have described them,

[1] The Macmillan Company, New York.

we shall require a photon of more than a billion electron volts for creating a nucleus or an entire atom. Neither any apparatus of ours, nor any natural radioactive substance on earth, provides us with such photons. Perhaps they occur among the cosmic rays, but if so, they are not at our command. But energy enough to create a single electron is contained in much more modest corpuscle of light, one possessing but half a million electron volts and photons such as these are available at will. . . . In 1932, such particles were discovered and the manner of their discovery suggested strongly that they had just been born out of light in this very way. These positive electrons were found among the cosmic rays. When we expose a plate of dense matter to a stream of photons such as these, we find electrons springing two by two from the plate, negative and positive leaping from the same point, and when we assess the kinetic energy of the members of the pair, we find that they add up to the sum which was foretold. A photon has died in giving birth to each of the pairs. This then is the reaction in which electrons are formed out of light. May not the reverse reaction occur, in which a positive and a negative electron meet each other while roaming through space, merge with each other and form a corpuscle of light? The fixity of matter itself has vanished, for we are able to convert its substance from the form of electrical particles into the form of light. No element, nor matter itself, nor light itself, is permanent. All that is perpetual is something of which they are all made, incarnating itself in all of them by turn, and passing unimpaired from form to form. For this immortal substance the least inadequate name, I presume, is 'energy,' but the name is of little concern. To this have we come by applying the methods of physics to the rubbing of amber and to all that followed from it; how great a way, from so humble a beginning! The stone which so many builders rejected became the cornerstone of the temple; the little effect

which seemed so trivial to so many of the wise became
the key to wisdom, and supplied a physical meaning to
two of the most ancient tenets of philosophy. Atomic
theories existed long ago, but ours is the generation
which, first of all in history, has seen the atom. The belief that all things are made of a single substance is old
as thought itself, but ours is the generation which, first
in history, is able to receive the unity of Nature not as
a baseless dogma or a hopeless aspiration, but a principle of science based on proof as sharp and clear as
anything which is known."

I have given this extract at such length because it is of
such high importance. If, as now seems likely, laboratory
developments will vindicate the theory of a single substance underlying all manifestations of material Nature,
we shall have to grant that the assertions of the Hindu
philosophers on this point, made thousands of years ago,
are not worthless primitive beliefs, but results of the
insight practised by keenly perceptive and concentrated
minds.

If God be Light, and if all material objects without a
single exception—whether you take your own physical
body or the chair upon which you are sitting—if all these
are nothing but condensations of that radiant energy of
Light, do you not see that God is, therefore, everywhere present? It is not merely a poetical fancy, but a
literal fact that you cannot run away from God, no matter where you go. The whole material world is built up
out of God, and is filled with Him, and you are near and
within God all the time. There is no escape from Him,
go where you will. He is infinite.

Is this not, after all, a more satisfactory conception
than the theological notion of a God who is just a glorified human being, a God made in man's image who arbitrarily does what He wishes with human beings and
universes? Is it not better to believe, and not merely to

believe but to be able to prove intellectually, and not
merely to be able to prove intellectually but to know
intuitionally, that God is an Infinite Power, the Power
back of all other forces and back of every materially
created thing; a Power which is everywhere present and
therefore within us and always within reach, because
wherever you go, God is *there*.

That, I believe, is the conception of God towards
which we are moving, and which is not so very far away.
Thus the circle will complete itself, and the most ancient
teachings about God will come back, but they will return strengthened and buttressed by scientific support.
They will be strong because they will be built up not
only on the basis of faith, of intuition, but also of intellect and reason. God is worth worshipping, and such a
concept of God can be safely held, because it is not
merely a relative one which is going to be changed or
displaced. It is the final and the ultimate conception which
man can hold. He cannot conceive a higher one, therefore his mind will have to come to rest on this notion
of God. And that is the God, the ever- and everywhere-
present Light, which the world will find through its own
use of intelligence and its own search for Truth.

And now, look at the question from an angle with
which you are all perhaps more familiar. When people
practise meditation, whether they are religious mystics,
so-called occultists, or whatever they may be, eventually
they begin to have certain visions and experiences within
their own hearts and minds. You hear that the more fortunate of these mystics have visions of blinding light.

"The ultimate aim in the trance practice is to find the
vision of God as Light. This Light is so intensely powerful that were it to be seen suddenly without proper preparation, one could be blinded through reflex action on
the optic nerves," said a Himalayan adept to me once.
Mystics who have this experience feel themselves to be
immersed in light, and they say this is the highest realiza-

tion. You can read other descriptions in Bucke's book, *Cosmic Consciousness*, and in the literature of the medieval religious mysticism, where the meditator, or the mystic, seems to be engulfed in a sea of light, and with that light comes a sense of extraordinary freedom and understanding, of happiness and peace and stillness.

And so, because that seems to them the highest experience which a man can have, especially to mystics who look for God, you will find that when these people return to ordinary consciousness and begin to describe their experience, because they have not been initiated by a competent teacher into the esoteric training, they often report having had a vision of God amid the Light, or of hearing an inner voice, or that certain things have been revealed to them within the Light. In other words, they look upon the Light as a state or condition within which they had to look for something, to find a form, the form of God. They did not know that the Light Itself *was* God, and it was not necessary to expect or to look for any image, any picture, or to hear any voice.

Moses approached the burning bush, and God spoke to him. The burning bush was aflame. The flame was the Light of God, but the voice which came to him was not the voice of God—it was the voice of his own mind, inspired, yes, but still the mind. Because God is Infinite Power and cannot be compared with human beings who speak, nor can He be limited by definite shapes. You cannot think of God as Infinite Power without a shape, and then proceed to imagine that He can be so limited as to converse with you. What really happens in those reports of voices or visions is that the mind of the mystic is so illumed by the Light which he is contacting that it draws his consciousness into the planetary overmind, which may give him accurate guidance or prediction, or do all sorts of wonderful things—but he is still in the region of mind.

Remember that it is the Light alone that is God. And

yet, although this Light is God to the mystic and the meditator, it must be understood aright even by them. If it is not correctly understood, that experience, instead of being a help, might become a hindrance. I mean that if you want truth you must be prepared to stop at nothing until you find *Ultimate Truth*. You must not stop by the wayside because you have made some wonderful discovery. So long as you think that reality is to be found in any *experience* you are deceiving yourself.

For most of us, if not for nearly all of us, such an experience would be sufficient. Still I must frankly tell you that it is not the Ultimate, and after this glorious experience comes on the path of meditation, another path is sooner or later found to open up, and that is the Esoteric Path—a Path which leads to the Ultimate Reality, to Absolute Truth.

In that Path there is neither Light nor Darkness, nor experiences, because you then learn to transcend time. Experiences which begin must also have an ending. You must find the Eternal which has no beginning and no ending. When you have found it, then you have found That out of which God Himself draws His own Substance. You will then merge with God into the Ultimate Reality.

You see now how far removed the true concept of God is from those barbaric notions which we so often meet in various parts of the world. Yet even those notions have been helpful to different people who cannot find a higher understanding at the time. Everything which helps you, wherever you stand, is good for you. That is why the man who knows the Truth has no quarrel with anyone. He knows that everyone finds just that amount of Truth which his experiences in life have brought him to, and he sees just what he should see at that stage.

Even though different people have different thoughts about God, it does not matter so long as you understand that these are merely thoughts, and depend upon the place where the individual stands. You then know that man is evolving through his various thoughts and ideas to the ultimate and highest concepts of God. When you discover that, then all ideas melt away and you become *harmonized with God* instead of thinking *about* Him. Thought is a shadow, something secondhand, but *to be* means that you unify yourself with God, and then you can really know Him. So you must give up thinking *about* Him and begin *to be* God, which means to become one with Him. Then knowledge and intelligence merge into God.

Thought puts a veil between you and God. When you can tear aside the veil, then you merge into God. It is possible for everyone to find his way back to God because God is present in each of us. But we must begin to search and look, and the right place is within, not outwards. You must first look inwards and find the sacred atom in the heart—the spiritual self within. When you have found your inner spiritual self then you can look outwards again, and you will find the sun—in other words, the Universal Self. You will see God in every thing and every body—*after* you have seen God in yourself!

Thus, after following other gods, after believing in a multitude of deities, man finally understands that there is but one Spirit behind all creation, and after believing in a personal spirit, a personal God, he ultimately realizes the truth that the highest deity is impersonal and universal.

CHAPTER III

A SANE RELIGION

IF YOU examine the definition of the word "religion," you will find that it is derived from the Latin word meaning "to bind." To bind with what? Obviously, to bind with God. Obviously, that which binds man with God is religion.

As you look around at the state of orthodox religions in the world today, would you say that they have succeeded in binding mankind to God? If you are frank and honest, you must admit that they have failed to do that. And, since they have failed, let us try to see why.

First, you must understand how religion develops historically. Religions originally centre around one man, one personality who receives in some way a revelation or an illumination from God.

Then he either writes this revelation or gives it out by word of mouth to a number of people—generally to many, because if he is aware of his mission as a prophet, he will try to interest as many as possible. Having reached all he can, he finds a few who understand him, and those few constitute his disciples and his apostles. The others, or the masses, are merely his followers.

When such a soul descends into the public view, he does so with a clear sense of the mission which has been given him by God, namely, to bring a new spiritual impulse to the world. He knows full well that it is not his own personal power or wisdom which is the motive factor, but that he is an instrument through which the

Higher Power will flow. Knowing that, he can say, as Jesus said: "It is not I, but my Father which has sent me." He becomes God's messenger to mankind. If those who hear him are wise, if they are at all intuitive and understanding, they will accept him. If they are stupid, dense, or materialistic, they will reject him.

It is a peculiar thing that the force which embodies such a project of God is like a two-edged sword. It will either help those who hear him, or it will hurt them. If they reject him, they do so at their own peril. They will be punished, not by an arbitrary mandate of God, but by their own higher self.

If, on the other hand, they accept, then they will receive the blessings of God and the fruits of the Spirit. But that is no concern of the messenger. He has only to deliver the message: the world may take it or leave it. In accepting it, the message will bring many joys and blessings, and perhaps some dangers; but in rejecting it, there will be many hurts and many dangers. You have only to study history to find verification of this.

The special followers or disciples of a prophet will receive not merely the actual teaching which he gives them, but also what is behind the words, namely, the spirit which is flowing through him.

Hence, if the disciples have the right attitude of absolute faith which rejects doubts, they will receive their reward through the spirit which flows through the prophet and through his words, and this will bring them nearer to the fulfillment of the true purpose of incarnation. There is only one reason why we are here on earth, and that is to find our true Spiritual Self, our true Inner Being. Unless we do find this we come back again and again, and suffer until we do find it.

A prophet's work really consists in the planting of seeds, the growth of which will be seen by later generations. When a prophet has completed his work he disappears, and then we see the beginning of organized re-

ligion. In his own lifetime the prophet is not interested
in organization; he comes to give not any material thing,
but that which will remain for centuries in the hearts of
those who are sensitive enough to respond. Nor does he
come to found any external organizations; these are
started by his followers, and generally after his death.
The disciples get together, as they did after the death of
Jesus and of Buddha, and form a brotherhood, or a
church, something to keep them together and give an
outward expression to the Inner Teaching and Presence
which they themselves have felt.

This is the beginning of every church and every external religion. In the days that are nearest to the founder,
the religion is generally pure. It is expressing that which
the prophet came to teach. As time goes on, however, it
degenerates, and often becomes merely organized super-
stition. It begins to lose the spirit, and becomes stronger
in the letter. The followers start to quarrel among themselves as to what he actually said, or what he meant by
what he said. Gradually they have rifts, and subsequently
they separate.

That is natural, because they are arguing over the
body, not over the spirit. The real thing—the Inner Spirit
—will remain for a time. It may last many centuries, and
then gradually it will begin to fade away and ultimately
disappear. No religion will endure for ever. That which
is *behind* religion alone endureth for ever and will always
find new incarnations.

The original visions and revelations of the great sages
have become mutilated by their ignorant followers or
narrowed by their bigoted zealots. Yet we need not be
disheartened if we find that religions tend to break up
and disintegrate. This is inevitable. They rise, grow, and
then fade. So if you understand that they are merely
obeying a law of Nature, then you accept this, and know
that when one religion dies away, another will come to
take its place. If you look around the world today, you

will see that most of the existing orthodox religions have begun to follow, more or less, the same downward arc. They are disintegrating and losing their followers. There is no doubt about it.

Why was it that the early Christians went so joyfully to their martyrdom? They were thrown to the lions,—burned alive. How were they able to endure such sufferings?

They were so close to the time of Jesus that they had his sacred Presence as their support. This enabled them to endure their martyrdom, so that when they were faced with death itself, their consciousness was taken out of the body completely, and they had no sense of suffering; their minds were elsewhere. Their bodies were tortured, but they themselves passed away as in a trance, with no consciousness of physical suffering.

But, before they passed away from the body, their faith had to be tested, and if their faith was strong enough, a Higher Power came and released them by withdrawing their minds from their bodies. In hypnotism and under chloroform the mind is withdrawn from the body and the most drastic surgical operation is not felt. The Divine Spirit also gently withdraws the mind, and the same result is obtained.

Today, no one feels a call to be martyred for any religion. It no longer binds man to God, because it is no longer an instrument used by the Divine Power. It is now a mere man-made organization depending upon human instruments.

Ancient scriptures and philosophies are of inestimable value and should occupy a treasured place on our bookshelves, but this is not to say that Truth has spoken only to those vanished men.

It is impossible to live entirely in the past when we seek for Truth. The present is just as real, just as useful, on this quest. Therefore, we should use these ancient books, but not be used by them. We should subscribe to everything within them that passes a universal test of Truth, but reluctantly and hesitantly dismiss whatever cannot pass this test.

This does not mean that we set ourselves up through false pride above those ancient lights, but it means that we value Truth as a spirit and not its relics left in books. Therefore, we cannot slavishly accept everything merely because it was given forth by some illustrious person of the past.

For one thing, we know that those records have seldom come down to us in all their purity, but have been tampered with and interpolated by ignorant and prejudiced men. So we must take these ancient books and scriptures as valued helps on the quest, but refuse to be shackled to any one of them. For the real quest must finally lead us within ourselves and not into the printed pages of a book. We first have to lose faith in all bibles before we can really believe in them.

Spiritually we live in "the twilight of dubiety," to borrow Charles Lamb's phrase. Religion is a subject surrounded by mysterious shadows.

Nevertheless, we must have some sort of religion. If we cannot accept any orthodox cult, we have to work out some sort of relation between ourselves and God, and I would like to put forward a few thoughts and suggestions as to what seems to me a sane religion for the modern man.

First of all, religion must be a personal thing,—a relationship between yourself as an individual, and God the Infinite Spirit—not between you and any organized institutions. The latter are man-made things, and they are not God. God is a spirit, so you must find God as spirit; it is a purely personal relationship that you have to seek— something that needs no external demonstration. No church, no temple is necessary. You can find it inside your own heart and in the secrecy of your most intimate feelings. It is not something to argue about or to discuss with other persons. They cannot help you.

The only way in which religion can be established is by worship, not by argument or discussion. You must worship God in your own private apartment; you must set up a certain attitude of thought and emotion towards the Infinite Spirit. What better attitude can you adopt than true worship, which is, first of all, to be humble, and to feel as a little child in the presence of that Great Being who is the Supporter of the Universe.

Humility, therefore, is the first step, not only in religion, but in every study that is worth while. As soon as a man thinks he knows all about a subject, or even half of it, he puts that much limitation between himself and the attainment of his goal. But if he adopts the attitude of a child who knows that it knows nothing, then he is teachable and it is possible for him to learn something.

Do not, therefore, go into worship with the idea of *dictating* to the Infinite Spirit what it shall do for you or what it shall teach you. Do not ask even for benefits. If the Infinite Spirit is wise, it ought to know what you need. You must give it credit for that much intelligence. If you know what you need, how much more should that greater Being know!

Thus, humility is the beginning of your worship. It is not necessary to pour out endless praises. God does not need this. And you are not to request anything unless it be spiritual—more light, more understanding, more strength. A peaceful life must also be a prayerless one. To have realized that all good is the hidden basis of existence, is to leave no room for requests.

By quieting the body and the thoughts, you prepare the conditions in which the Infinite Spirit will speak to you and manifest Itself to you. Your effort to do this is a form of worship, and God will come to you in that great silence. He cannot come to you if you are too busy thinking of your personal problems.

If you make an effort to silence your mind, that means you are beginning to forget your personal life. The personal ego is nothing but the totality of your thoughts. If you were to write down every thought that occurs to you during the day, and add them up, you would have an arithmetical sum, the total of which you might call your "personality." If there were no thoughts there would be no personal ego. The silencing of thinking is the stilling of the personal self.

§

Before you can begin to worship God you must forget yourself, and before you can forget yourself you must learn to control your thoughts and silence your mind. It is a very difficult task to do this completely, but it must be done—at least to some extent. If you can still the mind only fifty per cent you will have accomplished something. But you can make the effort, and after you have tried for a while, one day you will begin to succeed.

You will have fewer thoughts during your meditation periods. When God sees that you are making sufficient effort, He will come to you and you will gradually begin to feel His Presence. You will sense an atmosphere of divine stillness, and the few thoughts which remain will probably be exalted ones.

The Infinite Spirit is everywhere—why are so few people aware of it? Why is it that men seem so shut off from the Presence of God? The first and most obvious reason is that they have sunk so deeply into their bodies and intellects that they have lost the habit of remembering what they really are, and where they really belong. They have formed the habit of thinking of themselves as bodies and intellects. The Infinite is there, present in them, and everywhere, but, having lost the habit of remembering that they are really Spirit, there is no hope for them unless they can find some person to remind them of what they have lost.

Such persons play the part of ministers to mankind. If religion were effectively performing its function, every clergyman, every priest, would be a minister of God to remind man of what he really is. Preachers must become prophets before they can amount to anything worth while. The fact that humanity seems so hopelessly lost in matter is a sign that the priests are no longer cognizant of what they themselves are. And so we have blind leaders of the blind. That is the true reason why religion has failed today. The Infinite Spirit needs an outlet, a focus through which it can pass into the intellect of man if he is to be reawakened. The Spirit is everywhere present, but must be concentrated through some outlet to be effective. Electricity exists, but unless you can convert and concentrate it through the generator it will not flow through the wires and light your lamps.

Similarly with the Spirit. It must find a medium, a wire through which to flow and reveal itself to those who need light. If Spirit is to help human beings it must find an outlet through another human being. So, when God chooses to make His Presence felt, He usually does so by using some individual as His channel.

This brings us back to the third element in worship. We do need ministers, but they must themselves have found God. If they have not they cannot help us; if they have, then they are necessary to us, and become as links between ourselves and God. Thus, the third condition of worship is an intermediary between yourself and God who will be a focus until you yourself are sufficiently strong and illumined to do without outside help. When that time arrives the intermediary will humbly withdraw and leave you, because he does not wish to stand in your own light, nor between you and God. But until you can directly find God, he is there ready to help you. Therefore the third condition in true worship is an inner link with someone who has himself found God.

So, if you have these four qualifications: humility and

a childlike attitude to begin with; forgetfulness of your personal life for the time of worship; mental quiet; and your own personal relation with some human intermediary who will help you to effect the connection with God until you are able to obtain it for yourself, then you are prepared to worship. You will have increasing forgetfulness of the personal life and increasing moments of the divine stillness when you will feel that within that silence there is a Higher Power descending upon you. That is the secret of true worship—the sense that you are being taken up by a higher power.

Do not look for anything psychic, or for marvellous manifestations of an occult nature. They may come, but do not value them above the divine. Those things will only prove a hindrance to your worship; they are sidetracks which will take you away from the path of true worship. If you follow them they will lure you into fascinating bypaths, but that is not real worship. When you find true worship, something within you will tell you—something impersonal, infinite, and non-material, for you will during a brief interval lose the sense of your body.

In that moment when you feel that you are being taken up by a higher power, the answer has come to you, and then you are really worshipping. When you feel this, you must let yourself go; do not resist or hinder it by making any effort of your own. Just let yourself go and let this Power take you wherever it wishes. It will not take you to any place, but it will take you out of your personal self, and partly out of your physical body, and to a large extent out of your intellect.

It is possible that at such times—not always, but perhaps occasionally—you will see a Light, a great Light which envelops you and which appears to extend into fathomless space. It will seem to permeate you. You will apparently float into and become one with it, so that you will not know whether you are the Light or whether that which you were has disappeared.

If this experience comes to you, do not be afraid to let yourself—your personality—go. There is nothing to fear. You may feel that you are going to vanish into space— that there is a danger of death. Even if there were danger of death, it would be worth dying for such a revelation. But you will not die; this is only a temporary experience. It will not come to you often, so accept it gratefully when it does come.

That Infinite Universal Light is as near as you will ever get to *seeing* God. You will never "see" God otherwise than as Light; God is infinite and is Spirit. He can only appear to you in an infinite way, with no apparent finite limits. The nearest thing to Infinity that we can know is space. You cannot see to where space extends. You *think* you see the horizon, but if you try to approach it you will find that it always recedes into space. Space and light are the only emblems by which God can manifest Himself to you. Light is the form of God, space is His home.

If God reveals Himself to you as Light, be thankful. It is a blessed and beautiful experience. It will not come to you often. There is an explanation as to why you cannot expect to have this great vision frequently.

If you were to see God as the great Universal Light, you would see Him as something other than yourself— that is, as something outside of yourself, although still *inside* your mind. You might feel yourself as part of this Light, but it would really be outside yourself, and so, you would still be *seeing that Light.* In other words, there is a relationship of duality; God is regarded as something apart from your own self. To see—whether it be an angel or a material object, or even God Himself as Light—is to see something *outside* of yourself. The very act of "seeing" connotes two things—a "see-er" and that which is seen—which means duality.

If God has rewarded you by giving you the vision of His Substance, and if you continue your efforts to worship Him, He will wish to lead you a step farther. He wants you to attain the Highest which it is possible for man to attain. And what is the Highest? It is to discover and know that *you, yourself are spirit.* To see God "outside" of yourself is still seeing Him as *apart* from you. The vision of the Light which you have is a vision which takes place within your own body. When you see the Light, you are still on the highest mental plane. You must rise higher.

Therefore, after He has shown you the Light, God withdraws Himself, as such, as Light, and leaves you free to find your real self. You must then no longer look for God as *Light*, but as *your own self.* You must find God henceforth not as something in vision, but as *being*—as something which you *are.* You are a ray of God. To know God is to be God, not to see God. To see implies duality, the relationship of one who sees and that which is seen, but *to be* implies no relationship whatsoever, only the fusion of the ray with the Sun. This is the highest state of spiritual unity to which you can attain.

§

When you find your real self, then you are truly worshipping God. But you cannot reach this state through your own effort; it can only be reached by grace—maybe through the help of a teacher. When you have proved yourself completely devoted, and your mind has matured sufficiently, you may earn that grace, and then you will find the Sun from which emanated the ray that you are.

When, therefore, you have fulfilled the fourfold condition—childlike attitude of humility, forgetfulness of self, stilling of mind, and connection with some human intermediary who is competent to lead you to God—then you may worship, and your worship will be in silence and secrecy. The Voice of the Silence is better than the voice of the priest!

"Noise is unpleasing to God. Men! pray in silence,"

was the admonishment of one of the sacred books of Amen-Ra, the Sun God.

Let go of your dearly-held dogmas, enter into the sublime Silence, and wait for the dawning of Light. It is useless to use verbal prayer, excepting under stress of great emergency; ordinarily your worship must be conducted in silence. This is true worship which will bind you to God, and because it binds you to God it is *real* religion.

It is not then necessary for you to subscribe to orthodox religions or go to church. You may do so if you wish, if you think it will help others by setting an example to those who need this form and for whom it may still be necessary. It is left to your discretion. Religion is intended to loosen man from his material desires, to cause him to work not only for material things, but for superphysical things. When the *real religion* has been found, everything else will only be a substitute and even a degradation. Real religion will bind you to God, and that is the true essence of worship.

How will this work out in your own inner reaction towards life? First of all, you will adopt the attitude of good will to all men, because you will know that everyone has sprung from a common origin. We are rays from that Unknown Sun, and when you understand that every living creature, man or animal, is a ray from the Primal Light, and has therefore in essence just as much of the divine as you have, you will treat it with respect and reverence; and because that is so, no matter how people may act, or what they may say, or how much they may have forgotten their spiritual nature and origin, or how beastly their behaviour, you will realize that they only do this from ignorance.

You can have only one attitude towards your fellow men, and that is to understand who and what they are and to see them as *that*, behind the temporal personalities which they are expressing. You can have only pity for their ignorance, and a desire to help them if only one step

ahead towards the recovery of what they have lost—their
divine memory.

The best way for you to help others is to know that
they are essentially divine. The only way you can do this
for the masses who do not understand direct spiritual
terminology, is through good will. No matter whether it
be the worst criminal or the greatest saint, both are
equally deserving of your good will. That is the first
active expression of true religion. Good will will not be
limited—you cannot reserve it for the good and hide it
from the bad. Therefore the second manifestation of real
religion is *tolerance*.

Tolerance means understanding the plan behind the
universe. And that plan involves the evolution of all creatures. Just as matter has evolved out of Primal Light, so
human beings themselves must grow and evolve amidst
stumbling and falling. They are all standing on different
rungs of a ladder, and if they are on the bottom rung
today, they will later be at the top. So we must be patient.
Nature has tremendous patience. She waited millions of
years to bring you into being as a human, and she is
willing to wait millions of years to make you perfect.

So, if Nature, which is only an expression of God, has
such tremendous patience, you can begin to copy her in
your relations towards your fellow human beings, and no
matter how they may act towards you, try to have a little
of that patience which is *tolerance*. Tolerance should extend to everything, but this does not mean that we should
say: "All right, if this town is being managed by a gang
of criminals, let them manage it; we shall be tolerant of
them." If fate has put you in a position where you have
a public service to perform, whether it be the humblest
duty of voting or whether it be acting as governor of a
state, you must do your duty and see that order and justice are available for all. Good will and tolerance must be
combined with common sense.

The third essential is *hope*. Hope means that you know,

or at least have a tremendous faith, that behind the worst conditions and circumstances there is still a divine plan working. You know, amidst the blackest despairs of yourself and mankind, God's will is being done. Browning said: "God's in His Heaven, all's right with the world." All's right with the world—yes, in the *highest* interpretation, because God is everywhere; He has not deserted us, and whatever happens is for the ultimate evolution of mankind.

If you have faith in a divine plan back of all things—which includes your own life as well—you will maintain an unbroken hope. No matter how desperate things may seem with yourself or with the world, still you must hope and hold on, knowing that the wheel will turn. It *must* turn. The worst experiences are sometimes means of completing unseen good, and the hardest sufferings have a positive and constructive element behind them.

Our life is simply a spiritual education, and suffering is part of this. We must keep up hope, whether we suffer or whether the world suffers, and realize that nothing can endure permanently. All suffering must come to an end, as night ends when dawn arrives.

Hope also means believing in the presence of a divine power which is here to help you if you want it. If you want divine power you must look for it. It may not always help you in your own way, but you may be sure of this: if you approach it rightly, without dictating, it will help you.

Now we come to the fourth and last of the determinants of real religion, and that is *service*. Not in the sense that we should run about and fuss and make ourselves a nuisance to everybody. We must reach an inner dedication, a desire to be constructive in life, and to do something worth while for mankind, no matter how small the service be, how limited the scope. You must learn that we are all one in origin and you should express this on the material plane through good will and an inner attitude of service. I deliberately say "inner," because it is for each individual person, according to the circumstances in which destiny has placed him, to find out how or whether the *material* expression will have to come; but the inner attitude will be the same for all, and that is dedication to the higher powers to serve mankind.

What form the outer service may take does not matter. You may be a labourer, and your field of usefulness very limited. If you have the right spirit you will find that it will not matter what you *do*, but *how you do it*, because the attitude you take towards your work and the efficiency with which you try to do it will be the expression of your religion. You may be hired help or the president of a republic, and still your inner attitude will be the same.

Whether you have a big canvas to work on or a small one is not your affair. That is given to you by destiny. But the inner attitude *is* your affair. This self-reliance is the only true worship for mankind. All other religions are but ladder rungs leading up to this supreme knowledge.

We are living today in an age wherein the psychic forces and the mental forces which are hidden behind the scenes of evolution, are extremely active in stirring the strong emotions and passions of mankind. Because destiny has ordained that the accounts of nations shall be settled, these accounts have to be paid off, and whether they are paid off in full or only partially depends entirely upon them. By a change of heart and mental attitude, half of the evil destiny could be swept away at once. But if we cannot change or do not understand the need of a change, then the blind forces of destiny must go on and do their work.

To achieve this settlement of destiny, everything which is hidden is being brought out, everything that is at the bottom is coming to the surface, and we see some things in the soul of mankind which are fine, but also many things which are ugly and even ghastly.

Because this is a closing period, a transition from one age to another, the psychic forces for good and for evil are more active and more open than ever before. So you may see many things that you will disapprove of, and people may say or do things that you intensely dislike. The pressure on the mind of humanity today brings about either active like or active dislike, love or hatred, and it almost forces mankind into two camps, each actively hating the other.

The blind psychic forces are trying to reproduce their own conditions on this material plane; they have created a world divided into these two camps, each actively hating the other. It does not matter what political names they give to these camps. What is important psychologically is that half of mankind is being urged to hate the other half.

How can we be tolerant, you may ask, under such conditions? Here again, we must use common sense, and above all wisdom. Jesus once said, "Be ye harmless as doves, but wise as serpents." He definitely meant this to apply to conditions such as those under which we are living today. When you find yourself face to face with an individual or with a group who represents the destructive forces in Nature, you must then apply the second half of Jesus' counsel and be as wise as a serpent. When you are with those who represent the constructive side, then you can afford to be as harmless as a dove.

Always be tolerant inwardly, understanding that the hidden forces are expressing themselves in the only way in which they *can* express themselves. They are blind and destructive because life and experience have brought them to that point. So you must pity them in their ignorance, and to that extent be tolerant. But if duty of any sort forces you into active relationship with them and you must come to some decision and action, then you must be as wise as a serpent, and do what your good sense dictates. In this way you will not do violence to your tolerance, but *within* your tolerance you will resolutely perform your duty.

If you realize what the essentials of religion are, you will find all that you need to know. If you must play your part in society, or go through the rituals of orthodox religion, you may do that. But the real religion is beyond these things. It is not only real but *sane*, because it demands nothing from you which intelligence cannot accept. It demands no blind adherence to dogmas which even the merest schoolboy senses to be untrue, nor does it demand allegiance to customs and habits which are antiquated, futile, empty, and unreasonable. Therefore it is sane and rational, practical religion.

Something within us is unsatisfied and calls for a higher existence. We must seek our own spiritual experience instead of living on the results of others. We must pray, not for more truth, but for more will to live out the truth we already have; not for God to love us, but for ourselves to love God more and to help Him by letting Him act through us, through our bodies. Within the heart dwells the supreme divinity; often we are made to know that it reigns supreme; but unless we live out the will of that divinity in our daily outward lives we are not true disciples of it.

CHAPTER IV

THE MYSTERY OF THE KINGDOM OF HEAVEN

THE Sermon on the Mount has peculiar importance over all the other sayings of Jesus. It embodies most of the messages he had to give. Before it can be correctly interpreted it must be understood that he was talking from a plane far removed from that enjoyed by his hearers. Jesus had to speak to the people in language which they could understand. To talk to them as he might talk with others on the same plane, would have bewildered them. And so he spoke in parables, in similes, and in symbols.

The Sermon on the Mount represents the first culminating move on the part of Jesus to present his message to the world. Before this vital event in his career he was subjected to great temptation. He went into the wilderness and was "tempted of the devil." The "devil" then, as now, is that adverse element in Nature which seeks to keep man's consciousness imprisoned in lower forms of matter. That adverse element has existed from the very beginning of creation. It is nothing new, and it has its place because it gives us the opposition we need to bring out the latent strength within us. Without that strife we could never grow. Evil has its place, but it has to be overcome. And this is a battle which is not entered into once and finished with; it continues from plane to plane. As our experiences increase we gain more understanding of the forces which are at work in life; and as we understand them we can consciously take our stand and work out our incarnation until we finally attain full liberation.

Jesus had first to live through human experience. He did this in his early years. Then he had to live through superhuman experience, and the experience on the path of initiation, before he could really satisfactorily undertake His self-imposed mission. He could have had his personality exalted and given a position equivalent to that which is today occupied by the leaders of totalitarian states. He refused. He was not interested in exalting his personality. He had something else to do. Because he passed that final test he was ready to begin his work. He gathered the people together and gave them the most famous of all addresses: the Sermon on the Mount. The essence of this Sermon is contained in the beatitude with which it opens. I have commented on it in another chapter.

It was difficult for people who had been told to hate their enemies, to receive this doctrine which says: "Love your enemies, and bless them that curse you." It takes courage to switch over from one outlook to a higher one.

However, the tests of life are the same as the tests on the path. They come about naturally, through the ordinary course of events, and whole peoples are tested, just as much as individuals, and certainly every word from a teacher like Jesus becomes not merely a word but a force —almost an ultimatum which challenges people. Those who meet the challenge satisfactorily gain a great reward. Those who cannot, are left behind. And in that sense Jesus brought a sword on earth, and the force which worked through him, the challenging force, descended upon those who refused to accept his message when brought into touch with him.

There is a scientific law concerning the practical side of the process of attainment. Jesus said, "But thou, when thou prayest, enter into thy closet, and when thou hast shut the door, pray to thy Father which is in secret; and thy Father which seeth in secret shall reward thee openly."

Where is this closet to which he refers? It is first in our brain, whence it is brought into our heart. The heart is the centre of spiritual consciousness in man, and the head is the centre of intellectual consciousness. To pray in secret is to come down from the intellectual into the spiritual, from the personal into the impersonal. We must bring all our consciousness, all our energy into the heart, because it is the threshold of the higher self.

"After this manner therefore pray ye:

" 'Our Father, which art in heaven, hallowed be Thy name.' "

Jesus had, just prior to this, said plainly: "When ye pray, use not vain repetitions." Therefore he could not have meant that these words of the Lord's prayer were to be mechanically repeated day after day and for ever and ever, when he had almost in the same breath told the people not to repeat vainly. Yet despite his clear command, the Christian Church repeatedly reiterates the words of the Lord's prayer. He taught, as a guide to prayer or meditation, that nothing must be set or fixed and formal, and that repetition was vain.

" 'Our Father, which art in heaven, hallowed be Thy name.' "

Our Father, which is in reality, in the eternal. We should forget self utterly, and in this self-forgetfulness is the secret of success in beginning meditation or prayer.

"Hallowed be Thy name."

There is no name which we can give to God, or to the Overself, in any language. What does it mean, then?

In ancient Egypt the name of a person, or the name of a thing, was regarded as having major value, so much so that great care was taken in selecting a fit and proper name for anything or anyone. The name of God will never be found because it is a silent name—it cannot be uttered verbally—it is found in the silence alone. It is, therefore, a holy name. It must not be uttered; it must not even be whispered; it must be found, heard, and spoken only in the silence. God's name is the only name which is holy. "Hallowed be Thy name," means "Too sacred for utterance is Thy name." We must not utter it. It must be found, heard, and spoken only in the silence. We must silence our thoughts and our feelings, if only for a few seconds, when we want to think of God, and in that complete silence we are hallowing the name of God.

> "Thy kingdom come. Thy will be done on earth as it is in heaven."

God's kingdom has already come. It is here, it is the one kingdom which is forever coming. But until we realize this ourselves it has not come to us. Our attitude of aspiration or of prayer is the desire to realize the coming of the kingdom. This does not mean that we shall have a perfect utopian state on this material earth. That is not what Jesus meant. Jesus was interested only in spiritual things, and to him the material world was an illusory world. The kingdom which has to come is not of this earth; it is the kingdom of heaven, that purely intangible and invisible kingdom which everyone must find for himself, and in one place alone—in the heart.

"Thy will be done on earth as it is in heaven." The ego must become so unified, so surrendered to the Overself, that there is only one will, the Father's. Then it will be done on earth. The earth is the body; the heaven is that timeless state within which the body lives.

> "Give us this day our daily bread."

What bread do we need? Do we need food for our body? We shall have that anyway. So long as we are alive, we shall have our daily bread, and if the time comes when we are no longer to have daily bread, then we must accept that; it just means that the fated hour of death which has to come anyway has come now. It could not mean that Jesus came to our planet to ask people to pray for that which they are going to get anyway. He meant a different sort of bread. The "bread" mentioned in the prayer is but a symbol of the bread which we really need. What is bread? That which keeps the body alive. Jesus was not interested in the body; he was interested in the soul. What will keep the soul alive? The daily awakening to reality and to truth, as against illusion and falsehood. So long as we live in illusion, so long as we are deceived by false appearances, we are spiritually starving. To feed ourselves we must reflect deeply and meditate deeply, if only for a few minutes, as to what we really are and what we are here for, until we get an intuitional understanding of that reality. If we do this for ten minutes each day we are asking for our daily bread and receiving it.

"And forgive us our debts as we forgive our debtors."

This is again an illustration of the law of destiny which, it is well to remember, is the greatest force dominating human life today. Destiny is always at work. We need to remember its power, because by remembering we shall know just how we must act towards other people.

"And lead us not into temptation, but deliver us from evil. For Thine is the kingdom and the power and the glory forever. Amen."

These words do not accurately represent what Jesus said. It may be that we shall find a correct report eventually. The person who is seeking God must not be afraid of temptation, because it is through temptation and through tests that he has to fight and win his way to that which he seeks. It is not that there is anything wrong in temptation itself; everything depends upon the inner state or heart and mind of the person who faces temptation. But what he makes of that temptation is the thing that matters. If he is afraid of temptation, then he is merely resisting what will give him more strength when overcome. To be led into temptation or away from temptation is of no value to us. We have to face our problems ourselves because by over-coming them we grow in power and understanding. When Jesus said, "Deliver us from evil," he did not mean "de-liver us from temptation." The temptation must come— we do not have to pray for that—the adverse elements are there to do their work and they will see that we are led into temptation. The evil is not the temptation; it is the inability to understand what forces are represented by temptation. There is no such thing as a universal temptation, because that which tempts a man at one period of his life will not tempt him at another. So there is no fixed definition of temptation. What we need is to get a state of mind which will enable us to understand and to rate the forces which are ranged on either side in this conflict.

"Take no thought for your life, what ye shall eat, what ye shall drink, nor for your body what ye shall put on."

Did Jesus mean that you should become negligent, neglectful of your duties, of your means? He did not. He meant that we should cease worrying, cease being anxious, let go of all disturbing thoughts, and resign all problems to the Overself, to the higher power. By logi-cal, rational thinking you may find a human solution, but by ceasing to think, by taking no thought and relinquishing your problem, the higher power is then given an opportunity to deal with it.

To take no thought means to still the mind; to sit and enter into real meditation. Thereby the Overself is given a chance to come and take thought on your behalf for you.

If you surrender your problem with the idea of receiving some particular solution, then you have not surrendered, for to surrender your problem means literally to take no thought; it means to hand it over and without anxiety to wait for whatever happens.

With your personal burdens and your personal problems, many of you are in the position of the man travelling in a railroad compartment carrying his package on his head and refusing to place it on the floor and let the train carry it for him.

Perhaps you believe that you must carry all your own burdens, forgetting the higher power; forgetting that in its wisdom it gives you whatever you need. In surrendering to it your personal problems you must be prepared to accept what in its wisdom it sees fit to give.

If you place your problem in the hands of the higher power the right solution will aways come, and whatever is will be for the best.

This is not blind faith. It is something more, that which is born out of the inward quest through continuous inward search, that which causes you to know that you should obey the injunction to

"Seek ye first the kingdom of heaven, and all these things shall be added unto you."

§

The mystery of the kingdom of heaven is a poetical and symbolical phrase, which to different minds will mean different things. But there can be only one ultimately true meaning. Heaven to some means the after-death state. To others it means that which you can enjoy in the present life of happiness. But neither of these two meanings adequately covers the depth of this phrase.

If you believe that the kingdom of heaven is a state of prolonged bliss which you may enter at some time after death, you overlook the fact that man in his mental and emotional nature cannot change so fundamentally. For only the mind and the emotions survive death, and these will remain precisely as they were during life. If we grant that the state of heaven is an after-death state, then obviously it is not an eternal state, because it had a beginning and therefore it must have an ending. If it depends upon the death of the body for its beginning, then it is something which is connected with the body, even though negatively, and something which has no external being of its own. Every condition, every object, which has a birth must have a death. That kind of heaven could never be the eternal heaven.

A further proof lies in the pictures which orthodox religions in both the Western and Eastern countries have painted of heaven, describing it as a place peopled by the same beings who lived on earth, and who carried with them their same earthly natures. That is a very imperfect heaven, filled with very imperfect beings. If you restrict the meaning of heaven to such a state it will be purely ephemeral. It could never be a permanent state. But certainly he who invented the phrase "the kingdom of heaven" could not have referred to a purely ephemeral, faulty, and imperfect condition as being the ideal and the goal of life.

Many consider heaven as a perpetuation of the pleasure of earthly existence. But that, too, is an impossible condition, because life here in this material world is a mixture of pleasure and pain; never is one separate from the other.

Heaven as a state of permanent happiness and perfection obviously must be an eternal and unchanging state.

If it is something which is born today and dies tomorrow, then it is imperfect, ephemeral, and fugitive. It must be something that is unchanging and eternal, not pseudo-eternal.

Second, heaven must be something *real*. If it is just a dream or a psychic or mental hallucination, then it is not *real*. Reality means that which *is*, not that which seems to be. Every state or condition of matter in this material world is illusion, because it is not what it seems to be. Ice is not really ice. It may melt off into water. Water is not really water. It disappears into steam, vapour. Similarly, every state of the mind, that is, every set of ideas, every series of mental pictures, is illusionary, because they, too, come and go. A dream during sleep is nothing more or less than a series of connected ideas, but when you awaken you see how unreal the whole thing is. Similarly, a heaven which is based on a series of mental pictures, such as a psychic heaven, a spirit heaven, an orthodox or religious heaven, must be an illusion.

What is left? Neither matter nor mind can constitute heaven. But there is something which exists *behind* mind and *behind* matter, from which both grow, and to which they are returned, and in which they are rooted. That you may call Spirit. Or you may call it the Overself. It is something which is without shape and form, but out of which all forms are created. The nearest element to that state is light, because light has no shape, and no form. Light is what the mystic beholds when he sees God, and Light is what the scientist must find when he seeks the origin of the universe. And yet Light itself is a veil upon that state—it is not the state itself. It is the last of the veils.

The heaven of orthodox religion is a place where forms and people appear, and because of that, it is an illusion. A true heaven can only be in the world of reality. All forms belong to illusion, because all forms are condensations and limitations which spring out of reality, and which cannot exist eternally. The matter of which, for instance, a chair is composed, takes shape or form as a chair. When that matter is analyzed by the scientist he discovers it is energy, a series of electrical radiations. And later he will be able to trace it still further.

So we can see that the original substance, and the original energy behind matter, can take on myriad forms. They are real for an hour or for a thousand years, but eventually they must disintegrate. If heaven is worth anything, and is what Jesus meant it to be, it is something which does not change its nature and disappear and disintegrate. It must be something which is really eternal, and that can only be in the non-material, non-mental, and non-form worlds.

This conception of heaven leaves us in a great void, in a seeming emptiness where no idea, no thought even, can enter. That is the nearest the human mind can get to describing heaven—a great void where nothing and nobody appears, yet which is the supreme reality.

What is the advantage of attaining such a state? First of all, it is the very purpose of incarnation here. It is the reason why we have been born, and until and unless we attain that understanding, we shall have to continue the weary cycle of birth and death. It must be found in the flesh, not in any spirit, psychic, or mental world, or even in dreamless sleep. The Spirit, the Overself, symbolized by Jesus as the kingdom of heaven, must be found here on earth in the full waking consciousness.

Deep sleep is the nearest approach to heaven which the average person can reach. What, then, are the conditions which we find in deep sleep? First of all, the personal self disappears. There is no ego, no *I*. Second, the mind disappears; there is no mental movement, no thinking, no ideation during deep sleep. Third, the world itself disappears. You are left in a great void. These three conditions must be found. And yet something more! When you understand the mystery of consciousness you will really know what the kingdom of heaven is. *There*

is only one consciousness—not three—not a material, plus
a mental, plus a spiritual consciousness, but One alone.
One Light shines through the human being, and that
Light is divine.

Thinking, moving, acting in this material world are
merely different manifestations of spiritual consciousness. When you let a light shine through a window made
of coloured glass, the rays which appear on the farther
side will seem coloured, yet on your side they will be
white. So when the light of the Overself shines through
your intellect, it does not change its nature, it only
changes its appearance. It manifests as thoughts and
ideas, or as physical energy, but it still remains spiritual
consciousness. It cannot change its real nature. The light
from a white glazed lamp which projects its rays through
a yellow-coloured windowpane is not emitting two different kinds of rays—only one and the same. If you had
a red glass screen placed just beyond the yellow pane,
you would then see two sets of rays, different in colour.
Behind the original lamp-glass the third, or rather the
original, white light, would still be shining. Can you say
there are three different lights? No, for ultimately it is
really one and the same light manifesting through all
the three.

And so with the consciousness of spirit. The consciousness by which you work and move and act
throughout the day is essentially spiritual, only it is coming through some dim and rather remote windowpanes,
through the intellect, and through the body, and we do
not recognize it as the inner light. That is why meditation is needed. Meditation is the process of *interioriza-
tion*, of withdrawal. Now, if you imagine the coloured
light which is beyond the red glazed screen indrawing
itself into the glass, then coming behind it, indrawing
itself still further, then returning behind the yellow pane
and then ultimately reaching the original white lamp,
you have the perfect picture of what meditation is. It is

the same with consciousness indrawing itself, by forgetting the five senses, from the external world, which is
the home of consciousness in its most remote state, and
sinking deeper and deeper into itself through reverie,
then coming to the mind, or intellect, and indrawing
itself still further. Behind that it finally comes face to
face with itself, its own pure white light, and it is still
the same consciousness that it ever was.

You hear people telling of astral bodies, of different
states and different kinds of consciousness, but these are
only illusions, not reality. These different conscious-
nesses appear to exist, but really there is only one. If
you grasp the full significance of this you will see that
just as the scientist finds that there is only one substance,
which appears as matter or energy or light, so there is
really only one consciousness, which appears as waking,
dreaming, or deep sleep. All of these are but variations
of the original consciousness.

The Overself is the foundation upon which your waking experiences, your dream experiences, and your deep-
sleep experiences are built. It is not only the foundation,
but it is that which communicates existence and reality
to them. It is the gold thread which runs through them
and which still remains, even if the three are banished.
It is the innermost white light of spiritual consciousness.

If the kingdom of heaven is an eternal or absolute
state, and not a relative one, it can have no dependence
whatsoever on any of those three conditions of waking,
dreaming, or deep sleep. They depend on *it;* it does not
depend on them, but only on its own self; otherwise it
would not be absolute.

Why, then, is it necessary for us to obtain realization
of the spiritual self in the waking state? If you withdraw
consciousness from deep sleep, what happens? You will
discover that there is nothing to be conscious of, nothing to be aware of, no one to be aware of anything.
That is because you have entered an absolute state where

there is no dependence, no relativity. The word "consciousness" as we normally use it, hardly applies to that state, because we always think in terms of someone being conscious of something else,—in other words, of a personal self and its consciousness of some object. The personal self is nothing more or less than the totality of all your thoughts and feelings. If you banish them, as in deep sleep, there can be no personal self. Therefore you have to pass through and transcend the deep-sleep state in order to find the Overself, because thus alone can you transcend and pass the personal self.

If you do that, what becomes of your personal consciousness? It disappears as a form, as personal consciousness, but that in it which was the mainspring, the reality within it, that subsists. It subsists as *liberated consciousness*, impossible to describe other than by metaphor and simile or by negatives. It is the true eternal kingdom of heaven, which cannot pass away, and cannot perish. It does not depend upon the limitations of personal being, nor upon existence in a mental or material world. It is entirely self-sufficient, and there is no time in that state, nor sense of time.

People do not understand what the word "eternity" means. They usually picture a state wherein they themselves, the personal selves, are going to sit down and do nothing, and so they think of it as a state of perpetual boredom and monotony. Of course, that is just their imagination thinking it to be "eternity," but that is not what it really is. The moment you strike out the personal self, there is no one remaining to enjoy eternity. You disappear, and so to think of anyone settling down to enjoy eternity is an impossibility, an illusion. They wonder: "How will I live in heaven doing nothing?" But when the personal "I" disappears, that problem will also disappear with it. The kingdom of heaven will be reached.

It appears to be the divine will that man must experience the depths of illusion in order to find the heights of reality. We have to pass through the circle of dream, deep sleep, and waking, in order to find the centre of the circle, the immortal, eternal centre. Now, the mystery of the kingdom of heaven is a mystery because we do not realize that we exist within heaven every moment of our lives. Hence it is a paradoxical mystery. If we had that realization it would be no mystery, but then there would be no kingdom, no inner self to search for, nothing to lure us away from the imperfect state, which is the normal human state. It is a "mystery" because we have covered ourselves over with thoughts and desires. They have covered us as the embryo is covered by a membrane, and cannot be born until it breaks through it. So we have to break through the membrane of thought and desire which are outwardly objectified as the material body.

Here again you see the need of meditation, which is a stripping away of that membrane by removing yourself from the domination of thought, desire, and the body. The effort to turn inwards in meditation is an effort to free yourself from these coverings, and to find the true self within. Meditation, in the sense of turning inwards, is an effort to untie ourselves; hence its necessity. If that effort is not made, and if one does not realize its necessity, then life is indeed a mystery. The greatest secret of life, the kingdom of heaven, is the greatest mystery within the cosmic mystery. The most important purpose of our existence is to understand it.

We are so covered over that most of us do not even make the effort to free ourselves. Hence there must arise amongst mankind those who point out the way, those who are spiritual and religious guides. Whether well known or little known, these guides appear from time to time to show man that he need not remain a prisoner unless he chooses to. So mysterious is the human state that without external help it is almost impossible to fathom this mystery for ourselves. Therefore the help arises. It may come anywhere, in any part of the world. Someone, at some time or other, must inevitably appear to keep mankind from forgetting what he is really here for.

Jesus said in speaking to his personal disciples: "Unto you it is given to know the mysteries of the kingdom, but unto them which are without, I speak in parables." This meant that for the few—the comparative few who were ready to follow him—the membranes would be torn asunder, and the state of the Overself would be revealed. For the others, and particularly the masses, this could not be achieved, but something else could be done. He spoke to them in parables, as a means of starting them on the beginning of the path which would ultimately lead them to the kingdom of heaven. They were not ready for the ultimate Truth, but they had to make a beginning, and so they were given codes of ethics, moral injunctions, spiritual aspirations; and a few higher principles were laid down for their information.

Parables are for children who are not yet mature enough to perceive the Truth, and what is more, to stand amidst materialistic environments for Truth. Those who are grown up sufficiently, who want Truth ardently, and above all who want it for its own sake and not for any benefits which it might bring—only they are ready to become disciples. And so Jesus revealed only to them, to those that were ready, the mysteries of the kingdom— which means the mysteries of their own spiritual nature. He gave them insight into their own eternal being. And he gave it to them quickly, without parables and without circumlocution, because they were ready.

Why were they ready? First of all, because of their *faith*, their intense and complete faith in him and in his doctrine. Second, he explained: "Except ye become as little children ye cannot enter the kingdom." So the second condition which made them ready was *humility*.

They were humble inwardly, which meant that they were teachable. The average man is not humble; he may outwardly appear to be so, but inwardly he sets up mental resistance and barriers, and builds walls of prejudice against truth. Humility consists in having a perfectly open mind, as though you were new-born, and being able to receive with complete faith not only the words of those who know, but what is still more important, that which is behind the words, which is Spirit.

In addition to faith and humility, there was a third condition which made it possible for Jesus to open the mysteries of the kingdom to his disciples. That third condition, as vitally important as the other two, was their intense longing and overwhelming thirst for truth, for complete light to be shed on the mysteries of life. With these three qualifications it was comparatively easy for Jesus to open the door to his disciples, and so they found *who* and *what* they really were. Then in their turn they began to teach the masses. Every person who has these three qualities, faith, humility, and longing for truth, will eventually find his way into the kingdom. If these qualities are sufficiently developed, sooner or later the divine power which takes care of this universe will lead him to the appropriate teacher. If such an initiator is not available, then the divine power Itself will directly initiate him.

Generally it is a law of Nature that the divine power must be made manifest through another human being. Because you are human, because you are living in the flesh, you must find another human being who is also living in the flesh, through whom the higher power can manifest to you.

The Overself is everywhere present in the universe, yet we are nearly all ignorant of it. It is everywhere around us, but few seem to find it. Why is that? It needs a focus or outlet on this material plane through which it can reach you. That outlet is nothing more nor less than a human instrument who may have no power or virtue of his own, but who may nevertheless be a channel for the Overself. As Jesus said: "It is not I, but My Father which is in heaven which doeth these things." But still he had to be there. There had to be prepared an outlet, an instrument, a channel through which the Father could speak.

It is partly because there are so few of these human outlets, so few fit instruments through which the Father can speak, that you find mankind today in such appalling spiritual ignorance and darkness. There are many so-called spiritual teachers, but unless and until they have completely penetrated into the kingdom, they can give forth only their personal ideas, thoughts, and opinions. These latter may be very exalted and helpful, but they are still not the real power and expression of the Overself, merely because they are mental.

Those who have attained the true understanding of the mystery of the kingdom are very rare in this day and age, so rare that one might search through many countries and not find one. That explains why we have now what is almost a dark night of the soul of mankind. However, there is a good side to the picture, and that is this: When man through this intense darkness suffers sufficiently—because his ignorance will always cause him to act wrongly and thus bring needless suffering upon himself under the law of destiny—when he feels the pressure of this suffering, he will cry out. For what? For relief, which means peace. And as this yearning for inner peace grows, becomes stronger, there must be an eventual response from those existing within the universe who can answer it, and the more intense the call, the more powerful and more wide-spread will be the help which will be given.

Everything in this universe has its appropriate place and every event has its appropriate hour. All major events must happen in accord with destiny—the working of cause and effect—and at the right moment, there will always be an answer. If, seemingly, we find vast spaces where there are ignorance and darkness and utter materialism, and at the same time, yearnings and longings for spiritual light which are apparently unsatisfied, we should know that suddenly and miraculously there must eventually appear here and there those who can give the answer. It *must* happen; it is a law of Nature. We need never despair, but we should be patient. The history of mankind is, and perhaps will ever be, a history of alternating day and night, of the ebb and flow of materialism and spirituality.

I said before that one of the qualifications which attracted the disciples to Jesus, and which ultimately was responsible for initiating them into the kingdom of heaven, was their ardent love of truth—truth in the highest sense. What does such truth mean? It means wanting to know what is man's place in existence, a desire to understand the real meaning of life, why and what we are here for, and what is the real basis of this universe. It is not curious that man, once he is awakened, develops such a longing to know and to understand. It is because each one has potentially, within himself, the state of the kingdom of heaven; and if he has lost awareness of that state, what could be more natural than for him to long to return to it? However unconsciously, he feels that he is missing something, but he does not know what, and so he searches hither and thither for what he has lost. He searches in every material condition and worldly experience first, and then he searches through mental experiences, but is never fully satisfied. Something eludes him. Why? Because he is searching in the wrong place. He is searching *outside* of himself. Body is not his self, mind is not his self. He has to dive deeper than that. He has to find the Overself and then he can discover the answer which eludes him.

So you see that the longing for Truth is really a longing to return to that state which we have lost apparently, but which we really *are*. This longing may be covered or buried for years, for lifetimes, under the trials and temptations of earthly existence, but somewhere it will always exist and must reappear. And it *must* reappear because man will never find Truth, ultimate and final Truth, in the material world. The scientist is finding this to be so. He is pushing on and on, he is coming up against the very limits of matter, and eventually he will be driven through the exploration of the mind into himself.

It is the same with every search for happiness. You may try one thing and then another, but eventually you shall be driven back to the only eternal refuge within yourself. After you have found this refuge within, then you have found the kingdom of heaven.

The paradox is that after you have found your peace and happiness there, you may go on with worldly existence and enjoy it if you wish. There is nothing lost because you are now inwardly detached, but you are no longer deceived. Withdrawal from the world is entirely an inner process, when you understand the truth. It is something deep within your heart. It has nothing to do with outward gesture and demonstration. Monks who flee from the world in an effort to find spirituality will doubtless find something, but not necessarily true spirituality. They may find peace.

If you want to find spirituality you must find it whilst living in the world, yet not being of it. In other words, being inwardly detached and renounced, but outwardly living and enjoying as other people do, not held in your heart by material things, not mentally imprisoned by them, but able to renounce them at a moment's notice. If you can do this, you are free; you are no longer a slave.

In the ancient Egyptian mystery schools attached to certain temples, people who sought the mystic knowledge or the higher spiritual life and were admitted, were trained for varying periods of years. After this training— unless they were ordained for service in the priesthood— they were sent back to normal everyday life in the outer world to live as other people live, take up a career, marry and have children, and so forth. Life in the world might go on for many years after the training in the mystery school. And then one day the call from the temple might come, and they would be asked to return immediately and resume monastic existence. If they had learned their lessons fully they would return readily, because the world could not keep them captive, no matter what attractive environment they had created for themselves. Even had they reached the highest position in society they would have had to reject and leave it at twenty-four hours' notice, and go back to the temple. Thus they were in the world, but not of it. If the world had captured them, they would not have had the strength to go back; they would have failed to pass the test.

But those ancient mystery schools and those spiritual training systems do not exist today; they have disappeared. Life itself has become our mystery school. It is training us and teaching us.

Life is our modern school. We find our sacred lessons and our divine initiations through daily living. We enter our battleground here. It is not only a battleground of material and economic forces, but also a battleground of the soul. We may try to live out our life in the world fully and completely, and yet succeed in spiritualizing it. There is no reason why we should not discover the kingdom of heaven here. It is not necessary to withdraw from the world, but it is necessary to withdraw from *enslavement* to the world.

This state of being which Jesus called the kingdom of heaven is entirely an inner state. Primarily, it has nothing to do with the outer life. Whether you eat meat or not, whether you are married or a celibate, has nothing to do with it. The kingdom of heaven is a state of inner being and you will find it *within yourself*. It has been called by so many names at different times and in different countries, that people have often become confused and violently argued amongst themselves about religion. Through all history the followers of one religion have criticized or condemned the followers of another. If you put religion aside, you will find that the philosophers of the East and those of the West have given so many different names to the Absolute. The Absolute of the philosophers must be the same as the kingdom of heaven of the Christian religion, and yet you find these men arguing, and vainly, because they never come to a conclusion as to what should be the proper goal of life. They argue because they do not know. There is only one *experience* of the highest state of life, and this is the same for all men at all times and in all countries. There are many different experiences on the way which bring you to it. But when you attain the Ultimate, the Reality Itself, and not your *idea* of it, then there can be but one universal cosmic experience. Only those who have had this enlightenment perceive Truth; all others merely perceive their own opinions of Truth.

It is obvious that anyone who has attained that highest perception could never argue about it with another person who has attained it. They would just recognize it as existing in each other. Jesus and Buddha would have smiled understandingly at each other. But those who follow them—and sometimes even in their own lifetimes—not having themselves attained that transcendental experience and that divine understanding, begin to argue and sometimes even go to the length of persecuting those who disagree with them. Why? Simply because they have not experienced reality. They argue and fight about their *ideas* of this experience, what *they* think it is or should be, what should be the way of life of those who wish to follow their spiritual leader, and so on—all

merely personal opinions. They do not *know*. These
controversies and arguments, in fact, all discussions
amongst those who do not really know what they are
talking about, are frequently futile in purpose and sterile
in result.

The only way to settle these questions is not by argument or discussion, but by *getting the direct experience*
of divine illumination. And that is a personal thing. Each
person must obtain it for himself or herself. Then only
will you find out what is really meant by the kingdom
of heaven. This attainment is not quite so hard as it
seems to be, because you are not seeking something a
hundred thousand miles distant; you are seeking something which is here—*right here*—inside yourself. You are
not seeking something which is alien to you, but rather
your own inmost nature, *your essence*.

Why, then, should it be so difficult to find the kingdom? The difficulty lies in the persistence of strong
mental habits which we have brought down from former incarnations, habits of false belief and of ignorant
thinking which keep us tied to the "not-self." We are
the creators of those habits; but since we have made
them, we can unmake them. If their elimination were
dependent entirely upon our own efforts, it might no
doubt be a very difficult process to get rid of them, but
we have help. *The higher powers exist. They will help
you, but only after you have made strong endeavours
of your own.*

CHAPTER V

THE SEVEN BEATITUDES

WHAT do we find at the end of the quest of the Overself? Towards what is all this search and aspiration leading? Why are we so interested in these higher matters, and what do we hope to discover if we do succeed with these spiritual practices?

The goal has been pictured for unawakened humanity by the teachers, seers, and prophets of the past in different outlines. To us the simplest way is to say that it consists in fulfilling the purpose of human incarnation upon this earth. That is why we are here today—to find our lost awareness of the divine self, self in its largest and loveliest aspect, whilst passing through this transient terrene life. We haven't lost this self, remember, we have only lost *track* of it, which is quite a different thing. We have retained awareness of other things. We are always aware of the body and we are generally aware of the intellect, but we are not even momentarily aware of That which animates both.

In the opening portion of his Sermon on the Mount, Jesus has pictured the lofty goal and lofty rewards of this quest. The nine sentences in which he delivered these beatitudes should really be reduced in number by coupling the first and second on the one hand, and the last and penultimate sentences on the other, because of the intimate connection which exists between them. Thus we arrive at seven beatitudes which give a con-

densed statement of what is to be found at the end of
the quest, and a concise description of those qualities
which flower into fullest bloom in the final stage of the
quest. These affirmations are not a mere set of abstractions, but are expressions of forces latent within the
very core of life itself.

The very first words in this Sermon are:

"Blessed are the poor in spirit, for theirs is the kingdom of heaven. Blessed are they that mourn, for they
shall be comforted."

When a great seer like Jesus spoke, the hearers of his
age were content. But the modern mind, and particularly the modern Western mind, is not content with such
bare assertion. It wants to know why? How? Where?
It wants every minute detail fully explained. It wants
reasons, facts, proofs, explanations, and arguments. Not
so the Eastern mind, which is content to state conclu-
sions without showing the process of patiently accumu-
lating the testimony and reasons for them. It speaks
down from a higher non-material plane to us. We are
left wondering at its revelations, which are unacceptable
only because we cannot follow the steps which lead up
to them. Both attitudes are true, both are useful to adopt.
We must reconcile them.

These words of Jesus have puzzled many people. Even
if you rearrange them and say, "Blessed in spirit are the
poor," they might be slightly easier to understand, but
the riddle still exists. What does this sentence really
mean? Does it literally mean that everybody who is materially poor, who is financially poverty-stricken, is a
blessed person? You will understand what Jesus could
have meant, only if you understand correctly what poverty means from the deeper standpoint, and what the
spirit means, and what the kingdom of heaven means—
then only will you know the meaning of this phrase in
truth, and not merely as it appears on the surface.

Their meaning can be understood only from the esoteric standpoint. The esoteric doctrine is not something with which the world at large is acquainted today. Fragments of it have found their way into the world, but the complete philosophy has not. To find the esoteric viewpoint one must have been initiated by a competent master, a competent adept. Real initiation means the beginning of a new life, a new outlook, and a new understanding, and it is brought about only after you have learnt something of the art of meditation.

Everyone who practises meditation and tries to withdraw the mind from its external surroundings into the divine element behind it, can succeed in his efforts only by banishing the most powerful of the thoughts which remind him of the existence of the material world. Amongst these, some of the strongest are connected with the things, the properties, and the persons that belong to his outer life. Unless he can banish these thoughts and temporarily forget their very existence, it is impossible for him to achieve the state of mental stillness which constitutes advanced meditation. If, however, he does succeed in conquering these thoughts during meditation, this detachment recapitulates itself after he has returned to daily living in his attitude towards possessions. An inner renunciation of material existence will then hide behind his outward attentiveness to it. He lets go of things in his heart and in this sense only has become poor in heart.

So long as you have any possession, whether it be a material possession, or a mental possession, or an emotional possession—so long as you have such possession exclusively dominating your consciousness, you are not "poor in spirit." If you have possessions and cannot let go sufficiently to forget them utterly and completely at the divine call, then you cannot reach this point and proceed with meditation. To become "poor in spirit" you should, in consciousness, be able to renounce the world. Yet you may have these possessions and they may not dominate your consciousness. In that case, you really have achieved spiritual poverty. You have to feel strongly from the depths of your heart that, however attractive the world is, however attractive your possessions are, however attractive your friends and relatives may be, the whole thing is nothing but part of a passing show, and the manifold happenings, the various events, are merely moving pictures that come and go. They are temporary, fleeting. They have no real abiding power.

Now when you understand that everything that passes through your mind is thought or idea, and therefore an illusion, you are ready for the ultimate discovery, which is usually kept secret in the Orient because one must have a certain amount of mental courage to face it, and few people have that, by reason of the kind of training they receive.

This ultimate discovery is that life, the universe, human life, are nothing but a dream, a phantom, an illusion. It is like a motion picture—it has no reality in itself. It is just a mental picture passing through your consciousness. This whole world around you has the same value as the dream you dreamt last night—nothing more. When you awoke you knew it was a dream, but until' you awoke, to you it was reality.

It seems so appalling to say that this world which seems so solid, so substantial and so real, is really dream stuff, and yet that sense of the dreamlike character of the universe and of human life is so easily proven. Take the whole of your life up until this morning. Where is it? Where has it gone? It has gone into the memory. It has become a memory.

Those years when you lived so intensely through the greatest exaltations, the most poignant emotions, the strongest passions, and the most terrible sufferings— where are they now? They are just a memory. But what is a memory? A memory is a simple thought—an idea in your mind; it is no more than that, at best a mental picture.

If all your past years have been a passing show of fugitive, transient thoughts, what of your future years, and the present in which you are living now? Will that not be the same, because the present will become the past, and the future will become the past also; so, since the past, present, and future constitute the whole of your human existence, what is left of your life? It is nothing but a series of thoughts which come and go; therefore, from the highest standpoint, they are illusory.

Thus, when you awaken into Truth, you see that human life and the entire panorama of the universe is the same as a dream, just ideas passing through your mind, and you dismiss them for what they are. You know a dream is a dream only after you awaken from it, and only then do you believe you have awakened to the real state. You had to have a standard of comparison. So life here seems real until you have a standard of comparison, and that standard can only be Reality itself.

But what *is* Reality you ask? To understand this question, you must first understand what thoughts are. Thoughts, ideas, memories, all mental pictures, opinions, fancies, images, desires, feelings, and passions, all these are ideas in the mind. You can't have a feeling or an emotion about anything unless you think of it, so ultimately all these things are ideas in the mind. But these ideas are constantly tumbling over each other, coming and going like fugitives.

To understand what they are, is to understand what lies behind them. Try to imagine a thought existing without you, without your being aware of it. It simply couldn't happen. So you see *consciousness*, or *awareness*, is a fundamental part of the nature of thought.

Now, if you withdraw the consciousness from the thought, the thought disappears. But what happens to your consciousness? That still remains. Now, if the consciousness still remains, and has been the substance of the idea in your mind, you will discover that it was the consciousness alone which gave reality to your thought. Therefore consciousness, in its own pure state, *is* reality. If this consciousness is reality, then it must be spirit and truth. However, you must be careful to remember that consciousness itself may take various forms, so if you wish to find the Ultimate, you must find the final consciousness, which means Absolute Consciousness.

You can, by narrowing down your attention through concentration, bring it to the size of a pin point, and for the moment become that pin point of consciousness. Likewise, you can by concentrating upon the heavens above, spread out your awareness to fill the skies. But all these are mere forms of consciousness. If you want the real consciousness as it is in its ultimate nature, you must free it from every form; you must free it from every idea. That liberation of consciousness constitutes the attainment of real life.

When you understand this, you will know that the whole of life has only the value of a dream, a passing, cosmic dream. You see clearly and fully through its illusory character, and then you can become detached from it all; you can renounce it all. You see the truth about it, and you refuse to be so caught up in it that your spiritual sight is blinded. It needs no professor to prove this point. If you can detach yourself thoroughly so that you understand the ephemeral value of your external life, then you are "poor in spirit" indeed, and then only are you fit to take this initiation.

Such a detachment has nothing to do with outward appearances. Outwardly you may be very rich, or you may be very poor; that does not matter. What does matter is, what is your *inner attitude* towards your riches, or towards your poverty? If you are dominated by either, you cannot enter the kingdom of heaven.

Moreover, the praise of outward poverty is not necessarily spiritual. Asceticism may readily be practised by
those individuals who feel a deep call to it, but it is not
and cannot be a social idea. We need simplicity, but not
asceticism. External gestures of giving up worldly possessions are impractical in the West, and not really necessary. The attitude of mind towards the world is the
only change necessary. The kingdom of heaven is nothing more or less than a condition of inward freedom.
If you are afflicted by possessions to the point of being
anxious about them, or burdened by them, if you are
fearful about the future, or regretful about the past, or
if you are equally afflicted by your lack of possessions,
then you cannot attain this freedom.

What really matters is your inward reaction to outward events, and that alone will determine whether you
are "poor in spirit" or not. If you detach yourself sufficiently deep within your heart from the experiences of
life, then you are ready for the kingdom of heaven,
then you are blessed, and then your inner state will be
heavenly.

Of all who achieve this detachment of spirit, Jesus
says "theirs is the kingdom of heaven." That Jesus
meant just this may also be seen from another statement
wherein he explained that "the kingdom of heaven is
within you." Renunciation of the world is really an inner change of outlook upon it; an outward gesture, such
as becoming a monk or a nun, or such as giving all your
wealth to the poor, is not what Jesus meant.

When you thus understand the transient nature of
external things, when you realize how illusory they ultimately are, you are ready to receive the blessing which
Jesus states shall be yours. The opposite of illusion is
reality. Hence the reward which awaits you within the
kingdom of heaven is the finding of reality. This means
that you will live in an element which is ever-enduring.
Everything else that we know, whether it be this vast

material universe that surrounds us, or whether it be a desire or a memory or a thought which flows through our minds, appears to be real, but it is real in a purely limited and relative sense only. It comes and goes; it is transient. It is born, endures for a while, and then disappears. Death and change are the ultimate conditions of life in the material and mental worlds, but the reality which you find when you finish the quest will not come and go; it is time-defying, and hence *eternal*. It is the underlying substance which forever *is*. It is overwhelmingly difficult to describe, and I can only say that when one penetrates into the realm of the Overself, its reality becomes self-evident, it needs neither argument nor explanation.

I call it reality because everything else is but a second or third reflection, a manifestation and an appearance from it—real enough while it lasts, but the lasting period is temporary and dated. Something in us is seeking either consciously or unconsciously for that stable, unchangeable, enduring element which is the hidden secret of existence.

You will see the temporary realities, the material appearances, understand them for what they are, use them for what they are, and yet keep your consciousness within the Absolute, which is the kingdom of heaven. If you looked beneath appearances and sought that one hidden reality, you would be free of your fears. It is illusion which causes fear, and you have fears in life because you are deceived by it, as a man walking in the night through an Indian jungle might mistake a coil of rope for a snake. If you really knew that life in the essential is a benevolent power, you would fear nothing; even if suffering came, you would not fear it. That higher realization would put an end to misery. If you pry beneath the appearances of the world and find the reality which underlies it, then all your unsatisfied wants and ungratified desires collapse and disappear. You have found that which is the root of everything, which can support you adequately throughout life, that which you know to be eternal. It is absolutely essential to learn the truth about the appearances of life and the world if you want to get rid of fear and misery.

The few who think and the many who feel deeply grow more and more discontented with our mechanized, materialized existence. The illusion of progress has bewitched us. We have learnt how to make a hundred thousand things which our unlucky forbears never possessed, yet we have not advanced very far towards happiness. We have piled up our wants, but most of them are for material objects. We have yet to learn the lesson that the mere ownership of *things* can never supersede the conscious ownership of our own heart, our own mind, as a way of happiness. We are unable to subordinate things to ourselves, but yield ourselves to them.

We ought to distinguish inward fact from outward fable. Man is really engaged upon an inward pilgrimage, and whether he performs it on foot or flies in a giant aeroplane, his outward speed gives no measure of his true progress. We are accustomed to the mean and mortal perspective of the purely ephemeral, when we might have the wide and eternal expanse of the divine to solace our sight.

§

Jesus says something which has been often misinterpreted and misunderstood, because its purely literal significance has been taken.

"Blessed are they that mourn, for they shall be comforted." This sentence is really a continuation of his previous one, for it deals with precisely the same subject, and is also intended to reiterate and re-emphasize the vital necessity of making a right beginning. The only right beginning in the spiritual life is to "see through" the illusion of material life. Hence I have coupled these two phrases together and counted them as a single beatitude.

Who are the mourners? Those who mourn for the dead? To weep and to mourn over that which is lost, or over those who are lost, is not going to bring you comfort unless you mourn in the right way at the right time, and for the right purpose. To mourn for the dead, whether it be dead people, or your dead past, or your dead possessions, or your dead ambitions—to mourn for the dead will bring you no comfort whatsoever unless you can let them go within your heart.

Before anyone can find the comfort of the kingdom of heaven, this state of utter detachment must be found. If it cannot be found voluntarily, which is admittedly most difficult, it often has to be found involuntarily, so that those who are destined for entry into the kingdom of heaven not infrequently have the experience of finding themselves stripped of all their possessions, whether they be possessions in the form of living persons, as relatives, husband, father, wife, and so on; or whether they be personal belongings, as money, house, furniture, and so forth.

Very few have the mellow wisdom and ripe understanding and ready courage to face the hard truth that this world is only a camping ground. We are not here to live forever, and therefore all mortal possessions and earthly glories should be wisely used and wisely understood; they should not make us captive. If we cannot grasp this, then we risk having to be stripped of everything and thus made to mourn involuntarily. We are really birds caught in the net of external existence, glorying in our captivity. If, however, we can face this truth and retire from our servitude of finite things, if we can fight the battle out within our hearts and thus arrive at a state of detachment, then the combat need not be fought out again in the world. It will not be necessary to lose everything; the loss has already occurred deep within us, and an outward loss need not again occur. Such persons are the *voluntary* mourners.

Those, therefore, who mourn for what is lost, in the sense that they have let go of all belongings, all relatives, within the depths of their heart—those for whom all possessions and all people are as dead—they alone are the mourners whom Jesus refers to in this sentence. They have had to give up *inwardly*. That they shall be comforted, is his definite promise; that they shall be given a new treasure.

Such mourning is worth while, because through it they find the eternal reality, which makes them really blessed and comforted. However, if those who have neither the wisdom nor the strength to be prepared in the depths of their hearts to arrive at this inner detachment from ephemeral things, and who consequently have to endure the stripping process through misfortunes which life generally brings, will try to convert their trials and their troubles into stepping-stones leading towards this detachment, then even they also shall be comforted and their involuntary mourning will not be without value.

They must begin with faith, and time will gradually bring them to a realization of these truths. Their first step must necessarily be an act of faith, of trust in the words of Jesus, but such faith does not mean blind acceptance; it is an intelligent faith, which is really a sensitivity to something within which assures them that there is a higher power and a higher reality. They will get, eventually, glimpses which will assure them of a goal worth reaching.

If, having this opportunity of birth in the flesh, birth as a human being during the few years which are passed here on earth, we do not take the opportunity of fulfilling its higher purpose, we have foolishly wasted our incarnation. We enfeeble ourselves clinging to transient, material things. We are not gaining true life. We are gaining death. What is the final end of life—to eat,

drink, sleep, and make merry? It is only to become
aware, aware of *Who* and *What* is behind it. If we do
not grasp this opportunity, we lack wisdom; we are foolish. Here we all are, apparently caught up in this great
wheel of life with its endless revolutions through births
and deaths. *Now* is our opportunity to seek the eternal
Overself, for the sense of separation from the divine
centre within must always make man restless and un-
poised. That is why the millionaire, who is able to get
everything in this world, *still* seeks for happiness. I have
met both millionaires and ragged mendicants, and I
know. Certainly I know that I could not live without
this sense of a divine Presence ever near me, ever around
me. Without it, life would hardly be worth while.

There is, however, a still subtler reason why Jesus
used the word "mourn" in this connection. Mourning
has forever been associated with weeping; indeed, in
Oriental lands the two terms are synonymous. When the
awakening soul is being led into the state of inner detachment, it reaches a point where spasms of physical
weeping not infrequently make their appearance. When
the heart yearns for the return to its spiritual home,
tears possess a peculiar importance; in fact, Jesus possessed the power to intensify these spiritual yearnings
in the hearts of his disciples, and such intensification
would generally bring about frequent outburts of inner
anguish or audible weeping. Even today living adepts
possess the same power and usually apply a similar
method to hasten the progress of their disciples. Such
tears are therefore to be welcomed. Hence, it can truly
be said that those who mourn for their lost spiritual
homes are really blessed, for the grace of God has fallen
upon them.

But apart from that, it is worth noting that no one
finds the kingdom until after he has walked the path
of tears. I believe in tears. Weeping, like the proverbial

laughter, is good for the soul. Goethe was right, uncannily right, when he wrote:

"Who never spent the midnight hours
Weeping and waiting for the morrow,
He knows you not, ye heavenly powers."

Prolonged weeping provides us with initiation into wisdom. There is no doubt as to that. Tears of regret for past errors, tears of despair for coming calamities, tears of physical pain, tears at the sheer treachery of so-called friends, tears of parting from those who are loved,—let them all fall; they bring wisdom. Let them soak into our hearts and let us not despise them or try to force them back.

Jesus goes on to say:
"Blessed are the meek, for they shall inherit the earth."
I have frequently said before that the first step on this path, and equally the last, is humility. But that humility does not mean a feebleness which places you under the feet of other people; it does not mean a cringing attitude in the presence of other human beings; it does not mean a whining supplication for favours, as a beggar whines for alms at the street corner; and it certainly does not mean a cowardly fear of the world. All that is despicable. True humility means that you are humble towards the higher power of the Spirit, but towards nothing else. You have to be as submissive, as reverent, and as childlike as possible towards divinity; but towards the world at large, and towards humanity at large, you may be as strong and as bold and as self-reliant as you wish.

A certain temperament is required of you. It is the temperament which combines veneration with receptivity. The would-be disciple must approach the Overself in a spirit of humble readiness to learn. You must not come to impose your own personal ideas, or even to get them verified. For the time being you must suppress your own prejudices and surrender your own criticisms. To be truly humble is to have this sense of a higher existence calling to man; it is to sit like a child on the shore of the Infinite, filled with awe and wonder and worship. This is the meekness to which Jesus referred, and if you can attain it, then by a wonderful paradox the world becomes yours.

Yield yourself to that higher power which secretly governs the world, which holds this earth within its invisible grasp, prostrate yourself before it, and then there will be little on this earth which it cannot do for you.

You begin this path by cultivating an inward attitude of awe and veneration for your diviner being, by being inwardly meek; you finish it by becoming a channel of the cosmic power, i.e., you "inherit the earth," as Jesus puts it.

The Overself is the Power behind all power. When we find this one secret Power, we need seek no other. For all others are finite, but this is infinite. He who possesses such an inner strength, which makes him independent of environment, can find freedom in a prison cell. Thus arises the strange paradox that the reward of humility is power; power in the sense that you have found a state of being which is at the root of all existence, which is the ultimate creative cause of both material and mental conditions. You have found the secret source of all other powers.

There is only one Force in the universe, but it bifurcates itself, and then bifurcates itself again, and still again, and so on, until it shows itself in the form of many apparently different forces; but trace them back to their original source, and they are found finally to be one. People call this God, the Creator. It dwells hidden back of all other forces. When a man can humble himself sufficiently to acknowledge his spiritual ignorance, his emotional weaknesses, and his mental limitations, when he can do all this in the right spirit, he is making himself ready for the divine visitation.

You will consciously contact this power by becoming its instrument; you will intelligently cooperate with it. You cannot use the divine power, but it will use you. That power is able to manifest in every possible form and on every possible plane. Working through you, it makes you a conscious constructive part of the great elemental creation of Nature so that you no longer act by your own personal understanding and strength alone, but as its agent. You become literally conscious of this higher power acting through you, sensing a Force which is beyond and above that known by the vast majority of men. In the sequence you will see miracles happen before your eyes, whether they be material, mental, or spiritual, because that power has no limitations, no bounds.

When we understand the purpose of incarnation and the purpose of evolution, and when we work consciously with the higher power, we become co-agents in the great universal work which Nature is trying to accomplish. Then our own power becomes sublime and immense. That power becomes your reward when you permit it to work through you. No one can dictate to it. You must submit and surrender, and then let it work as it wishes.

§

"Blessed are they which do hunger and thirst after righteousness, for they shall be filled."

What does righteousness mean? It does not mean what our friends of the narrow world and narrow minds think. It has nothing to do with what the world thinks about you. The world is not competent to judge as to what constitutes righteousness, and what does not.

A thing is right when it is correct. The French language uses one and the same word to indicate either the quality of righteousness in a man or the quality of correctness in a measure. Both measure and man are right when they exist in truth. Hence, to hunger after righteousness really means to hunger after the adjustment of one's self to truth.

In this revolutionary age, when so many of us are tired of the old formulas and teachings worn threadbare, thoughtful persons subscribe to no special cult or creed or shibboleth, but want the Truth that transcends them all. This is the mysterious El Dorado which lies beyond the borders of common knowledge. It is a fabled land of which many have written, but at which few have arrived. Personally, I love the wisdom of antiquity. I am fascinated by the ancient religions, the ancient philosophies, the ancient literatures. But I deplore and deny them the moment someone tries to use them as chains to bind around my feet and mind. That is the paradox: loving the old, I must yet express the new. And there are many others who feel as I do, who seek to understand in a *modern* way why we are here and what is the purpose of life.

Righteousness means that you have aligned yourself with the purpose of your own incarnation, which is the realization of the truth behind it. If you hunger after that goal, if you feel consciously or unconsciously that you are here for a sacred purpose and that you want to fulfill that purpose, if you have the keen hunger, the intense aspiration to discover spiritual truth, cost what it may, then eventually you shall be given truth, or, as Jesus puts it, you shall be "filled" with truth.

This means that if you never give up your aspiration, if you take up the quest and persevere, year after year, until the very edge of the grave if need be, then you shall be filled, then your aspiration will ultimately be fulfilled. God has implanted this aspiration in your heart because it is His intention to see it fulfilled at the preordained hour; so you may have to wait. Meanwhile, never give up your aspiration, never give up this quest of the Overself, and you will eventually find that it has been worth the waiting. Whoever will pursue this path of introspective inquiry, whoever will have the courage to detach himself for a while from his personal woes and joys, such a one can verify for himself the truth of every one of Jesus' words. He can obtain the fullest demonstration and the clearest experience of their reality.

To hunger and to thirst, in Jesus' sense, is never to desert the quest, no matter what happens to you. "If the way which I have shown to lead hither seems very difficult, it can nevertheless be found. It must indeed be difficult since it is so seldom discovered. For if salvation lay ready to hand and could be discovered without great labour, how could it come about that it should be neglected almost by all?" said Spinoza.

We have much faith, but little faithfulness. Many men believe in an ideal but few follow it to the far end. Achievement only follows struggle. The discipline of life is ever present. Every man has a problem behind him. If life were smooth from year to year we would cease to evolve. The world represents opposition, waiting to be conquered. He who would achieve must overcome, and not yield.

How strong is your desire to know Truth? Truth is so subtle and elusive that unless you have that keen determination, that keen longing for it which persists year after year, you will never find it. No matter what happens, you must not let disappointments in life keep you from your quest, but you must continue your search, no matter what comes, and if you do that you will eventually attract that which you seek. However, you must seek truth for its sake alone. You must be prepared to avoid sidetracks. If you seek it expecting material benefits or psychic experiences, you are looking for that which is fleeting, and you will miss the truth.

Truth is the highest goal, because from that mountain peak you can see everything else *as it really is*. You can see that many stages which you have thought of as the goal, are nothing more than successive steps. It will show you how so many half-truths and quarter-truths and imitation truths have posed as whole truths. It will give you an understanding of the truth about yourself, about life, about the universe as a whole, which will eliminate all doubts.

You will never again have a single doubt about the fundamental basis of these mysteries. If you were to experience one doubt in the course of one year or even in the course of ten years, you could not have found spiritual truth. When you have found Truth, you will never know even the possibility of entertaining doubts or contradictions in your mind; you will feel absolute certitude, fixed and unalterable. Such is the nature of Ultimate Truth.

> "Who steers right on
> Will gain, at length, however far, the port."

The material world is the great lethal chamber of the soul. Only spiritual heroes can arouse themselves sufficiently to escape from its stupefying effect upon consciousness.

The mind of man has drunk the cup of Lethe and lost the bright memory of a diviner life, till all around him seems as unstable as foaming water and as forlorn as the sea at night. The agony of his starry loss presses upon his unconscious memory and drives him to seek satisfaction in religion, philosophy, mysticism, and other expressions of the abstract. It will resolutely pursue him to the end, hide where he will, flee where he likes. The more life darkens, the more imperative becomes the need of light. This is why there is a voice which affirms itself anew in every deeply thoughtful man, and which brightens his heart with a great hope; a voice that says he *himself* is deathless, whatever overtakes the body; that a Power which is ultimately benevolent sustains the mighty universe; and that unless his life takes this Power into the reckoning of all its thoughts and actions, he lives to little account.

From one end of the world to the other, from far-off Japan to familiar Europe, from the toiling factory workers to the leisured men of wealth, all peoples are consciously or subconsciously seeking this Truth today.

The veiled portals of the Infinite Truth stand before us all. Multitudes of men pass before them, stop for a moment, and gaze despairingly or cynically at them, and then pass on. A few—brave and venturesome spirits —whose tremendous hunger and thirst for truth impels and inspires them to step out of the conventional throng and dare to advance up those shining steps, ultimately find their reward. They disappear within those curtained doors, far beyond our ken, and return satisfied, "filled," and serene.

§

The fourth of Jesus' beatitudes is:

"Blessed are the merciful, for they shall obtain mercy."

How true, whether taken in the literal sense, or interpreted in its hidden significance! Whatever you give out in the world or to your fellows, will inexorably be reflected back to you. That is an iron cosmic law. The one who is cheating another, cheats himself. The man who is always cruel to others will one day find that others are cruel to him, and if retribution does not come in this birth, he will find it in the next. There is no evasion. Forbearance is paid back to us in forbearance. Similarly with mercy, with justice, with honesty, and with all the other human qualities; whatever you give out will sometime and somewhere be reflected back to you, not by any arbitrary force or deity, but by yourself—your own higher self which awards your good fortune and decrees your punishment—for no one else really does.

Destiny and justice are always on the job, and however long delayed the accounting be, it is nevertheless
inevitable. We may rise in battle against the notion of
a blind fatality pursuing us all our lives, but we must
yield in acquiescence to the notion of reaping that which
we sow.

Everything that we show forth returns to us; therefore we must be careful as to what we do to others, because the law of destiny is always at work, always send-
ing back what we send out, paying us in our own coin.

When you try to understand the inner significance
of this law, you will understand that it implies acceptance of the doctrine of reincarnation, which in its turn
compels you to accept the doctrine of the relativity of
morality. Human existence is a ladder stretching from
bestial ape to benign angel; each rung in the ladder is a
separate incarnation on earth. We learn slowly, painfully, as we climb higher. For the ultimate glorious goal
is unavoidable and must be achieved, even though a man's
own self-earned fate be used as an instrument to effect
this education and thus fulfil a higher purpose than his
own.

One implication of this doctrine is that it is not enough
to say "this thing is good, and that thing is evil, and I
shall take the side of good." Nobody knows what "good"
is, nor what "evil" is. Both these terms are wholly relative. Something might be good for you at one stage,
yet bad for you at another stage. What is "good" for
the primitive man is frequently "bad" for the civilized
man. The same ethical code which lifts the savage man
into advancement, and is therefore good and helpful to
his evolution, will later become for the evolved savage a
hindering, retrogressive, and evil code. The code has not
changed, but, at a higher stage, it handicaps him and
keeps him backward. We cannot label anything as good
or evil other than in relation to the particular circumstances of a particular person at a particular time. The

stamp of relativity is imprinted upon human life. So be tolerant towards others, as Jesus enjoined in this beatitude.

But before you can *really* be tolerant and merciful, you have to know just what is wise and what is foolish, what is right and what is wrong, what is duty and what is not, what is good and what is evil at any time and for any person, and to know that you have to know the whole universal plan; and you have to see just where everyone stands on the ladder of reincarnation in this amazing cosmic drama. You have to perceive the unseen, non-material currents which are working within the universe, and you have to know the beginning and the end of it all. When you know all this, you can truly practise mercy, then you can truly deal with the different events of your personal life, or of your national life, as they happen, without the illusion that there is a universal prescription which will suit everyone.

§

The fifth of Jesus' sayings is:
"Blessed are the pure in heart, for they shall see God."
It cannot be correctly understood if you do not know the spiritual significance of purity, and what the term "heart" really means. Purity must not be limited to the usual narrow connotation. It is immensely greater and grander than that. It means that you should be purified of the personal ego and of the personal desires— all those personal greeds, passions, and hatreds—which keep you chained to earth. When they attain any strength at all they keep you imprisoned.

There is a mystery hidden here. The divine atom of the Overself, the soul which links man to God, is hidden away in the human body on the right side of the physical heart. Everyone who aspires to "see God," as Jesus here calls it, must pass through an initiation, through an experience where his attention is drawn into the centre of his being, into the heart—in fact, where his consciousness is temporarily reduced to a pin point. If you could measure a pin point, you might know how subtle this experience is. When he has become almost as nothing, as a pin point existing in the centre of the heart, then and then only has he achieved the state of true purity.

Why? Because, before you can descend to this point, you must be willing to let go every desire, and every thought, and every idea which is likely to hold you back—which is likely to draw you back in consciousness to this material world. You must reach the point where you can regard your personal desires with the eyes of equanimity, even though you have not eliminated those desires.

So you see that the word "pure" in the eyes of an adept or of an avatar like Jesus, does not mean merely what the world usually associates with the word "pure." That is, it does not have any special reference to sex, as conventional usage has made it have. It has reference to *everything* that can be defined as personal.

The man who is unduly selfish, who is immured in greed, who is full of wild desires, cannot get this experience, for he is unable to give up the personal ego. Purity is a quality which comes by relinquishing the personal.

You have to release yourself first if you wish to pass your mind into the divine Overself-atom within the heart. This is accomplished during a profound stage of your meditation, when you have to bring the mental energy down into the breast, and pass it through this microscopic secret atom where your divine self resides. You cannot do that unless you can forget your proud personality for the time being, unless you can be ego-free and desire-free. It is only through such self-forgetfulness that you can achieve divine self-remembrance.

You must analyze life and practise discrimination. The thoughtless attachment to transitory external things constitutes your bondage, mistaking a thing for what it is not, living as though the personal ego were going to live for ever. One day death will come, and everything material will vanish. What, then, is the use of living only for transitory things? That is bondage. You must let them go if you want to penetrate into the tiny void of the Overself within the human heart. To be pure means that you become empty, empty of everything personal, so that you can pass through this tiny portal of the sacred heart-atom, which is the narrow gate that Jesus speaks of elsewhere. If you cannot free yourself, then you cannot pass through the gate and see God. To see God you must find the God *in you*, the Overself in your heart, because it is impossible to see That without becoming It. There is no duality in divinity; you can see God only by uniting with Him, and this you can do only after letting go of everything that keeps you from such unification.

A man can see only a reflection of his face; he can perceive a mirrored image of it, but never the real face. He is that face, and if he tries to see it, he can see only a picture of it. Similarly, we have God within us as our deepest self, and if we wish to see it we shall see only a mental picture in vision, never the real Divine Soul itself. This vision would stand outside the inner self, although remaining inside the mind, as something apart. But although you cannot truly see the Overself, you may truly *become* it. Hence your first sight of God will be when you feel that you *are* the ray of God in your own heart.

§

Jesus says next:
"Blessed are the peacemakers, for they shall be called the children of God."
Who are the peacemakers? They are those advanced souls who have reached a certain point in their inner

evolution. By constant aspiration, by frequent meditation, by constant reflection on the purpose of their incarnation, they have reached the point of comparative
mental quietude and control. Their dominant ruling
principle is not greed or hatred or passion, but a higher
quality. They live more from within than from without.
Thus they have found peace for themselves and automatically transmit it to others.

This quest may not bring you happiness in the orthodox sense, usually understood as the fulfillment of wants,
but it will certainly bring you inner peace, the starry
solvent of all woes. Those who are disturbed by strong
desires for anything have not yet found peace. Happiness means different things to different people. Its definition depends upon what they need, what they lack most
in life. Usually the provision of that lack constitutes
their idea of happiness.

We forget, however, that such fulfillment may not endure; it may go again. Wealth has frequently taken to
wings, as the history of the past generation shows, and
romance often comes to birth only to be entombed later.
Fortune is a fickle jade, whilst even regal lives have
flitted out of existence like particles of dust.

There is, however, such a condition as coming into
tune with the Infinite, which you can always rely upon
as producing an inner sense of utter satisfaction, of lacking nothing, of perfect contentment. Your desires have
come to rest in the Overself, like tired children nestling
in their mother's arms. They do not trouble you, simply
because there is so much inner peace that they fall back
baffled and quieted. How can they move when all within
is motionless, how aggravate when all is sublime stillness? How restful and how happy to be free from the
torments of desire! Just to abide in quietude! No matter
where you are, to be free of restless desires, to be ever
at ease! Here is a calm that is unbroken and eternal, and
not dependent upon the state of your finances or on the

state of the world peace, but only on the eternal reality which is ever-present within yourself. This is true peace. The desire for constant excitement disappears from a man into whom the quietude of the soul has entered.

I have more faith in a philosophy which gives a man peace, which makes him laugh at the things he once thought vital to his existence, than in one which teaches him to call small desires great ambitions. The first has some fun in it, is full of a true sense of proportion, but the second is dark and drear. This rich repose is the only thing which cannot disappear again, once it is won. It is worth more than conventional happiness, for you can keep it with you no matter what be the external condition of your life. Clothed in a beggar's shabby rags, or wearing a princess's gorgeous gown, the peace remains unbroken. It will be the basic fact in your life.

You will not be wholly dependent upon circumstances or externals for your inmost satisfaction. You will find that entirely within yourself, and having found it you can carry it to outer things. You can rule them. If pleasant things come your way, you can still enjoy them; if they do not and troubles arrive instead, the peace will not be lost.

You will feel that there is a stable state amidst the bewildering changes of our epoch. True inner peace is something that is not going to be rudely disturbed some day; it is an attainment on which you can rely for ever and ever and ever.

Do not imagine that the attainment of spiritual peace is *only* to be found in the mystic trance or the yogic meditation. On the contrary, you will find it everywhere and anywhere after you have really finished this quest. Trance is merely a *stage* on the path to the Overself. It is not the Overself itself. Several mystics, yogis, and aspirants who have reached an advanced state, reach what we might term the penultimate plane where they have extraordinary ecstasies, great inner bliss. In that

state, which they believe to be God, which they believe
to be the highest, they think they have found the Overself. They have certainly come close to it, but they have
not found it. If they stop there, they are still in the
world of illusion. True, it is the most exalted illusion possible, but it is still illusion—using the word "illusion" to
indicate that which is temporary and which is an appearance. They must go further. They must go further
because ecstatic bliss begins and ends. The extraordinary
bliss of that state cannot endure. It must come to an end,
and then it may be followed by that sad reaction, the
so-called "dark night of the soul." All ecstasies must
ultimately die. But if they can seek further and deeper—
and that can only be done through the help of a competent guide—then they can find a peace which is unbroken and unbreakable.

From that peace there is no return, no lapse, and
when you have once found that reward, you will carry
it with you wherever you go. You will never lose this
marvellous calmness, whether you are working hard in
an office, facing fire on a battlefield, going to your death
on a sinking ship, or accepting the enthusiastic plaudits
of a crowd; whether you are a king whose throne has
tottered and fallen, or whether you are a commoner who
has suddenly been raised to the throne of a king. Your
hold on it will not weaken under any circumstance. That
is the kind of calm you have to find. The goal of this
quest is not accompanied by tremendous bliss, but it is
accompanied by tremendous peace. Mystic ecstasies are
indeed sweet on the way and give you encouragement,
but you must not dally and try to eat sweets all the
time. The elations of the mystic must pass, the ecstasies
of the artist must vanish, then the calm composure of the
sage will remain.

Neither meditation alone, nor trance alone, nor mysticism alone can confer the possession of this real peace.
You must come out of all three eventually, and when

you come out there is your fleeting visible universe confronting you once again and demanding your participation. Whoever has mastered the seventh stage of the quest can pass into profound self-trance at will, if he pleases, but that means less to him than the capacity to act in the material world as others do, whilst still being fully conscious of the hidden spiritual peace.

You will cease to trouble unduly about the opinions and criticisms of other people when you become conscious of the value of yourself. You will no longer permit yourself to be irritated or hurt by unpleasant persons when you find yourself clothed in an armour of sublime independence. In short, true peace will make you free.

You have your realization of harmony even when people say you are a fool or speak badly of you. You may even be fulsomely flattered, but this will make no difference. If people want to flatter you, they may, but you remain inwardly indifferent. The moment you accept flattery, you must also accept criticism. No matter what is said about you, whether it be praise or pillory, you will not accept it. You must let the past go and let it take care of itself whilst you live on the pin point of a moment. Live there for ever and ever and ever, then you will have true peace. So let the past go. What is it now but a memory, and what is that but a thought, an idea? It has no enduring reality. Your future is still only a thought; therefore it, too, has no reality. Let it take care of itself. What about the present? The present seems real. We cannot deny that. But let us advance the calendar until tomorrow. Tomorrow you may think of this moment, this present moment—what will your thought be then? It will be nothing more than a memory, an idea, and will then have the same value as all your other thoughts.

Hence this present reality is still only an idea. So the life you are living now is only a mental one, not material.

If I tell you that the world is only an idea in your mind, it includes also that world in which you live at this moment. So it is true wisdom to live in the present as though it were the eternal. Live in the eternal Now; live on the pin point of a moment. And what is that? A pin point has no measurable value, because the point fades off somewhere and disappears. It means that you live in the empty ground of your innermost being, where all is void. That is your real home and you should live there, yet you may send the frontal part of your attention to engage itself with the world. You just send a messenger, a part of your mind, and that deals with the outer world. But *you* still remain in that inner timeless void. Having attained this peace, you are utterly unconcerned, detached.

You can do this only after a course in the successful practice of yoga, because yoga is the emptying of the mind of all things, i.e., the creation of a mental void. When you have found the void, then you must hold on to it, even when you deal with worldly affairs. Even though an actor lives another personality on the stage, somewhere at the back of his mind he is always conscious of who and what he is. Similarly, you have to act your part in life as the personal self, but at the back of your consciousness remember who and what you are. Thus you attain to peace. In your innermost being hold firmly to this void state and let the personal ego live on as something that is but a part of you. Always remember that it is not the essential *you*. Always, in the back of your mind, remember that.

Rest in that inner void, and whatever you have to do will be done just the same. But it will be done spontaneously through you, and there will not be the belief that you as the personal self are responsible for doing it. It is just the current of life which is carrying you along. If you have to kill a man impersonally as a soldier defending your country, you will just do it. No evil destiny will be made, because no destiny can enter the void. You will have perpetual peace, because there is nothing to trouble you in the void. People who believe that they have to carry all the burden of their personal lives cannot find peace. If, however, they could understand that back of the mind there is the great stillness of the Witness-Self, and if they try to find it, and do find it, then they would know what it means to be inwardly calm whilst outwardly active in the world, and yet not of it. I know of no more important boon than this—the attainment of true felicity. If few attain this seraphic state, it is because most do not seek for it.

Jesus called those who possessed this attainment "the peacemakers" because they have established their self-harmony and made peace with themselves, for there is no inner conflict within their hearts any more, and the everlasting tension of a life divided against itself has ceased. And, of course, Jesus alluded also to the fact that, naturally, they carry that peace to others. This has nothing to do with patching up the quarrels of other people. Jesus did not mean that, because it is merely one of the by-products of inner peace. He had another and profounder reason for calling them peacemakers. The void within the divine atom of the heart is literally filled with stillness, utter peace. This hidden threshold of the Overself reveals itself by the extraordinary quietude which the mind feels when approaching it during meditation.

"They shall be called the children of God," continued Jesus.

The Father is the Overself, and all those who have entered into communion with it, those over whom the Overself is throwing its mystic light, and who are reflecting this light, little by little, through their lives, are its children. This relationship is not something which applies to today but not to tomorrow. It is a constant realization because it is eternal. One such child of God was Brother Lawrence, who lived as a monk and worked in the monastery kitchen. He never lost the sense of the divine Presence. He did not have to pray or to meditate for it. It was always there even amidst his labours. He explained that in that Presence there was settled unbroken peace. "The time of happiness does not differ with me. From the time of prayer, and in the noise and clutter of my kitchen I possess God in as great tranquillity as if I were on my knees," he said.

§

"Blessed are they which are persecuted for righteousness' sake: for theirs is the kingdom of heaven. Blessed are ye, when men shall revile you, and persecute you, and shall say all manner of evil against you falsely, for my sake."

Here again, I have combined these two sentences into a single verse, because they are so closely related to each other. Thus we arrive at the seventh and final beatitude. There is a profound reason why Jesus placed this particular thought as the final one. In the mysterious mathematics which governs the cosmos the number seven is the number of evolutionary culmination, the number of spiritual completion. It will be noticed that both in the opening and the final beatitudes, Jesus mentions the kingdom of heaven, which is the eternal reality. He who has attained this divine Consciousness thereafter identifies his own interests with those of The All. The welfare of all living creatures is close to his own heart. The subtle unity of life behind the myriads of individual lives is known to him by personal realization. Hence his own attitude towards everyone is that of perfect sympathy. To this rule he can make no exception. Just as the sun shines upon the good and evil alike, so does the man whose heart dwells in the kingdom of heaven radiate his own light upon the good and evil equally. That is, he exists within the element of divine love.

Thus, it is not until your own life becomes divine that you discover the divinity behind the lives of others.

When you realize Truth—when you discover the Universal Self, or the Overself, when you realize and know it truly, then you will discover that there is only One Self, One Being—then you will know the real meaning of love. You will have a tolerance and sympathy that "passeth all understanding."

Love that comes from understanding is the highest expression of love, and is not based on mere emotion or sentiment. Love based on understanding is the ability to put yourself into harmony with every creature, to know how all think and feel, and to do it with complete sympathy. Out of love's reservoir of wisdom you think and act in perfect harmony with all living creatures.

Love is a much-abused word, but I use it in the best possible sense, which means simply this: that you will experience harmony with the entire universe, with all living beings, with all manifested creatures. You will love them all because you have found within them the same divine essence that is in yourself. They all spring from the same root, and that root is the one Overself. They are humanly kindred and divinely related to you; through the Overself you can understand them perfectly and sympathize with them perfectly. There is really only one Overself, and in finding it you find the Overself of the other person, and when you find that, you automatically enter into perfect harmony with the other person, *whether that person knows it or not.* Hence you will both give love and receive it. You manifest towards that person an attitude which is identical with the feeling that you manifest towards your own personality. There will be complete and perfect harmony with all persons in the sense that others are not basically different from yourself.

This is the seventh fruit of attainment. Real love exists when there is true inward identification with the life of another entity. You will inevitably make the interests of all beings as dear to you as your own. A great compassion for suffering, ignorant mankind will arise within you. The welfare of all creatures will be yours. No narrow nationalism can circumscribe the love for his fellow which an adept feels. The wide world is his home. Moreover, you will also receive love—not from all, although you give it to all, but from some who are sensitive enough to discern your unvarying inner attitude towards them—though they be only a few. But you will certainly receive it from all in one sense, because all are seeking for this divine life, whether they know it or not. In seeking it they must necessarily and inevitably love you, however unconsciously, if you have found it, because you automatically make available to them a pathway to that which they seek. You need make no outward effort to help them. Your mere presence will suffice, because you are an outlet from the world of the Infinite to your finite fellows. If they are seeking consciously then they will understand better, and maybe love you consciously.

But why did Jesus warn his disciples to expect persecution? Why did he, on another occasion, send forth his twelve apostles into the world with the strong warning: "Behold, I send you forth as sheep in the midst of wolves: be ye therefore wise as serpents, and harmless as doves." The wandering Galilean teacher plainly meant that it is not enough to be good only, not enough to be harmless only. You have also to be as shrewd as one of the shrewdest of creatures, the snake.

Why?

Because this entire world, this vast universe, and the panorama of life which moves across its face is the interplay of two cosmic forces, involution and evolution, creation and destruction, so-called good and so-called evil. Out of the hazy atmosphere of cosmic beginning rises the endless procession of these twin powers. They are always at work and will be till the universe disappears. You must perceive how, by this strife, this constant interplay and inevitable conflict, this bewildering conflict of forces, the wonderful current of life flows through the most variegated scenery, and thus receives the richest experiences. Thus man is *made*, his character is formed by his struggles with the adverse element in Nature, and opposition is ultimately turned into opportunity. His recreant steps will finally bring him to the divine goal. Thus history is converted into something more than a mere string of isolated events, more than a fortuitous chain of happenings, and more than a dismal catalogue of ruined empires.

Now we are better prepared to grasp why Jesus warned his apostles to expect trouble. The adverse element in Nature exists either to destroy the handiwork of divinely constructive minds, or to oppose the light-bearing of divinely guided ones. No true prophet, no true apostle of Divinity, ventures forth into the world and carries through a sacred mission of spiritual help and spiritual service without arousing the hostility and antagonism of these dark forces. The latter find blind and unconscious human instruments through whom they may thwart the unselfish activities of illumined men. Not infrequently such misguided enemies are aroused to criticism, falsehood, slander, malice, hatred, and finally to acts of personal violence, such as was evidenced in Jesus' own crucifixion.

Not that Jesus feared death. The man who knows the truth about life does not deeply care whether he dies or lives, because he does not identify himself with the body. Death to him means no more than birth. The one life is eternal. It has never been born and can never die. It will go on and on and on. Realizing this infinite peace, why should the knower of Truth unduly cherish the body? He is quite prepared to part with it at any time, for death has lost its terror.

The long line of mystics who have been martyred, and of prophets who have been punished because they dared to speak the astounding truth from their hearts, explains itself. The highest truth dissolves the power of creeds and destroys the arrangements of castes; it comes to deliver men and to unfasten their self-forged chains. Why wonder, then, that the worldly-minded ones, who hold entrenched places, fear the divine voices and seek to still them?

No man who dares to promulgate a message received from a higher source, who dares to express a vision not of this world, can make these known without having to suffer a host of criticisms, a vast number of misunderstandings, the sharp arrows of the envious, and the bitter falsehoods of enemies. But, if he is sincere, he will have emerged for the sake of a few from the calm, cloistered retreats which are ever open to him. They will be ready to receive gratefully, understandingly, and sympathetically what he brings to them. It is for their sakes that he endures the wounds and hurts which are caused him by the others. He attempts to make no converts. He emerges to acquaint people with certain facts, not to convert them. For

> "A man convinced against his will
> Is of the same opinion still."

But we are in the midst of world-throbbing events. The despairing cries of millions of men and women, the agonized questioning of thousands of perplexed but sincere souls—rise to the high places and call tumultuously at the very gates of Olympus. Up from this blood-stained planet rises a red cloud which reaches the eyes of the gods; it moves to the accompaniment of never-ceasing cries, which likewise reach Olympus.

The Buddha is depicted on all statuettes with long drooping ears because, as a god in human form, he possessed the superhuman sense which heard all the uttered agonies of mankind. And so we need not be surprised if lesser beings than Buddha hear the world's cry and come among us to bring their peace and truth and love in response.

Those are the seven rewards which we may hope to

find when we finish the quest. But remember, it is really all one reward, one divine state of being. The intellect examining it, analyzing it, criticizing it, cutting it up, produces these seven aspects. There is essentially this one state, and always, spontaneously, it meets whatever is demanded of it by every circumstance. It cannot cut itself up; it is all-comprehensive.

After all, words are merely labels and names. There is only one ultimate Consciousness to be found, and the variety of names makes no actual difference to it. What the scientist calls the Unknown Reality, what the Buddhist calls Nirvana, what the Hindu calls Liberation, what Jesus called the Kingdom of Heaven, what the yogi calls One-Pointedness, what the mystic calls Union with God, and what the sage calls Self-knowledge, are all precisely the same, i.e., clear and conscious realization of what you really are. This brings with it the fulfillment of your purpose here on earth in every way, physically, mentally, and spiritually. It is transcendental being, a life above that of matter and mind. If we find this higher life—and really there is no "if" about it, because there is no escape; it is the only final destiny open to man, even though Nature is patient and will wait millions of years for its accomplishment if necessary—when we find it, we shall gain the beautiful condition described by the Master, Jesus, in the simple, finely-phrased beatitudes.

What useless cargoes of words our books carry! What is all our intellectual accomplishment in comparison with this spiritual realization? The belauded literati of both hemispheres appear as pygmies in the parade of life alongside those divine men who have found themselves. H. G. Wells has somewhere said that the great and universal truths were so few that they could be written on a post card. If any man was ever able to condense them into such small space, it was Jesus.

CHAPTER VI

PRACTICAL HELP IN YOGA

MEDITATION in ancient days was practised as a vital part of daily living. In most ancient cultures it began with the early-morning worship of the sun. The sun was but the symbol of that Great Light which man hoped to find within himself. After seeing the visible sun he would close his eyes and search for the inner Sun, for the inner Light of the Overself. The practice was a necessity of life in those days, and it is still a necessity.

Because we have forgotten to look inwards for the illumination that is there, we are dismally ignorant, lost in spiritual darkness. We run hither and thither, but where do we arrive? Consider the ever-increasing hurry and distraction of modern life. God is not so much denied as merely crowded out. Just as when Christ came on the first Christmas Day there was no room for him in the inn, so now there seems little room for him in the noise and bustle of the hostelry of modern life.

In fact, those raucous voices which we hear in the world today, those terrible voices of blind passion and cruel hatred, of irritability, strife, and misunderstanding, are the voices of men who have never turned inwards, who have lost understanding of their relationship with the divine soul. The only radical cure for this outer noise is to find inner silence. And once people learn how to find the inner peace, we shall surely have outward peace and eliminate senseless wars. It will come as a perfect and natural result, and it is the only way in which we shall ever find peace. The dreams men have of lasting external peace will never materialize until they find it within themselves. It is human nature in its degenerated state that creates wars. No piece of paper called a treaty will ever heal the world of war.

Meditation, the art of mental quiet—yoga, as the Indians call it—is perhaps the fundamental practice of this inner quest. It is essential to whoever seeks to find his spiritual self. The basic principle behind it is simply this: throughout the day we are so busy attending to external things and external activities that we never become aware of *who* it is that is attending to these manifold activities. We just become so immersed in them that we do not even try to know who is being immersed.

Meditation has as its primary aim the detachment of this entity or person who is acting, working, walking, moving, from the activities themselves, so that he might get a chance to be truly *conscious*, to know himself. Hence, the fundamental method of meditation is to direct attention deliberately away from these outward activities and to turn inwards in opposition.

Whether in work or at pleasure, we are constantly engaged in external activity. And by external I mean even mental activity, which although in appearance internal, is still external, because the working of the intellect is something which the being, or the true person, must regard as external to himself. In other words, *he* who thinks and he who acts is neither thought nor activity.

Therefore, if you wish to find this innermost being within you, you not only have to turn attention inwards towards the mind, away from action, but you must penetrate still further inwards away from intellect itself towards that which is *behind*. Unless we grasp the vital necessity for the practice of meditation, and attempt to do this, how can we ever hope to free ourselves from the surface life that enslaves us?

Many persons have misconceptions about yoga and meditation. They think that the practice of meditation is necessarily going to lead to marvellous supernatural experiences. Well, it may or it may not. They think it is going to develop occult powers. It may do that, and it may not. They also think that you have to undergo the most ascetic regimes of self-discipline in order to make meditation successful.

We who live in the Western world of Europe and America have neither the leisure nor the opportunity, and frequently not even the will, to practise such meditation for those protracted periods of time which the Indian yogis and medieval Christian mystics have given it. The arrangements of modern society permit us to have a very small amount of leisure time, and so it behooves us to make the best possible use of the short period which is available.

It is not necessary to spend the whole of one's day in mental quiet in order to find the spiritual self. From what I have seen during my frequent travels in the Orient, it is not even advisable, because prolonged meditation involves the hardest feat any man could accomplish. The immense strain of the effort to carry it on throughout the day is too much for most men, with the result that many among those who do attempt it, drift into laziness, selfishness, or hypocrisy. It is better to devote a short period every day, and to make that period *vital*, to render it really significant, and then to stop and get up from your meditation, than to become a drifter.

Many complain of lack of time. "I should like very much to practise meditation," they plead, "but really I haven't much time." After a close cross-examination we usually find that they are so busily occupied doing this and that, that they have no time to do the one thing that matters. The petty, the trivial, the frivolous claim their attention. They dare not sacrifice a moment from their round of games when the greatest game of all—life—is still waiting to be played. First things first. They lack time to come to themselves, yet they always manage to find time for whatever else they regard as necessary. They do not realize that a more necessary task than self-knowledge cannot be discovered.

If you cannot find the time for the divine, how can the divine find the time for you? The man who forsakes all thought of God throughout the day, ought not to complain when the time comes that he appears to be utterly forsaken by God.

Everybody has time for the things which he values most, and if you value mental quiet sufficiently you will find the time. It does not matter very much whether it is the morning, afternoon, or night. And it does not matter very much how short a time you give it, although perhaps a period of twenty minutes would really be the most practical minimum, merely because it takes so many minutes to get started, to get going, before you can enter the practice proper. Surely twenty minutes is not too long a period to ask from anyone.

But even if you did not have that—and I can hardly imagine any human being who is in such an unfortunate situation—then twelve minutes would matter profoundly, if you sat down and said to yourself: "During this brief interval I shall blot out everything. I shall forget my personal life utterly, and I shall turn inwards and seek that release which is to be found within." If you did that with sufficient intensity and the utmost determination each time, eventually you could not fail to find something worth while.

We do not grasp the tremendous value of physical existence or the importance of a wise use of our time. Heaven can be entered after death only if we have already entered it while alive. This is the value of life in the flesh; there is no other worth-while value that I know.

We must endeavour to find some fair proportion between activity and repose or we lose the only real good which life has to offer us. It is true that we rarely find ourselves in a position where we can indulge in the luxury of leisurely reverie. For this we are not to blame our stars, our environment, or our friends. We accept without question the society in which we are born; we submit freely when it impounds and imprisons us. To obtain a recognized place in society, be it that of commoner or king, we have perforce to pay the price of freedom. Those alone who are prepared to disregard the claims of ambition and the criticisms of society at the bidding of the true self, are entitled to time for reverie. And the gods so ordain matters that they get it.

There is really no restriction as to a suitable time or place to commence this practice. Begin it at once wherever you are, do it according to the rules prescribed, and try to dive deep into the Self.

§

Although it does not greatly matter which time of day or night you do begin this practice, still, if you have a choice, then it is better to choose one of three periods:

There is an advantage in practising in the morning, because the mind is freer, less burdened, and fresher. Moreover, if you succeed in breaking through the crust of personal and physical existence during the meditation, you will find something of that peace and stillness which envelops the deeper self. Then when you take up your day's activity, you will find that stillness and peace still persist as a definite echo, still linger with you as a sort of heavenly afterglow, so that you carry on your work in the midst of that beautiful presence. This is the particular advantage of practising in the morning.

Moreover, the period succeeding dawn is a period of great stillness in external Nature, and for those who seek the internal stillness of the Soul, it is consequently easier to practise more successfully then. The mind, at the moment of awakening, is like a delicate thread tied to the spiritual self. Therefore, the first activity of the day becomes of much importance. Let it then be nothing else but your effort to get in touch with this spiritual nature, for at this moment the effort will meet with least resistance. Do nothing else; do not attempt to dress even, for that will send the mind out of its naturally concentrated condition and set it jumping about like a monkey from thought to thought.

The second time which is helpful for seekers, is the mysterious hour of twilight or sundown, for the reason that Nature again experiences a hush, a pause in her external activity, during the union of day with night.

The third time, not so good as the previous two, is that of noon. At high noon we have the possibility for a few minutes of contacting the spiritual self again a little more easily than otherwise. The reason lies in a mysterious connection between the sun and the spiritual life of this planet.

But if your life is so arranged that dawn, sunset, and noon are not available for practice, then it does not matter. Find a few minutes any time of the day when you will be alone, quiet and undisturbed, and begin your attempt to put your mind in tune with the Infinite. It is advisable, if you can, to find an environment that will help and not hinder your practice. Such an environment would be one where Nature is beautiful, quiet, tranquil, where the climate is not too trying, because extremes of both heat and cold hinder the mind's effort.

After you have set aside a certain time every day, it is advisable to keep to that time. You will then automatically begin to meditate at that particular hour of the day. If you can do this, if you can stick to this regular time, do it; it will be helpful to you, it will eventually make meditation easier.

It is useful to keep one room reserved, or even the

corner of a room, no matter how small it be, as the place where you will regularly practise your meditation. If you can do that you will build up an invisible but real mental atmosphere within its walls. Every time you enter that room your mind will automatically revert to the tendency to turn back on itself. The room becomes your shrine, as it were. Every entrance raises your mental vibration without any conscious effort on your part.

It is important that you should not be disturbed during your meditation, hence you ought always to lock the door. You must bid farewell to the outer world for the period of your withdrawal; and again you must bid farewell to your own personal life with it. Try to let go of your particular burdens, your domestic cares, your business anxieties, your ambitions, hopes, and personal pleasures just for that period. Calm yourself and dismiss all thoughts about the family, surroundings, and worldly affairs, however exigent and necessary they may appear to be. Forget all the ties which link you to external activity. Now draw the blinds, or close the window shutters. Keep out the light, as the glare of light pressing upon the eyes will tend to distract you back to physical things.

If you cannot have a private room where you can lock yourself in and meditate, then meditate anywhere. You need not make an outward demonstration of it; you can sometimes meditate walking in the street. In fact, when you do become more familiar with meditation you should learn to practise not only at fixed and set periods during the day, but at odd times also, so that you can utilize those occasional scraps of time when there is nothing to do. You may be waiting somewhere to keep an appointment, or travelling at leisure in a train; use a few minutes out of those periods. Let your mind revert to the quest, but do it without making a fussy external demonstration. Don't let people know what you are doing; let it be your own secret.

Next, find the sitting posture which is most comfortable to you. If possible, sit facing north because the north aspect is best for all worship where the object is to *absorb* power, whilst the east aspect is best for worship to *give* power or adoration. Don't worry about adopting an Indian yoga posture. If you have experimented with such positions and find one that is easy, then use it, by all means. It will be helpful. If you have not found the folded-leg, squatting position difficult, there certainly is an advantage in its use. It will relax the whole body; it will diminish the flow of blood into the lower extremities, and it will help you to achieve what meditation is intended to achieve, because of its power to soothe the nerves.

Such postures, however, were particularly practised by the Orientals because chairs were seldom used in ancient times in the Orient, and the East, being so conservative, still follows the old custom. The cross-legged posture is the perfectly natural one in which to sit down, but we Westerners are unaccustomed to it.

It is difficult for Western people to adopt yoga postures, and it is not necessary. What is important is that you should sit down in such a position during the period of mental quiet that you can forget you have a physical body. If you sit in an awkward and uncomfortable position, then the body will constantly remind you of its presence, and that will draw your mind back into the external world again and thus defeat the purpose of meditation. So adopt whatever position is easy and comfortable, whether it is squatting or sitting on couch, chair, or floor.

Next, close your eyes, and close your mind to every impression from the five senses. As the slowing down of breath has a profound effect on the mind, so the very attitude of calm, unhurried preparation for meditation is a good aid to success. It creates the right initial atmosphere for real meditation.

§

Of what are you to think? Although there are so many different subjects which you might use during meditation, the first effort is primarily concerned with the development of concentration. This implies the ability to bring your mind to a one-pointed condition, thereby controlling all thoughts so that you can make them walk along a single track. This is the first stage. For the purpose of concentration it does not matter whether you do that by thinking of worldly things or of spiritual things, but since you are endeavouring to contact your inner spiritual being it is preferable that you concentrate upon some elevating topic, something that is going to carry you away from the outer world, some ideal or idea which will lift you into abstract realms.

There are different methods of meditation because we are all built in different ways. We have different temperaments, different mental make-ups, and different physical make-ups, and so we have to find the way that suits us best, the one which will offer the least resistance. It is not necessary to take some way which is alien to our temperament. If we do, we will not succeed. If you feel that by prayer or by aspiration, rather than by intellectual analysis, you can make better progress, then use that way. After all, remember what meditation is. It is not some magical hocus-pocus. It is simply a device to enable you to shut down the conscious mind—that part of your mind which is forever engaged in paying attention to the external world, and dealing with your wants and your pleasures. That is the part of the mind which is working with the five senses and which is constantly being chopped up into thoughts; that is the mind which keeps you enslaved to the notion that the material world is the only real world because you pay attention wholly to the outer world and the five senses. Meditation is anything that will enable you to obtain release from this bondage.

The artist who is absorbed in his playing of an instrument is meditating, because he has become so lost in the music that he has forgotten the outer world. This beautiful state has brought him to the inner world. It is not the final state, but it has brought him away from the material world. He has turned his mind inwards, although he has still to go deeper.

Anybody who engages in some profound reverie, no matter upon what topic, whether a worldly or spiritual one, is practising meditation, just as much as any yogi has ever done it beside the River Ganges. We must not delude ourselves. Many American and European business or professional men already practise meditation and yoga, but they do not know it. The difficulty is that they meditate upon their business affairs alone; they do not escape from the *purely personal*. If they used the power of concentration to turn away from their personal affairs, they might meditate quite successfully and find their way into the realm of spirit.

All the world loves laughter. It pays its comedians more than it pays its scientists. The instinct is right enough, for it is the instinct of escape from personal burdens. The method of meditation proposed here is simply another form of escape.

I have given in my little book, *The Secret Path*, an exercise on one such idea, a question, "Who am I?" You can speculate upon that theme and you can try to find the answer to it, if you wish. I suggest it merely because that is part of the most direct of all methods of spiritual self-knowledge, whereas other lines of concentration take only a circuitous or semicircular route towards this goal. They work indirectly and may embrace both material and religious objects and yet ignore the Self. Here, however, whilst you are trying to develop your concentrative power, you combine that very effort with the endeavour to come closer to your spiritual self.

The chief aim, anyway, in this early stage is to control

thought, to bring the mind under control; so after you have chosen your topic, you must try not to let the mind stray from it. The mind is a rebel, as you will surely find out. The great difficulty which confronts the beginner in the art of mental quiet is that of controlling the multitude of thoughts which ceaselessly flock into his mind. This difficulty is the eternal complaint that has been made since ancient times. Try as you will, the most extraneous and irrelevant thoughts persist in pressing in upon you whenever you sit down to quiet the mind.

When the mind strays away, as it will do so many times at first, then bring it forcibly back to your subject. The moment you find that your attention has gone elsewhere, wandering away from the path you have set for it, make it return. It does not matter that your thoughts have strayed away, because that is due to the inherent and natural restlessness of the mind, but what does matter is that you should recollect them as soon as you discover the change, and again think of the subject you originally set for yourself.

Ultimately, after much practice and many repetitions of this exercise, the mind tires of its rebellion; it tires of wandering away, only to be mercilessly driven back again; it yields and stays just where you put it.

This is the achievement of concentration, this holding of your mind on one series of points, on one track, and keeping it there. Success demands mental abstraction, the ability to forget your environment and to become withdrawn into your thoughts, so that for the time being you are living entirely in them. You will forget at times that there is a room all around you! You will become oblivious at times of the world outside. You know only that these thoughts exist in which you are immersed, and they are the only things that matter to you during this period of meditation. If you can do that, then you have mastered concentration.

It demands an intensity of purpose which is, frankly,

not at all common. If you have not sufficient intensity, then you must seek to develop it by continuous effort, by repeating this exercise day after day, week after week, and month after month, until it becomes easier. Even so, many people have been known to try it for years and still success evades them; still they cannot break this wandering tendency of the intellect. Abstract mental concentration is one of the most arduous feats of all.

If you find it so difficult that after many repeated efforts concentration remains impossible, then what are you to do? Well, you might try focussing attention upon a purely physical object. That will be easier for some people. Instead of taking an idea or an abstract theme, take a concrete tangible object. This means that you will have to keep your eyes open instead of closed, and you will have to gaze continuously upon it. It is not advisable to adopt that practice, however, unless every other attempt is a failure. Generally, visual exercises should be used only after you have mastered thoughts. They ought to come at that stage only, but if you find that you cannot succeed otherwise, then you can take up this practice in order to gain mastery over the mind.

It does not matter what you use as an object in this elementary stage, but it would matter very much if you were at the advanced stage. It does not matter whether you take a carved image of Jesus, a garden flower, or a shining door handle. Once you have selected an object, then you must concentrate fully on that, and on nothing else. Do not let your mind wander into thoughts about its qualities. You must not let your gaze be diverted from it. If you do, what happens is that, by reflex action, the mind becomes fixed upon the very object upon which you are fixing your gaze,—the mind itself will be focussed on it, as it were. Repeat this process sufficiently often and the wandering intellect will become habituated to this concentration upon an object and thus be brought to heel in that way.

Whatever it is, select one thing alone. Do not attempt to concentrate upon a multiplicity of objects. Remember, however, that the gazing practice is not helpful to all of us, and you have to find out by experiment whether it is necessary for you individually.

Remember always, the actual object of concentration is of less importance than the degree of attention and interest we bring to it. Thus, I have frequently found a suitable object in listening intently to the smooth chugging of wheels while travelling in an electric railroad train, the rhythmic vibration and repeated hum of the onward-rushing, comfortably-sprung train, inducing a sense of rest which, when carefully nurtured, soon develops into a deep peace, a lulled reverie which slips insensibly into a meditative condition.

Another physical practice which can be a distinct help to the development of concentration is that of breath control. You can try this as a preface to meditation: Watch your breath movement intently for a few minutes. Slow it down to about half your normal cycle—not all at once, but little by little, reducing the time with every succeeding exercise. You arrive eventually at about half the usual rate of the complete breath-cycle. That implies, for instance, seven in-breathings instead of fourteen, and seven out-breathings instead of fourteen. But in between the two movements, the inhalation and exhalation, just gently check your breath—hold it for a second or two, but not for longer. And during that brief interval, during those few seconds when you hold the breath, the mind will be held too. It will be held in suspension, as if it were fastened upon the breathing which it is watching, and that produces a state of inward concentration; then the mind will be successfully concentrated.

The fakirs in the Orient, under the name of yoga, often practise all sorts of physical contortions with their limbs tied up in queer knots, because when the body is held firmly fixed by will power in those postures, that alters and controls the breathing instantly. Once the breath is brought under control, by reflex action it controls the mind.

You have no need of struggling with any contorted postures. You can enter directly into breath control. Here again, although breath control has helped many people, it may not help you. You must find that out by experiment. If you discover that it helps you, then by all means use it, but always remember it is only a means to attain an end. It is not a prime object in itself, and once you have really attained the power of mental concentration, you can dismiss all the indirect aids, and go directly towards what you seek.

Another helpful preliminary practice to meditation is to play a little music upon a gramophone. The music should preferably be of a religious nature and, if possible, executed on the violin. There are several records which you can buy which have the correct effect on the mind; they exalt and uplift it, and then still it. Listen intently to the music, keep the mind fixed upon it, and when the music dies down on the last note, begin your meditation.

§

There is still another aid available to some fortunate persons. It is perhaps the most efficacious of all. This consists in the help of a competent guide who has himself mastered the art. That is well understood in the Orient, so much so that those who want to master concentration for spiritual purposes always resort to the hermitages of these guides, and stay there for a while. They know that by remaining within the mental atmosphere of the teacher the powerful vibrations of the latter will automatically send their own mind increasingly inwards. He will send forth, as it were, rays of that concentrative power which he has himself attained. Science is now finding that telepathy is a fact, therefore we need not doubt this possibility.

And so, after the first physical meeting, the teacher can always send this radiation to the student no matter where the latter is. He puts into the disciple's mind wordless deliberate bestowal of his natural presence. The student will receive the rays, and an inner urge will come to him to go deeper in self-concentration. With that there also comes definite help, definite power.

The teacher's mind takes hold of the student's mind, starts a centripetal current at work within it, and thus assists it to enter into the concentrative state. Such result can come only when the student and teacher are working together in harmony. The harmony is established when the student who has applied and been accepted continuously maintains the right mental attitude of devotion to, and confidence in, the teacher. Each time the student enters into practice of meditation, if he thinks for a minute or two of the teacher, by spontaneous reaction he will automatically bring back the concentrative power and inner drive which come telepathically from him. This enables the student to penetrate his self more deeply than he could otherwise have done, more deeply even than the breathing exercise or the visual exercise could have helped him. That is the real reason why we need a teacher, not only to show us and to tell us what we have to do—quite enough has been said and written for many centuries—but to give us some of the power and the strength needed to do it.

Thus association with those who are more advanced in meditation than ourselves is a definite aid to development. We pick up, as it were, the vibrations of their mental atmosphere. We receive an inward impetus to further growth. We receive from such personal contact a truer understanding of the admittedly subtle nature of the art of meditation than we are likely to receive from the books.

In this daily practice, you begin to get your mind working more easily along one track; you render it more and more concentrated, capable of becoming more and more inwardly absorbed and withdrawn from externals. At first it may be done under a sense of duty, perhaps a rather painful duty, because the exercise is irksome. After a while—it may be months or years—the irksomeness disappears, and you become accustomed to the practice. As a result of the repetition there comes a time when concentration itself becomes a perfectly natural, habitual state. You do not have to make a tiring effort to concentrate; it becomes perfectly spontaneous. The hard labours of struggling with wandering thoughts then become unnecessary. Still later there will come a time, especially if you are working with a genuine teacher, when it becomes neither irksome nor a mere matter of duty, but a distinct pleasure, a real joy, to turn inwards and bring the mind to its centre.

The question is often asked, "How long must I continue this course of meditation which you advocate?" The answer must always be, until you have attained its goal—self-realization—or alternatively, until you have met and become the pupil of an adept. The months, years, or even lives, you will have to give to it depend largely upon your individual destiny. What have you done in this way in past existences? That will naturally shorten or lengthen the period you must give it in the present. Old hands mature quickly; novices must take a much longer time.

You may one day, through your efforts in concentration, reach a point where you have acquired a tolerable degree of mental control. As a matter of fact, very few people reach this point except after years of effort. It is not easy, and even then you may not be able to sustain the concentration for a long period; perhaps half an hour is your maximum. If you can do that, it is quite an achievement. You will find the mind begins to yield eventually.

What are you to do next? You have now to prepare to enter another phase, which is meditation proper, and this is where you will discover the real benefits and find the real fruit of your years of effort. Hitherto you have had to struggle and strain. Henceforth meditation consists of working to still all your thoughts. Henceforth you are to seek to still the mind as a whole, to drop from your sphere of consciousness whatever it is that you are meditating upon, and yet to remain in that concentrative state, in that same inwardly-absorbed attitude which you previously had.

At this stage, you must ask who it is that is practising this meditation. Who is it that is trying to make the mind still? Then you must wait, reverently. The answer will be heralded by an intuition, a gentle sense, and something very indeterminate. You cannot force it. You must pay the keenest attention and yield yourself up to it. That is the higher meditation, when you *let* the interior world reveal itself to you. That is different from the ordinary yoga, where one tries by a strong effort of will to draw the mind toward the Self, to force the mind to unite with the Self. The ordinary yogi fights. He fights his thoughts until he conquers them. This is a different method, wherein there is no effort, straining, or violence.

Meditation should now change into the withdrawal from thinking, whilst remaining as alert, as intent, and as concentrated as when in the most profound degree of thought imaginable. You must seek to bring the mind deeper into itself, so that it comes to one point—not to a series of points, i.e., thoughts along a single track, but to the very beginning of that track, so that it rests there, suspended.

During this period of meditation you must learn the art of killing a thought immediately it manifests itself. One after another, thoughts arise in the mind, and if you attempt to watch the process as an impersonal witness, you become aware of the involuntary, or rather habitual process whereby these thoughts succeed each other in an endless chain. Holding steadily to your point of vantage, you remain a tranquil observer of the ceaselessly flowing

river of thoughts. Having thoroughly established yourself in this observation post, the next step is to withdraw
attention from the ideas that arise, refusing to follow
them up to ultimate issue, thus making an attempt to kill
thoughts at their birth.

You will undergo some curious experiences. You may,
for instance, leaving all visions aside, begin to feel yourself floating out of your body, or partly floating out of
your body. You may feel that you are becoming nothing
but space. Such sensations are very good, and are signs of
definite progress. They are signs that you are freeing
yourself from the body which has been the weight keeping your thoughts down to the objective world. Do not
be afraid when they occur. When, at this stage, an unknown force seems to pull the head downwards, do not
resist it, but let the head bow down low and rest on the
breast. And vice versa. If this force seems to raise the
head, yield to it.

There is also the possibility of getting sleepy during
meditation. If one is practising alone without the help of
a teacher, then sleepiness is definitely a difficulty, a hindrance to meditation, and you must try to overcome it
by sheer combative will power, because the sleep of such
a person at such a time is certainly not meditation, and is
of no spiritual value.

In Patanjali's ancient manual of yoga, sleep is listed as
one of the five hindrances to yoga. That is correct. But
it is a hindrance only to people who are practising without a guide.

On the other hand, if you are working with a competent guide, whether in a group or alone at home, and if
you fall asleep during meditation, then it is a help, and
one should yield to it. In the Orient this condition is
called "Yoga-Nidra," which means "yoga-sleep." It possesses a value immeasurably higher than that of ordinary
sleep. The teacher is trying to speed up your progress in
the art of meditation, and to force your growth some-

what as a gardener may force the growth of a hothouse flower. To do that he has to shut down your conscious mind forcibly. What you cannot do by your own effort of will power, he helps you to achieve, and a sleepy feeling will frequently result.

You will feel that you are about to fall into a doze, and you may probably do so for a few seconds. But you will wake almost immediately after. The sleep will be light, dreamless slumber, and just those few seconds will give you the effect of sleeping for hours in deep slumber. When that occurs, it will come through a strong indrawing during your meditation. You forget the outside environment completely, then you wake up and hover on the verge of it for a few moments, and may repeat this a few times. Your mind flits across the sleep frontier and flits back again. Do not be afraid of that momentary sleep. It will not hinder you. It will only help, for that puts a stop to your restless mental activities. A little forcible help is being given you. It is forcing your progress, and that is why it has to be done without your conscious co-operation. Yoga-sleep has a real value in your development. In the old days of the mystery schools, similar experiences were deliberately brought about as a part of the training. Now you haven't those schools, but as much of the training is given to you as will still permit you to keep your footing and balance in the world.

There is a very important step that is comparatively easy to achieve, and that is to think very slowly and concentratively, and whilst thinking in that way, to *sense* the stillness which is back of the mind.

You try to ignore the ideas arising and concentrate attention firmly upon the gap, or period, between the formation of two ideas. Persevere in this, remain stable in pure awareness, consciousness, and eventually disturbing thoughts die down in number and disappear.

The meditation of beginners is thus quite different from the meditation of those who are much more advanced on the path, because the immediate aim in each case is somewhat different. The beginner has to battle with all his thoughts in order to try to find a central line of thought. But when he becomes more advanced, the aim is not only to find the truth about what he is meditating upon, but to reduce the number of his thoughts. After having thought in the most active and concentrated way possible, he suddenly lets all go and comes down to that element in which the mind itself is functioning. That prefaces mind-stilling. Not merely thinking *about*, but letting all thoughts lapse. He must try to empty the mind of all thoughts and mental pictures, including visions.

When you have the courage to proscribe, not merely evil thoughts but *all* thoughts; when you dare to dismiss the endless seekings of the intellect as mere mental curiosity; when you can genuflect to the Supreme Silence alone, then do you become fit to face the God within. What you seek is a cessation of all thought, even if not for long. If you succeed in stilling all thought, you have achieved meditation, but in actual practice very few people can do that wholly. But please do not let that discourage you.

It is almost impossible for the human being who must work and act in the world to maintain suspension of thought completely for any protracted period of time. If you are successful for half a minute, or a minute, that is very important, because during that brief period you will contact forces which you might say are liberating forces that will affect your whole being throughout the day. It is not the length of time during which you enter the stillness that matters, *it is the fact that you have entered it*, even if only for one minute. When you are able to do this you will be conscious of your thoughts moving ever so slowly through the stillness into deep concentration. This advance in meditation can be reached by most people who are working without the personal help of a teacher. It means that the deeper part of the mind, that is, the inner mind, has come up into focus. Progress will give an increasing inner peace, but this is not to be construed as the Ultimate.

The stillness and peace represent the environing atmosphere, the condition within which your spirit can manifest itself. They are the emanations or the fragrance as it were, of the Overself; hence the nearer you come to your inner spirit, the more of this peace you will find, and the more of this detachment from your external self.

To sit in a state of attentive immobility, whilst you calm the mind and watch for the arising of the Soul—this is the true way of self-knowledge. Thus you have reached a highly critical position. It is very important to realize that now you are not to make progress by your own efforts, but by reason of what is being done to you by the Overself.

Immediately you imagine you are making progress, then you automatically stop it! Hence few people have got beyond this stage. They are so happy at having arrived at this wonderful calm which they find in meditation, and which they believe to have been achieved by their exercises, that they let a subtle form of egoism creep in, and as it creeps in quite unnoticed, the Overself retreats. So many people stay on this plane and never get any farther merely because of this fault of relying on personal effort.

One must remember that one has built up a conscious process that must now be turned into an unconscious one. Just as a person who takes up the art of piano playing is unable at first to give full attention to the melody itself, simply because he is forced to bestow the major part of his attention upon finding the correct keys on the instrument, so in this art of mental quiet, one is at first absorbed in the difficulties of a constant train of consecutive thoughts and resisting the impulse to turn attention outwards. These difficulties will disappear by practice, and when the full force of the attention can be bestowed upon self-abstraction, illumination comes without much effort.

Because one is here dealing with an extremely subtle state, every analogy which may help to explain it will be helpful. Therefore, this stage of the self-quest may also be likened to that of learning to ride a bicycle. The apprentice rider has indeed many falls from the very beginning, so many that sometimes he may despair of ever being able to retain his balance upon that pair of wheels. But if he persists and strives daily, he at length meets with success. What is the greatest secret which will bring him to such success? It is to look some distance ahead, to keep his eyes fixed upon the road in front of him, and not to gaze upon the bicycle itself. In just the same way, one must now begin to look into the depths of one's being, firmly holding the thought of the Overself alone, and not attempting to watch the working of the vehicle which is bearing one along—the mind. This is indeed a delicate task, but like everything else, it can be accomplished.

The practice of mental quiet is not merely the retreat of attention from the world for a few seconds. It means withdrawing with all one's being, with all one's heart, with all one's mind, deeper and deeper until the centre is reached, felt, and united with the Overself.

Now, you will be tested—the completion of the answer begun rests with you. Will you give yourself up to spirit as you begin to feel an inner melting? You must submit everything—your question, yourself, and your surroundings—and concentrate without any effort. Invite it as though you want it to possess you completely, because that is the only way the Overself can answer.

It begins by reaching you through your feeling. As this melting sensation increases, and you yield yourself more and more to it each day, you will reach a point where the melting will stop. Your feeling, which will seem to have reached a crisis, will calm down, and although you may have been on the point of bursting into tears, suddenly you will feel contented.

It is the sensation of your mental energy coming down into the heart that produces a feeling of melting, an inward melting, as though your very heart itself had begun to dissolve. When you get this feeling, then you may know that it is the first faint tremor of your Overself.

Just be content to rest in that silence, and let come what will. Learn to accommodate that sacred silence. Rest there, having nothing and being nothing, just waiting, but not waiting for anything in particular. Be content to wait gladly. You will not be able to progress farther by your conscious effort, but one day something will happen. It will be like a beautiful cloud gradually stealing into the sky.

When you reach a point in your meditation where you seem to come right down to bed rock and your thoughts have lapsed, when even your yoga-sleep has lapsed, and you can keep your mind utterly still, you must then wait for this exalted state to supervene. It comes of its own accord.

In the end you see that the whole universe is just a picture thrown on a screen. Your pictures are ideas of others, the universe, and yourself. The pictures are never still, they come and they go, always changing, but the screen remains fixed, unchanged, all the time. Your consciousness is utterly unchanged, whereas your impressions are changing all the time. So long as you identify yourself with these pictures you cannot realize that you are really the screen. *When you bring about the state of mental stillness, you are bringing the stream of thoughts to an end and giving yourself an opportunity of becoming aware of the screen. Hence the necessity of practising concentration.* Then you will find that your thoughts were as dreams. You will wake up and discover *life-in-itself.*

CHAPTER VII

PSYCHOSPIRITUAL SELF-ANALYSIS

"MEN travel to gaze upon mountain heights and the waves of the sea, broad-flowing rivers and the expanse of the ocean, and pass by themselves, the crowning wonder," wrote St. Augustine in his *Confessions*.

Yet for most of us the secret of man still remains to be mastered. What has lain dark in the earlier centuries remains unrevealed in the twentieth.

The majority of men will die without caring and without knowing whether life has a meaning or no meaning; whether man has something divine in him or is a mere skin-bag of flesh, blood, bones, nerves, and muscles. They are strangers to their own selves.

It is not a flattering thought for mankind but it is nevertheless a true one that we have formed mistaken notions about ourselves. Half our woes and most of our mistakes arise out of this fact alone. Before we begin to study for a career, it might be wiser to study ourselves.

It would be well not only to hear lectures, but to give them. What could be more useful and more novel than to go home and give lectures to yourself, to stand courageously and frankly in front of your mirror and confess your unpleasant shortcomings, your pitiful weaknesses, and your punitive ignorance? "Myself!" is your perpetual problem. There is more than one man beneath your hat. The story of Jekyll and Hyde is lived by nearly everyone. It is your primary duty to investigate self before you attempt to overcome it. You might then better understand how to achieve your task.

It would be interesting to pause for a while and ask yourself: "What manner of man am I taking about with me?" It would prove profitable to survey yourself as a stranger, to throw your personality across the room and gaze steadily at it. You will eventually gain a largeness and liberty you have never felt before.

Socrates sagely remarked: "It seems to me ridiculous, when I am not able to know myself, to investigate irrelevant things." For some two or three centuries man has been keenly studying the phenomena of Nature. When will he so keenly study himself?

Now that science has card-indexed the whole universe, perhaps it can spare a little time to probe into the mystery of man's deeper mind. If it probes enough, it may succeed in creeping slowly back to the mind's source, the Infinite, the One. Thus inward-bound, it may involuntarily turn its inquisitive thoughts into veritable stepping-stones conducting towards the sublime Overself, which shines forgotten in the hearts of men.

We possess an inward heritage of divine consciousness, sufficient to bring the world back to a Golden Age, yet it avails us not. Because we do not know ourselves, we know not this all-important fact. Our education has taught us something about everything, but little about ourselves. Had we been taught and trained to understand self, we could all be living today with serene minds and smiling faces instead of with the gnawing anxiety and frowning foreheads which are everywhere evident.

All lores and cultures which have succeeded in penetrating to the spiritual hinterland of man, place the unveiling of his mystery in the depths of mind and heart, because in them alone exists the link between his visible individuality and that which lies behind it. Hence your work must be to explore this profounder mental-emotional side and embark upon its investigation.

Whoever believes that such inner activity can result only in vain imaginations is profoundly mistaken. Everything depends upon the manner in which it is undertaken, the goal which is aimed at, and the guidance (whether verbal, printed, or interior) which has been followed, as to what kind of result is obtained. The latter may certainly be as valueless as the mist to a traveller, but it may also assume the highest value when the investigation is rightly conducted.

The purpose of spiritual self-scrutiny is to bring the babbling stream of thoughts to rest and then to penetrate consciously into the region of the Overself, to make its silence articulate, and to set up a relationship between a man's normal conscious mind and this mysterious all-powerful reality which is his divine counterpart.

There seems to be a great deal of confusion about self-analysis. Any attempt to analyze yourself must be, at the beginning, an intellectual one. In this it does not differ from the intellectual efforts of philosophers, metaphysicians, and other learned men who still subscribe to materialistic ideas. But something more is needed. I must try to make clear to you just where the purely intellectual work ends and where the really spiritual work begins. When you understand that clearly, you will then know better how to proceed.

There are certain chapters in my book, *The Quest of the Overself*, dealing with the method and matter of analysis of oneself. You must study these chapters carefully. They may seem dry. People put them aside hastily, and study the later ones which seem more "practical" and useful to them. Here they are mistaken. In so delicate and intangible a realm as the soul, right ideas are really important. Those particular pages need to be studied slowly in a certain way. If you come to them in order to criticize because of the prejudice you already

entertain against such ideas, they will of course be useless to you.

To criticize before investigation is a fault, and to believe before investigation is another fault. You ought to
read quietly, neither wilfully resisting nor blindly accepting. For there is a power inherent in true words.
Unto that power I readily submit this book.

It is not my intention to try to substantiate every
statement therein. I wish rather to put my ideas before
an already sympathetic and attentive audience so that
they may thus be conveyed with the utmost economy
of means, avoiding the sidetracks and circumlocutions
of unnecessary argument. In short, I want this book to be
of real service to those who are mentally and spiritually
ready to receive it. I do not want to coerce people, in
no matter how subtle a manner, to accept a position to
which the circumstances of their natural inner growth
have not yet brought them, or to waste the time of all
with a logic chopping that leads nowhere.

Therefore, you must adopt an attitude of intellectual
sympathy to these thoughts rather than one of suspi-
cious criticism, if you wish to benefit by your reading.
They are frankly given out as ascertained knowledge,
not as theoretical opinion; yet there is nothing in any
of them which is not reasonable, provided you utilize
that impartial and impersonal reason which refuses to
confuse familiar thoughts and observations with true
ones. In asking for this much I know that I am asking
for too much from many, and such need not follow me
further. I am well aware that people do not turn to a
path of this kind until they have exhausted the possibilities of conventional methods of ascertaining truth. Indeed, they come to it in dark despair, as a kind of last
resort. It is only to persons of this kind, who feel a keen
anguish through their inability to penetrate into spiritual
regions, who find no help in orthodox systems, and who

have perhaps had a heavy share of life's sufferings, that my pages are likely to appeal.

To read the chapters of *The Quest of the Overself* on self-analysis in a spirit of harsh antagonism or determined opposition, seeking to detect flaws and sit in judgment upon what are thought to be errors, will be good exercise for the intellect perhaps, but it will not bring you nearer to truth. The tendency to read in that manner has, unfortunately, been developed by modern education. Hence this warning to suspend, temporarily at least, the critical faculty which has been highly helpful in building up the fabric of modern commercial and scientific civilization, *but which becomes an impediment when used in the face of statements emanating from those who have really penetrated the spiritual sphere.*

You are not asked to be dishonest with yourself in your thinking, or to destroy your faculty of independent judgment. Indeed, anyone who is disinclined to exercise his faculty of reason will not be fit for this path. You are fully entitled to maintain your existing viewpoint, for your personal experience of life has brought you to that. You are not required to desert what must necessarily seem to you to be of proved worth. I wish rather to make it plain to you that only when you have become dissatisfied with your present viewpoint, can you be expected to take, for the time being at least, the rationally presented viewpoint of those who have had a higher and more extended order of experience.

You are asked, in that case, to reflect without suspicion again and again upon the statements which you come across in your perusal until you can grasp the standpoint from which they were made. You are asked to be unbiased and to assimilate, experimentally as it were, an outlook which you have not hitherto entertained and which possesses a power of its own to awaken the intuitive faculty and give it greater energy within you.

Contemplation, no less than culture, dignifies you. This path begins with a starting point which is common to all persons throughout the world. It begins with a practical research into yourself. Religions, races, customs, classes, and nationalities create natural or artificial differences among men, but each and every individual cannot escape from the fact of his own self-existence.

It is not possible to condense this method into terser or better phraseology than that which once adorned the graceful portal of the beautiful Greek temple at Delphi: MAN KNOW THYSELF! For as the wise Greeks declared, we are all rays of the central spiritual Sun, and just as you cannot separate the golden orb from its individual rays, so you cannot really separate the Absolute Being from the individual human souls emanating from it. Because of this fact in Nature, the way to the discovery of your self-divinity exists unbroken for each one of you.

For if man is a mystery to himself, he is a mystery that can be solved. Man's greatest achievement will be not to build a longer bridge or to fly more quickly through space, but to know himself.

The most exact method of arriving at the true nature of self is to follow a process of elimination, i.e., to distinguish between self and not-self.

There is one warning—and a strong one—which I must utter. If you take this path of self-enquiry to be a dry intellectual formula, then you will make a vital mistake and meet with failure in your attempt to practise it. You must mingle aspiration with your practice. You must be deeply devoted to the One Self you seek. You must undertake this task of self-analysis in the same mood as that in which the Nature lover contemplates a beautiful landscape. You must believe that there is something wonderful, indeed holy, to be discovered by the proper performance of your task, even though your interest is to be entirely centred in yourself. Your ordinary mentality must therefore be collected and concentrated.

Your first step should be to free yourself from the age-old obsession that sense impressions constitute the self. This is done not only by self-analysis, but also by yoga practice in actually withdrawing mind from the senses, which method has been explained in the previous chapter.

The first analysis begins with the physical self. Enquiry is essential to find your true relationship to this body. And so this analysis in the book has been given, and particularly worked out and phrased in such a way as to make your mind dislodge itself during the time of practice from its habitual attitude towards the body.

Once you have really mastered the requirements, there is no need to keep on duplicating the intellectual path you have travelled. But you must be absolutely sure that you understand the leading points. They are important. Not only for your own intellectual satisfaction but because, also, when rightly handled, they become a means which will help your awareness to penetrate underneath your habitual intellectual relationship with the body.

This analysis is given so that you may begin to look upon your body as something distinct, separate, and apart. The body is there and it is yours, but you must learn to detach yourself from it so that you can understand it is not you.

Because you are so familiar with the body which you carry around, you take it for granted that it is yourself. You must try, during the period of analysis, to take up a less familiar attitude. Then you can begin to see where this body really stands in relation to your true self.

There is no doubt that you exist. You know that you are here and that you are a conscious being, but you have habitually taken it for granted that the self was the body. To it you have given a name. That name

distinguishes it from others. This in itself helps to confuse you on your quest. So long as you continue to
identify yourself by your name, so long will you continue to identify yourself with the body. The right way
is to start without prejudice on this quest. You must
try to forget yourself and your name during your periods of enquiry and meditation, and just *be*, without
being anybody in particular.

Whenever you say "I" you automatically refer to the
body. Just as it is not advisable during this meditative
enquiry to think of yourself as bearing a name, so it *is*
advisable, if you must use the word "I" in your thoughts,
to call it "*the* I." In other words, you must make it impersonal and put the definite article before it. By doing
this you detach your thought of egohood from the body.
You know that as long as you remain alive that sense
of selfhood will continue.

Even if half of the body were cut away, and you
continued to live, the consciousness of self-existence
would remain undiminished and just as powerful as before. That is perhaps one of the most elementary proofs
that consciousness of the ego, the "I," is not inseparably
bound up with consciousness of the physical body.

This "I," the ego, can and does sometimes separate
itself from the body without any purpose or effort on
your part. It does that, for instance, when you are very
"absent-minded."

If you are deeply sunk in a train of thought you will
not even hear the words of someone who is speaking to
you. The sense of hearing fails you. This shows that
you really hear with the mind.

The fact that sensations of pain and pleasure may not
even be felt when the mind is immersed in something
else is one sign of its independence of the body.

Unless the self gives its attention to the body, it
becomes abstracted, withdrawn into itself, that is, into
mind. The physical ear is thus but an instrument, and

so the self which hears is obviously more mind than body. The body is not *you*. It is not the soul.

Constant reflection upon such truths is an excellent means of helping you to gain that recognition of who and what you are. Whilst you are engaged in such reflection you are turning inwards.

Another important point which may seem trivial is, that although you habitually say, "my body," never do you think of saying, "My body is going to cross this room." Why, then, do you refer to the body in possessive terms? Consciously you are not aware of it, but something in you makes you automatically refer to it as belonging to you. If a thing *belongs* to you, then it is not you.

What is that something, then, which makes you unconsciously and unreflectively take such an attitude towards the body? Definitely, it is none other than the self itself.

Insofar as it is united with the mind, the self automatically tells you the body is merely your instrument. It is only when you become physically conscious that you think the body is you. You can say that it is linked up with the self and constitutes a part of the self, but you cannot say that in its totality it represents the self. Otherwise you would not consciously have the attitude of feeling that you possess the body when you use such a term as "my body."

In dreams you appear just as in your waking periods, and your characteristics may be the same. How much less are you in dreams? Just mind minus body. What is the dream state? It is nothing but a mental state. It is the mind functioning within itself. It is a series of ideas passing through consciousness. If self can detach itself so fully from the body as to relive again in dream, which consists of a series of thoughts and mental pictures, then dream is nothing else but mind. Do not, however, make the mistake of thinking that when I say self and mind are synonymous, I mean the ultimate Reality. Behind the mind is still something more. But from the standpoint of the body there is a reality, and that reality is the mind. A dream, if it were sufficiently analyzed by a scientist, would be proof that man is mind apart from the body, and that the soul is nothing else but mind.

In deep sleep the body is totally insensate. You have then no consciousness of the ego. The body does not say "I"; neither does the mind; there are no thoughts. When you awaken, the self reappears. If the self were only body and nothing more; if there were no spirit in man, no soul, nothing to survive that temporary death of self which is sleep, you would never be able to go to sleep; in the state of deep sleep *you* would have full consciousness. The body could not lose consciousness without dying, if the only consciousness it had was of itself. The fact that you can completely lose the body consciousness in sleep and still continue to exist is proof that the higher consciousness has totally left the body, while the self lives on, away and utterly apart from the body. That is precisely what does happen; the soul, which is the mind, does withdraw from the body in sleep, just as it withdraws from the body in death. In the deepest stages of trance and hypnotism the mind is expelled, literally driven out of the body, and curious things happen. Sometimes it transports itself to distant places and reports what is happening there. This could not have occurred if the mind or the self were permanently a part of the body. If the body constituted the sum of your self-consciousness, *you could never project the consciousness without projecting the body as well.* But the fact that the consciousness has been projected away from the body shows that it is something separable from the body itself.

If we merely look with an impartial and unprejudiced gaze upon our relationship to the body, and analyze it, we are *forced* to the conclusion that the self cannot be the body alone. The body may be a part of it, but the "I" is something more than the body, something subtler.

What, then, is left? Your thoughts and feelings. As our psychologists go on with their investigations of sleep and dreams, they will no doubt one day realize why sleep exists, and that it really is a matter of self withdrawing from the body. That is what it is. The trouble is that most people will never stop to analyze and reflect over this relationship of themselves to the physical body. They take it for granted. They will not enquire.

If you should pursue this course there would be no hope for you until you began to enquire and to ask whether the body really represents the whole of yourself. But with the beginning of enquiry and investigation there is hope; then you can begin to find the truth. That is why analysis is important. You must do it intellectually at first, to get the right mental attitude.

We shall leave the body and turn next to the feelings.

Feelings, emotions, and emotional moods are parts of your interior constitution, but they are not that one part which subsists through your life unaltered as the "I," the ego. The fact that the same person within a period of, say, ten years can completely change round and exhibit opposite feelings, shows that the feelings cannot be the self, because the thought of "I" and the sense of "I" still continue unchanged. In a single day you may be extremely happy in the morning and very miserable in the evening. Through this variability have you changed? No, it is the feelings which have thus changed, not the "I." The sense of self-existence remains; it has not altered a bit. So there again we must be rather acute and analytical to see the difference between the "I" and the feelings. The "I," therefore, must be something separate and distinct from the feelings. So we still have to find it.

Let us turn, then, to the mind. Egoism, individuality, desires, and memories, in the ultimate, are mere phases of the mind. They are thoughts. As a matter of fact, there is no difference between thoughts and feelings, except that thoughts change even faster. In the course of a day you may have experienced a thousand different thoughts. Did each of these represent your self? Decidedly not, because while they have vanished, departed, while they are *dead*, *you* continue to live. So, if those dead and vanished thoughts and those dead and vanished feelings cannot represent your self, there must still be something which gives you this sense of real *selfhood*, the sense of continuing to exist as your own individuality.

In deep sleep all thoughts disappear. If self were nothing but thoughts, it would also cease to be in sleep. Thoughts come and go, and yet something persists and mysteriously reveals itself again next morning.

You must therefore begin to separate self from mind. And this is the delicate turning point of your meditation, your self-analysis. First of all, realize that the mind consists of thoughts, and of that which makes you aware of these thoughts. The totality of all these thoughts throughout the day gives you, shall we say, the intellect. If you were able to stop your thoughts for a few seconds, you would still remain conscious. You would still be aware of that part which must be searched for; that which is consciousness. There is *something* in you which is awareness and which is consciousness, but which is not thought; something which yet gives you the sense of selfhood, the sense of *being*, the sense of individuality, and therefore which must be in contrast to the intellect; this is your real self.

When you look at a book, *what sees* the book? Is it the physical eye? Certainly the light gives the image to the eye, but the eye has to send a message along the optic nerve to the brain, and you have to become aware, conscious, of that message. Until you do become aware of it there is, for you, no book, no sight of a book.

In other words, the physical vibration in this physical organ has to be converted to something of a totally different nature. It becomes an idea in your mind, the idea of the book. Until this conversion takes place you cannot see the book. If you were to place a corpse in a chair and ask it to look at a book, it could not see it, though the physical eyes are there in all their fullness and perfection. But the mind is absent. The mind is needed to see. Somewhere in the winding convolutions of the brain the vibrations—messages of the sensory nerves—are converted into mental images, spiritual essences. How this transformation from physical to psychical is done nobody knows.

Mind is the knower, the seeing agent in you. The eye is but an instrument. Further proof of this lies in the fact that people who have certain abnormal faculties have been able to read from a book with the eyes blindfolded. Therefore, if the *mind* is the seeing agent, and not the physical organ, we should ascertain what is the real seeing agent behind the mind, if there is one. There is the thought, the idea of the book, and then there is something which is aware of that thought. That something we might call the real see-er, the real witness in the mind, and that must therefore be more really yourself than the mind, which is composed of ideas alone.

Without consciousness there could be none of these thoughts. That is a very difficult point which you will need to reflect over a great deal. Your mind is simply a stream of thoughts. Buddha pointed out that thoughts constituted the mind by streaming through incessantly. Now keep up the same line of thought. There are many different mental states, but one consciousness apprehends all these. In the course of a week you may have five hundred thousand thoughts, but only one consciousness keeps them going in your mind. These thoughts are just floating, fugitive things. That cannot be the ultimate. There must be, and is, the inner Light, because nothing else that we know could make us aware of them.

Because this ultimate Self is the knower of the changing, it must itself be without change. If you reflect you will see that this must be so.

What is it that registers all these changes, whether they be of the external universe or your own mental states? How do you know that you slept in deep sleep? Because immediately the sleep was over, varied thoughts came into the mind and by the contrast you knew that deep sleep was a relatively constant, unchanging state. This matter requires profound meditation. That which records the changes must be something which itself remains unchanged. If the *knower* himself were to be constantly changing he would not be able to know that these outward things were changing. How could you know that you have constantly changing thoughts unless there were something fixed and stable in you by contrast with which you could see and perceive the difference? There must be some part of you which does not change in order to give you the understanding that everything else does. That is a piece of deep analysis which you can use for your meditation. If you can reflect upon it in the right way it will help you to get the true concept of the Witness-Self.

You ought to sink yourself again and again into the stream of thinking which has brought us to this point, for you need to recognize its truth not as something imposed upon you from outside but as something which has its own inherent rightness, and therefore is born within you with the fullest power of conviction.

Using no other means than the facts of human life and experience of human thought in its varied phases, we have arrived in sight of the truth that the real Self we seek dwells in a higher dimension than flesh, emotion, thought, and time; that it hides somewhere behind the thought-emotion "I"; and that it must indeed exist beyond all our ordinary categories.

§

We have come to the threshold of this mysterious Witness-Self, which is nothing but awareness or consciousness. And here our psychologists become completely confused. The modern psychologist thinks that the mind cannot be emptied of its contents, that the mind and its contents are one. This implies that he believes thoughts and consciousness cannot be separated, that they are not two separable things. If these intellectual analyses do not convince him, it would be well for him to study yoga and find out for himself. If you practise yoga successfully, you can still your mind, you can stop the working of the brain for a short time, and in that experience you find that you are perfectly aware, but that you do not think. You are then Consciousness itself. You have found the Witness-Self. That is the answer of yoga.

However, there is great hope for the psychologists because they *are* investigating. They have taken up the right attitude of enquiry and they are looking for Truth just as much as any spiritual seeker. They have started from a different angle, but they must eventually find the Truth. And perhaps their way will be the better way because it will be the right way for our epoch. It will be the way of moving slowly, step by step, and proving each step, whereas the ancient way was the way of complete acceptance by faith. Man today is so much more critical, so much more intellectual. Scientists may lead the way from sheer materialism into the discovery of the Spiritual Self. If they continue to investigate they will ultimately find the Truth, for there is nothing else they can find. Their path is getting narrower and narrower. It is leading them inescapably towards the Spirit.

The final effort during your period of mental quiet

must now be made. The question, *"What am I?"* must
be put for the last time.

The meditation need not always be limited to the
"What am I?" theme. There are other themes equally
profitable as paths of enquiry to pursue, such as "Whence
arises the ego?" and "Where is the origin of thoughts?"
and "Who is the being who is meditating?"

All contents of consciousness have to be treated as
objects in this analysis. Everything, in fact, of which
you are conscious.

Now, that which is conscious of the object is Consciousness. Who knows this? What is aware of these
ideas? That by which they are perceived and that which
is not itself perceived. There is some ultimate observer
which observes all, but which is itself not observed.
Mind is the observer within the body, and that something else is the observer within the mind.

We say, "my mind." That implies something in the
background behind the mind. That something is the
Self, the Witness of the individual. What is it, then,
that constitutes the Self? Is it the physical sensations,
or the thoughts or feelings? The "I" contains all these
constituents, yet, as you have seen, is not wholly contained by them. You can detect it only through subtle
discrimination. To discover that, you have to identify
yourself with it.

Such discrimination must be made by you. That is
your work. You have to do it by reflection, by using
your intelligence and intuition to the utmost limits to
understand what you are *not* at first, then when you
have found that out, you perceive what you truly are.
When you have got rid of your false ideas and your
false imaginations you are able to see what is left. Behold, it is the eternal Overself!

The best way to effect your purpose now is as follows: It must, of course, immediately succeed the logi-
cal impasse which the meditation has reached. Throw

aside all further analysis, for you have reached the critical and decisive stage; cease all discriminative and discursive thought; and make your final prayerful repetition of the silent question, *Who am I?* Pause for a while in meditative, musing reverie without attempting to supply the answer. In short, you should simply question your inner self and then prevent your thinking intellect from working on the question.

After that, attention must dive deeper inwards, persistently trailing that elusive sense of "I." Having dissociated the latter from material and mental limitations, you must prepare yourself to follow it into the great silence that is back of the intellect; that is, to retreat into a realm that transcends intellect.

Intense inner concentration must act to reduce the number of your thoughts until the entire intellect is condensed to a single thought, which is none other than the thought, "I." Then this final thought should be pressed to yield the secret of its source.

When you were going through the intellectual phase of your analysis you had to think as sharply as possible. Clarity of thoughts and their formation into exact words was essential. They could not be vague and hazy. Now you have passed this phase and the intellectual sharpness can be dropped. Normally, your brain is thinking all the time. That means motion, activity, movement which is using up energy. To cease that movement even partially is to enter into spiritual peace. Truth can only be realized in the stillness and quiet.

If there were nothing really existing beyond this blank stillness, this mental impasse, this analytical cul-de-sac and utter void, there would and could be no answer to your query. Restless mind could never be stilled. Your questing heart would be for ever dissatisfied; the void remain a void. But other men have received an answer, the divine answer of the Overself. What they have received, you, too, may receive.

At this stage, when the intuition bids you yield up your intellect and commands you to thrust aside your thoughts; when it teaches you that the accumulation of thoughts constitutes a veil which shuts you off from spiritual reality, there will then ensue a great struggle, during which a part of your body will seem as if torn to pieces. Intellect, hitherto the venerated and trusted guide, hitherto all-dominant in your practices, now finds itself about to be deserted. Consequently it declares open war against the new invader, and is determined not to surrender its place upon the throne without a severe struggle. It is difficult at this point to see your way and you constantly oscillate between dawning intuition and resistant intellect, endeavouring to hold familiar ground and yet permit inevitable growth to take place.

This experience cannot be avoided and must therefore be accepted. What can be done, however, is to recognize the real nature of the struggle and to determine to ally yourself with the higher power that has sent its silent ambassador. You must realize that the path of humble intellectual sacrifice and mental recognition is now the path of wisdom, and act accordingly.

The first visitation of the Overself will come to you in a humble way. You do not know how, or why, or where it comes from. The first faint intrusion you will hardly be aware of, but gradually it will make itself felt. It will be something so soft, so gentle, that unless you are free from all preconceptions you are liable to choke it off. You must be utterly empty and void, ready to accept whatever comes. This holy influence will steal over you, suffuse you and fill you. This means that the emptiness of matter and mind is being filled.

The ultimate goal which lies before you is to maintain the mind in a condition entirely free of thoughts, without either falling asleep, losing consciousness, or degenerating into psychic mediumship. If the primal thought, "I," is held, stilled, pinned down, it becomes eliminated, for it does not exist by itself; it exists only by virtue of the divine light of the Overself's consciousness which informs it. With the nullifying of this single thought all those innumerable thoughts of the personal ego which have hitherto centred around it are seen to be illusion, whereas the sense of "I AM," the sense of being which informs it, is not.

How is it to be known? To know it is to be it. Everything else in the world can be known in other ways indirectly, but this is the one thing which must be known by becoming it.

At this stage of such becoming, the very "I" which seemed to be the centre of your existence, the ultimate root of your entire nature, dissolves, melts away into its mysterious background. The personal ego disappears, its limitations shattered as a rock is shattered by the growing oak, and it is replaced by a sense of existence which possesses eternal duration. With that change you feel an extraordinary sense of release, as though all the interests of the personality, its joys and cares, its hopes and fears were but a burden that had been hitherto carried blindly, but is now cast off. It is this strange and superior experience which transmutes the man into his own deepest nature, into the fundament of his selfhood. It is also among the highest experiences open to the human race whilst it remains human, for beyond it stretch pathways leading to the realm of angels and gods.

The true individuality of a man is the same in all; sacred, divine, deathless. In that elevated world to which it belongs there are none high and none low, for all there partake of the same sublimity, as drops mingled in one ocean.

To rest without thought is really a wonderful achievement, and as you discover its possibility you must seek to prolong those all-too-brief and precious moments when the mind, the "I," returns to its source, its primal divine element.

There is no fixed or formal period for meditation of this psycho-spiritual kind. You must be guided by your feelings. When you intensely live it you may take a full half hour. But there will be periods when you are weary of analysis. At such times it is inadvisable to prolong it for more than a couple of minutes. Eventually, when you are sufficiently grounded in the control of thought and in the understanding of analysis, you need not even bring it into your meditation. You can begin by affirming briefly, but with the utmost clarity of perception, that you are not the body, you are not the intellect, but you *are* pure awareness.

From there you begin your meditation, wherein you know the self as it really is, clarified, unmixed with thoughts and emotions which do not truly belong to it, and then you discover the mysterious being at the core of your heart.

Man is not chained to the finite self, but believes himself to be so. This belief is based upon an illusion. The illusion that the five senses are the conscious functioning agents of man's life, and that, therefore, the world to which they testify is a solid world of the utmost reality. The senses deceive him, and he deceives himself. When he claims his freedom, he shall find it. He needs to entertain such redeeming, liberating thoughts or he will never begin to seek himself, his real unlimited self.

Thus, in the last analysis, it is clear that it was the mind which involved him into matter. It is the mind that can set man free again. This is not done by running away to monasteries or mountains and spending one's life there; it is done by USING THE MIND TO ENQUIRE INTO ITS OWN OPERATION.

CHAPTER VIII

THE QUESTION OF ASCETICISM

THE notion once prevalent in medieval Europe, and one still prevalent to some extent in the modern East, that spirituality and activity are incompatible, is not entirely true. It is the spiritual and mental attitude which is most important. Body activities—we finally learn—are less important. The pith of the matter has been well expressed by Krishna, who was regarded as an incarnation of deity by the Indians of antiquity and is still so regarded today. He declared:

> "One untainted by egoism and unentangled, remains spiritually unaffected by acts done in discharge of duty. One discharging duties with this mental attitude is not touched by any activity."

Many were the hermits who fled from careers or worldly pleasures into monastery, forest, and mountain fastness, thinking that spirituality was only to be found in these sequestered haunts. And many discovered that they could not escape from their thoughts, that they carried their egoisms with them too, and that both the career and the pleasures which were supposedly forsaken were persistently intruding upon their minds. Thus, although they had apparently left the throbbing world, they were unable to escape the world's influence and attractions.

Were these hermits, then, more spiritual because they

seemed to have forsaken the material world? Did their physical lethargy signify a lethargy of ambition and desire? Do not daily-life experiences and problems become instrumental (if dealt with wisely) in perfecting the lineaments of the soul? The answer is self-evident.

You cannot become a saint overnight. You start as a sinner and may hope one day to end as a saint.

St. Jerome went out to a desert hermitage in search of the contemplative life, but finally returned with exasperated nerves and irritated mind, so narrow did he find the society of professional hermits.

When I was travelling in the snow-capped Himalayas, I went to visit one of the holy men who had made his abode in a hut which was perched on the side of one of the rugged heights. He was a grave, long-bearded old man who enjoyed a certain degree of fame and reputation in the Himalayan world. At the end of my visit he asked me to remain, but I told him I was in a hurry because I wanted to journey to South India, say my farewells, and collect my things preparatory to returning to Europe. He asked me why I wished to return to the West, and I replied that I had work to do there. He said, "No, it is only desire which can take a man away from the spiritual solitudes of these mountains." And then he quoted a formula not unknown to me. "God plus desire equals man. Man minus desire equals God."

I paid my respects to the old gentleman and descended the mountains into the larger world which I had deserted for the second time. To me he represented the ancient ideal of Hindu spirituality which saw nothing but evil in the world of busy men and busy towns, and nothing but holiness in the world of monastic retreats and natural solitudes. He was perfectly right from his standpoint, but I felt sure that I was right from mine, too. He alone can enter the world of activity with its trials and temptations who is not afraid of it but who has already mastered it within his mind. All others had

better keep away and remain untempted in peaceful hermitages or monastery retreats.

This criticism does not mean that you must never
forsake ambition and pleasure when the inner voice bids
you to do so; it means only that the true goal is control
of mind, and that a smooth-faced sanctimony is not
spirituality. Physical activity or inactivity is of secondary
importance in comparison with the attainment of this
goal.

The roots of our existence lie in the mind, and it is
therefore the mind which must be attacked if we would
really change our lives. Only where those roots are
burned by the divine fire of the Overself can we be as-
sured that they will never again germinate.

The evils of civilization are obvious and may be admitted, but they can be got at and removed. We do not
need to remove civilization itself in order to remove its
evils. For better or for worse we have eaten the apple,
the fruit of the tree of knowledge, and we cannot forget
that. Those things which are the causes of sin to others,
such as cold intellect and hot sex, may even become the
cause of uplift to the enlightened aspirant of our own
age. Both may become spiritually significant through
being associated with a technique of spiritual self-discovery. Instead of being stumbling blocks on the path
of higher attainment, they may become instruments of
this attainment to the wise. Says a secret Indian text,
"By what men fall, by that they rise."

Part of the training which had to be followed in the
Orient at one time was renunciation of the world. This
meant either complete retirement into a monastery or
hiding away in the mountains or jungles alone. It meant
giving up all worldly activity, including any attempt to
earn a livelihood; it meant renunciation of all human
ties, including family relationship, and rigid sacrifices in
many directions. Personally, I have slept on the rock
floor of yogis' caves as well as on the regal beds of pal-

aces, and felt equally as spiritual or as worldly, equally at home in both; in any case, it is not discomfort which conduces to the practice of yoga, not soft mattresses and elegant furniture which make a home, so much as the right atmosphere.

It is a mistake to imagine that the spiritual life can be found only in monasteries, hermitages, Indian ashramas, or similar places remote from worldly existence. Those who possess a natural predisposition towards an ascetic existence can profitably retire permanently into such institutions. To those who have an ascetic sense but no desire to renounce the world, I suggest occasional retreat plus the habitual exercise of small self-denials.

We who live amidst the achievements of technical invention and mechanical labour, who work for our livelihood amidst the everyday world, cannot hope to find sympathetic guidance from the ascetic recluses, unless they be sages indeed. Because they found their own wisdom by renouncing the world, they wrongly imagine that renunciation is the one and only means of attainment. Our epoch is not their epoch. Our application of truth, or even our rendering of it, may have to differ from theirs, and life is large enough to have room for both, thank heaven!

As long as your development is entirely under the shelter of a monastery or a mountain cave, you are free from every distraction and every temptation; it is then comparatively easy to find a measure of spiritual peace and of understanding. But I have heard of some men, inhabitants of Oriental monasteries, who, through the force of destiny or their own personal choice, have been brought to Europe and to America, and under the stress and strife of temptations in large cities where they have had to live for years, their spiritual attainment crumbled and broke. It was not a solid attainment after all, for when submitted to the acid test in the world of activity, it could not stand. I think the point is clear to you. I came to this conclusion: while living in cities and taking part in an active life would lead to slower spiritual progress, still it would be more solid. Whatever progress you made would not be illusory but real. It would not be progress untried by the opposition of matter. When put to the test it would not crumble, because it would be built on a substantial foundation. It would have already endured the strain.

As a matter of fact, the Far East has been influenced to such an extent by the modern West that these customs are rapidly disappearing there. Certainly it used to be easier for an Oriental, withdrawn from active life, from every distraction that might take his mind away from spiritual pursuits, to find inner peace. But peace is not the same as truth.

Institutions which harbour the ascetics of the world are not necessarily places of holiness made manifest. Anyone who has lived in such places sufficiently long to get beneath appearances knows how disappointing and disillusioning they can be. Despite the institutions being called monastery or hermitage or ashram, and despite the fact that the ambitious desires of the inhabitants are supposedly turned in a more exalted direction, there is often no fundamental change in their basic characters. Honourable exceptions exist, of course, in every such religious community, and shine out proportionately because they are exceptions. But let us not fall into self-deception—let us not imagine these places free of greed, sexuality, envy, backbiting, and petty unbrotherly feelings. The point is that in many cases they are mere miniatures of the outside world, the same feelings and weaknesses being exhibited, only on a more circumscribed scale.

The monastic ideal no longer appeals to modern men. The Western world at least is not attracted nowadays to the austere regime of asceticism, but is inclined rather towards balance than towards renunciation; therefore this point will concern the few, although it is still an issue—a disappearing issue—in some Eastern countries. I have found many fine things in these Oriental methods and I have found many shortcomings, and I am convinced that these methods of spiritual development were very successful in former centuries. But I am equally convinced that they are frequently useless today in their present form. I believe, however, that they could and should be readapted to the needs of modern life.

Asceticism makes men fanatical and unbalanced, with a tendency towards hypocrisy. Given certain ideals to live up to, which many of them find impossible after a time, they cultivate pretense, and as a consequence degenerate into religious hypocrisy, which is the worst of all sins. It would be far better for these people to renounce their religious lives and go back into the world. I know some of them start out quite sincerely. Why do they become hypocritical? It is because they do not realize that wherever you go, you take your feelings, your thoughts, your desires, with you. You have to learn to conquer them inside yourself just as much as if you were living in a city. You can't get away from it. Donning the yellow robe of monkhood does not free you from them, so of what use is it? You have to learn that real asceticism is a habit of mind, not of body. You have to learn that the body is not, after all, your real self, and that which you seek is something inside the body and certainly not the body. Not any amount of fussing about with the body is going to bring you into a spiritual state. Here again the need is balance.

§

But if I do not advocate a cowardly renunciation of the world—which is indeed utterly impossible to ninety-five per cent of Westerners—I do advocate that one should place one's worldly life on the most solid of all foundations. Our own active life takes up so much time and energy that it does render the spiritual relaxation difficult.

You should seek to simplify existence, to cut down your wants, and to diminish your cares, that more time and energy may be found for a divinely-lived leisure.

If you have such a passion for truth that you find certain social duties are standing in the way, then they ought to go. But so far as is possible, let them stay. If they become an obstacle, then they must go, because truth comes first. It is unnecessary to relinquish all social formalities. However, it is wise to eliminate the non-essential ones. Let your life be as simple as possible within your station, then you will have the mind freer to reflect. If your mind is wholly taken up with other things, how can you think about truth? To live more simply does not mean to become a barbarian. Try to find the golden mean and live free from useless desires. The moment you become obsessed by desires to play a part in society, there is always the danger that those desires will keep you too busy to attend to quiet thought and higher study. Do what you must do, but not a bit more.

You need a sense of proportion. The forces of creation did not bring this wide-flung universe into being because of one single person—yourself. Your presence is not necessary to the functioning of the universal machine. Similarly, society and civilization can very well get along without one for a time, and both will be the better for the change.

The first and foremost necessity in learning to control your mind is to have definite periods of spiritual retreat, to withdraw into solitude from habitual personal activities. Such withdrawals need last only a day or a week-end at a time. On the other hand, they may extend to a month or six months, or even to a year or two. The period cannot be predetermined or prescribed, but if you are progressing you will, at some time or

other, feel a pressing inner urge to throw off the shackles
of constant absorption in daily routine. You have heard
someone say—or you have said it yourself—"I wish I
could take a trip for a month or so and get away from
everything." That is a pressing inner urge, a spiritual
desire to unfold. Whenever possible, you should seize
an opportunity for freedom should it present itself, or
better still, you should endeavour to create it, even if
it be only for a few hours.

Men have become so steeped in material living, in
the struggle to earn a livelihood, and in the distracting
environment of great cities in which they find themselves
forced to live, that in the last half-century they have
become more and more obsessed by their material bodies. Work, living conditions in general, and pleasures
have become so definitely material that relaxation, in a
spiritual sense, has become a pronounced exception. But
in Asia and in some parts of Africa you will find that
reversed. People make it a business to have time to relax for religious and for spiritual reasons. I am speaking
of the masses. They realize that they have not only to
make a living, but they also have to make a life! It is not
a matter of becoming fussy about the condition of your
soul, but of getting a clearer insight into what you
really are.

You need not enter a monastery—the world today is
your monastery and the struggles of daily life are the
monastic discipline; it is not what you do, but how you
do it; not sitting in a hermitage that really matters, but
sitting in the deep centre of your own being. The wise
man can make the worldly life itself his hermitage, and
worldly activities his means of liberation.

It is at such times of withdrawal that you are able
really to relax and direct your mind into spiritual channels. If you live in noisy cities, you should escape whenever possible into the quiet solitude of Nature. Surrender yourself to the impressions which come to you from

the new environment. If you are looking for guidance in any particular problem, you will find it there more easily.

Even if you are but a humble toiler, unable to escape for more than a week or two during the entire year and for more than a few hours each week, nevertheless you may reap richly from the right use of even short periods of retirement. It is not so much a question of the length of time you are able to spend in spiritual retirement, but the way you actually spend the time at your disposal. You should use these retreats first of all for complete oblivion of personal affairs. Thus you prepare a suitable atmosphere for the impersonal soul of Nature to bestow some degree of illumination upon you.

The next step, during the time of your retreat, is to seek solitude as much as possible. Avoid the society of too many people. Each person you meet becomes a source of distraction and diversion from your aim—unless he be someone of superior spiritual stature. Each individual is surrounded by an atmosphere which he carries wherever he goes, which though unseen, is none the less so real that under certain conditions it will register on scientific instruments. This personal atmosphere definitely, but temporarily, influences others—at least some—who come in contact with it. Since the majority of people in the world are bent upon other aims than the highest which Nature (God) has set them, you must take care not to be suborned by these personalities. Too frequent mingling with them, whether in crowds or in social life, may lead to subordination of your spiritual aims to their materialistic purposes.

If you can be so fortunate during a retreat as to find the society of one who possesses a more powerful spiritual life than your own, then the withdrawal will indeed prove more fruitful than otherwise.

Do you see the difference I have drawn between complete fanatical withdrawal from the world, and occasional detachment? Self-control and self-discipline are qualities which can be learned in the world. The difficulties of asceticism are too pronounced, as I have seen them, and I believe the difficulties outweigh the advantages.

§

Those who are impelled to withdraw from the world into a monastic retreat of some kind are few nowadays, but those who feel the need of withdrawing into an inward peace of some kind are many. They can have their peace—and have their world, too—just by spiritualizing their life *in* the world.

The very act of withdrawing into the solitude of your own room or into the peaceful quiet and beauty of any sequestered spot for this practice of mental quiet is, in itself, a symbolic detachment from the active world. Certainly during the twenty or thirty minutes of retirement, if you use them correctly, you are as completely withdrawn from the world as any monk in his monastic cell. You need no further renunciation of the world than this, for all needed changes in your outer life will inevitably, if slowly, be made by you under the new influence from within of which you will gradually become conscious.

Temporary spiritual retreats must be a feature of the new age. Here men should go, not to spend their lives, but to gain greater strength and wisdom for their lives. I believe that such retreats as places of occasional retirement are much better suited to our time than monasteries.

Do not stay for ever in solitude. Keep up a balance, a rhythm with the world. What you will gain and learn in your solitude you must work out in society and activity. What you work out in activity will be the test of what you have attained within your heart. You must test these inner attainments. In this way you may test continuously, in a life of action, the integrity of inner achievement resulting from solitude. The centred mind creates its own country. I live in solitude though I walk on Broadway or Cheapside. Because I hold thought at rest in its infinite source, London or New York is as quiet to me as that solitary Indian hill where I found my Master. The wise path seeks a middle course between asceticism, which is so frequently a failure, and hedonism, which is so often a disaster. Let us enjoy the comforts and conveniences which the brain of man has devised, and the delight-bringing gifts with which Nature has provided us.

Withdrawal from the world will then be but a temporary affair. After a man has felt the radical change in his inner outlook, the transference of his spiritual centre of gravity from circumference to centre, he can and should like his own normal life and take up again his share of the world's activities.

We hear much of the need of practicing certain ascetic self-disciplines. Let us get our minds clear about this. Some say you must not eat meat, others say you must not drink alcohol; still others that you must not smoke, you must not have sexual intercourse; and there are even still more rigid and severe forms of self-discipline and self-torture practiced in the Orient, far beyond the imagination of most Western people; they were practiced in Europe in medieval times as well as in premodern America.

Now, why were these ascetic disciplines given to spiritual aspirants? I will tell you. They were given to the beginner in the practice of yoga and meditation as a forcible attempt to break his bondage to the external world. You see, the whole effort of meditation is to turn the mind inwards and away from the external world. Consequently, any powerful habit or any powerful emotion which tied one too strongly to the material world would reappear during meditation and dom-

inate him, rendering his meditation more difficult. The
pull of the external world exists in meditation just as
much as in active life; only in the first struggles of meditation he becomes more conscious of it, whereas in active life he surrenders.

When the beginner sits down to meditate, he is still
largely held back by all sorts of strong worldly feelings
and thoughts.

These ascetic disciplines were laid down to make success easier. The aspirant was told that, for a time at least,
he should give up the world and retire into a retreat of
some sort. He must forget every tie with the world,
everything that pulled him away from his inner self.
Remember these disciplines were given those who were
withdrawn from worldly life, who became monks and
nuns. They were excellent for those whom they suited,
but the fact remains that whatever progress you make
away from the testing ground of the outer world has
the possibility of being illusory. Reality is not merely
within you, it is also without you.

To find reality, that is, to find Truth, you will have
to find it not only inside yourself, by unification with
the inner Light, which is the first half of the battle, but
also in the universe around you. That is why it is so
often the case of those who have lived ascetic retired
lives, that when they return to the world they are not
strong enough to withstand its trials and temptations.
It is not advisable to indulge in extremes. Retreat for
any length of time you like, for two hours or two
months, but go back to the world and see what you
have really attained. See how strong you really are. See
how wise you really are. It is better to go back and try
to find the rhythm of solitude in the midst of activity.
Contrary to belief, asceticism is really unimportant in
itself, though often advised as a matter of convenience
for those who feel they must renounce a worldly life
in order to pursue a path of unhindered contemplation.

Thus you need not flee from activity into the refuge of hermitages, so long as you flee from it in heart. It is not essential to become a monk or to enter a monastery, in order to live the spiritual life. The true essential is to surrender your deepest desire to the Overself; thereafter you may continue to live and work in the world, as the blue-green lotus leaf remains dry though floating on the surface of a pool.

We are here to *live*, not to run away from life.

I say it is best for most of us to live normal lives, to stay in our places and work, but to run away and relax mentally and emotionally whenever we feel the need.

§

In the Orient it is taken for granted in nine out of ten spiritual circles, that if you wish to attain spiritual consciousness you should entirely renounce all sex intercourse, all sexual life.

Here in Europe and America, those who look to the Orient for guidance likewise hold up a life of complete chastity as the highest ideal.

Now we need a little common sense, and an understanding of why this restriction of celibacy and chastity has been advocated. The sex impulse is most dynamic in human nature, and therefore, because it is so far-reaching, some measure of self-control is necessary, even in ordinary human existence. In the case of a spiritual aspirant who wants to bring his mind under complete control a still greater measure is necessary. First, because such a powerful force in human character needs to be guided. Second, because man needs a certain amount of strength of will to overcome the mind, to control his thoughts, to practise concentration. The conservation of sex force helps to gain this strength. Third, to give him more control over his whole make-up, for if he controls sex he is more likely to control the lesser emotions.

That is why celibacy and chastity were more or less enforced upon most beginners on a spiritual path. The important point is, however, that an ascetic régime was given to beginners who had renounced the world, and who needed to economize all their forces, all their vital life substance, for this one purpose they had set themselves. In other words, they were monks, and for the monk the celibate life and the fasting life are the natural ideals.

But what of people who live in the world, through destiny or circumstances, who have to live a normal life like other people? Such people either are married, or sooner or later will want to get married. Is there then no hope for them? Is the spiritual path to be trod to success only by monks and nuns?

There is a strong predisposition in this generation—and especially in the younger generation—to let the sex force run away with it, to wallow in sexual thoughts, impulses, and acts. Such a condition of affairs, when spread widely enough and deeply enough, can have only deplorable effects. The misdirection of vital energies brings its own penalty. The hazards of sexual license are sins against our bodies. Wisdom and common sense are no less called for in the sphere of sexual relations than in any other; perhaps more, whether one has spiritual aspirations or not.

Morality has only a utilitarian rôle, but it receives an indirect and shadowy support from the ethics practised by spiritually wise men. In an age of looser sexual morality, one should also remember that although the conventional laws of morality may not originate from the highest sources, the law of spiritual justice ruling mankind should cause one to take a special care in one's conduct toward the opposite sex.

The man who lives a depraved life thereby renders himself unfit for this path, yet on the other hand absolute physical chastity is not of much value where it is accompanied by depraved thoughts. The call for frankness in sex, for a lifting of the mist, of the pretense and silence with which narrow minds have enshrouded it, is not necessarily a plea for immorality. Civilization has fixed a standard of decency and restraint upon this theme, which need not be thrown away, but the fear of acknowledging the existence of a vital function in human existence may well be thrown away. Sane realism is necessary and far healthier than theoretically refusing to face facts and life.

The attraction between man and woman is so powerful, and sex is such a dynamic impulse in human nature, that if it is not brought to heel in some way it can play havoc with one's life. But most efforts to eradicate it entirely usually result in failure and an aggravation rather than a diminution in the strength of the urge. The middle path is best, and that is the path of sane recognition of sex as a natural function and of the necessity of controlling the impulsive urges which it automatically and blindly brings about at recurring intervals in the physical body. Most of us are indeed but individual and unconscious mediums for this tremendous binding force which runs through all Nature.

We in the West are tasting these sweets of freedom. When we have had a surfeit we shall return to the middle path, to a saner life midway between the moralists and the immoralists. We shall not shriek with hypocritical horror at the mention of natural functions of the body, as at something mired in infamy, as we did in an earlier generation; neither shall we lose all decency and self-control every time passion rises.

The notion that the source of our nature is aboriginal sin and that sex is the diabolic element in our being, is scarcely creditable to the benevolent character of the Supreme Creator. Sex is as much a divine creation as any other element of man's make-up. Life runs in parallel throughout the universe; this duality which merges into unity is rooted in the same ground as everything sacred; and that which draws man to woman and makes him throw his arms around her, is nothing more or less than that force which draws the positive electrical pole toward the negative. Nor is that other notion which makes the functioning of sex entirely dependent on a conventional code whereby society lamely tries to protect itself much more creditable to man's own wisdom.

By brute force or by mental force, a man can dominate a woman, when the inner souls of both are suffering. In the true marriage, neither the man nor the woman dominates the other, although one of the couple will yield naturally to the spiritual superior. Through wise understanding and hallowed love they may become so complementary in time as to be one soul in two bodies.

Many married men have only half-wives. They find a wife for the body, but forget to find a wife for the mind. A wife should mate a man's soul as well as his flesh. Nothing could be more romantic than the illusions about one another with which many marriages begin. Nothing could be more tragic than the way in which these illusions are perforce dispelled when the marriages end.

§

When one really has high aspirations, then the quicker one obtains a sensible and self-disciplined adjustment of sex desire the better, for constant preoccupation with any one bodily factor is not going to help one's mind become detached from the flesh and soar into a more ethereal region.

A person who is unfit for total renunciation and who is sex-starved is more likely to concentrate his thoughts on sex and how to obtain satisfaction of his sexual instincts than on spiritual uplift.

To make a fetish of physical chastity—to suffer the torments of suppression whilst secretly longing for the pleasures of the flesh, to thwart one's strong instincts, to dam the channels of one's vital energies—all these cases call for sublimation. These would-be ascetics often end in becoming obsessed by the very thing from which they are trying to refrain. They begin to exhibit to the observant eye all those signs of frustration, neuroticism, and inhibition which inevitably develop where restraint does not arise perfectly naturally. Extreme fanaticism is abnormal and unnatural.

The monk who makes a fetish of celibacy to such an extent that he worships it and regards all those who are not in the monastic state as being inferior, that man has adopted a materialistic viewpoint of human nature. He is confounding people with their bodies.

You have to remember you are not the body, and therefore in the end nothing that you do with or by the body is going to affect your spiritual state drastically. You seek a spiritual consciousness, and no amount of altering bodily habits is going to give it.

Nearer to the spirit is the mind, and so the mind is where the goal is more likely to be attained. If this be true, you see it is perfectly possible for one to live in the marriage state and yet through control of thought to achieve the goal. Perhaps it will be harder than the effort of the monk. The monk will have less to resist. Although it may be harder for the married man than for the monk to attain spiritual awareness, success can still be his, because there is no crime, there is no sin, in sex intercourse *per se*. There is nothing in it but a perfectly natural function of the body. Let us not confuse the issues.

We need self-control, but not self-torture. We need sexual restraint but not sexual extinction, just as we need the illumined use of the intellect and not its ascetic rejection.

We must find a middle ground between both ends of the question. To renounce the world, to turn one's back on it as an evil thing, has been assumed to be the only path to spirituality. This is exaggeration. To accept the world, but to spiritualize one's existence in it, is another path and one which can lead to identically the same goal.

We need a sensible medium between sex obsession and sex repression. We want life in its fullness, for the Spirit is everywhere present, and not life in its narrowness as imposed by asceticism.

There may and will be certain critical occasions and periods when an aspirant has to withdraw entirely from sexual activity in order to concentrate the whole force of his being upon the "leap-over" from one phase of his inner life to the next, but these are temporary, and the faithful aspirant will surely be fully alive to the demand that is made upon him.

The successful practice of true chastity, i.e., in thought and deed combined, when it is a triumphant positive virtue and not merely an attempted negative one, when it refuses dissipation through innate strength, not through innate fear, and when lust has yielded to loftier desires, always brings great benefits of a physical and mental nature. This state also avoids the sufferings and anxieties that unfortunate sexual entanglements call down upon the undiscriminating.

Because the body is the sacred habitation of an undying soul, it should be treated with due respect. Its primal energy should be reasonably conserved and not made the sport of momentary changes, if higher attainments are looked for. If we have the courage and common sense to keep to such a balanced life as is here advocated, sex will then cease to be a bogey and its acceptance will no longer be a subversion of spiritual ethics.

So far as this particular path is concerned, you may live a perfectly normal, married, but disciplined sex life, and still achieve the highest progress in your spiritual practices. To be utterly and completely free of these hankerings is not asked of the seeker. Complete and total freedom comes to you only as the fruit of final liberation at the end of the quest, for it can come only when you have become identified with the Overself. But at least you should *want* to be free. At least you must recognize intellectually that your hankerings have no eternal value and that they are aims which can but give you temporary benefits. Some amount of external self-control is therefore required as a gesture that you do want the life which is more eternal. Some amount of indifference to material objects and material life is certainly called for. But this is quite different from extreme asceticism. The turning away should be basically an *inner* attempt.

The man on this quest will come to regard sex as a centre of energy and virility which, when sensibly curbed, gives him additional power for his mental concentration. Yet he will not look upon the sexual function as a sin or as a defilement to be eliminated from his life. Neither will he become hysterical, as so many do, when faced with this thorny problem of complete freedom versus complete chastity. Common sense is perhaps more necessary here than in dealing with any of the other difficulties upon the quest.

You should be very careful of adopting that extreme view which would adopt a "holier than thou" attitude in such matters. You cannot judge by external appearance, by the appearance of marriage or non-marriage as to what degree of spirituality any man has. It is what he is in his consciousness; that is the only thing that matters. If it were possible only for monks and fakers who have renounced the world to attain the Overself, then what hope would there be for the rest of humanity? None. You must keep balance and remember that the real work you have to do is a work in the mind. You must gain control of the mind so that you can get an understanding of truth, and those things are not bodily habits. So do not make a fetish of the cause of asceticism. It has its place, but it is a minor place. Keep it there, secondary and subordinate. Thus sex takes the place in spiritual life which you give it. It is relative. There is no absolute rule. To the struggling aspirant, it may be either a demon to be overcome or a force to be used for attainment.

"How can you reconcile sex and spirit?" the chaste defenders of an ancient doctrine sometimes ask. "How can you reconcile stomach and spirit?" is the retort. Nature herself is not conspicuously chaste, but mankind, of course, is ever improving upon her. The monk takes death to wife under the notion that so grim a companion is God-ordained, but he may be as mistaken as the ascetic who renounces the world and wounds his body with physical self-torture. No, complete celibacy is not essential, but decency and self-control always, inexorably, and universally are.

I would even go as far as to alter slightly Oscar Wilde's maxim on art and make it read: "There is no such thing as a moral or an immoral life. Life is well lived or badly lived, that is all."

You need not be afraid of the sexual instincts, and within the limits of right living and social decency you may admit them to your lives, but this is not to say that you need to permit them to tyrannize over you. You must regain control over yourself, and nothing is so hard as to regain control over sex.

You must not confuse causes with effects. Control of mind is a cause which ultimately leads to control of the sex impulses. To prescribe complete and permanent sexual abstinence as an essential ingredient of a method of acquiring control of mind may suit a certain number of people, but not many. Those who have achieved conquest of thought and reined in the mind will quite naturally and even effortlessly find a consequent conquest of passion. The mind is the real battleground, not the body.

Not by ascetically denying their existence nor feebly surrendering completely to them, may the average aspirant find his peace, but by treading a middle path which evokes neither after regrets nor torturing temptations. If and when he reaches a higher degree of spiritual attainment which places his individual will in harmony with the will of the Supreme Creator, he will understand and act in a truly holy manner at all times. Whether or not he forbears for ever thenceforth to touch carnal things or continues to live a normal, outward, everyday life is for him to decide. At this advanced stage, no one dares prescribe for another.

The man who lives the most dissipated life will check his feelings when he faces his mother. Why? He respects his mother. Some instinct rises up in him and checks him. So when you face the Overself, it checks your desires, it checks your thoughts and holds your mind. Your worldly passions, when you come into the presence of the Overself, are taken and checked and held by the higher power. Therefore, you have to practise asceticism, but you do it in a natural way. You work for the moment of realization, knowing that then alone can the real conquest of desire be achieved.

You may card-index all the qualities of the high soul, and then labour painfully to possess them one by one. But you who hunger for the Spirit and eventually receive it, receive every one of these virtues. Do not trouble about the long catalogue of the virtues. Cut away the roots of a tree and the branches will wither of their own accord; so cut away the root of all vices and they disappear of themselves. For when you discover the Overself, which is the root of all the virtues, you will find the latter growing up of their own accord. It is the rising remembrance of a grander self within our hearts which checks the beast and the reptile who hold our passions.

The driving urge that sends men into monasteries needs to be respected, however, for we must all subdue and sanctify the passions and energies, although there are different ways of accomplishing this. Some superior characters are born with a definite vocation for complete chastity and they will know no peace until they accept their destiny. They are quite right in what they do. But most normal people have not felt such a vocation, nor is it really essential, upon the path portrayed in my books, to become a monk or nun.

If I am in revolt against the orthodox yoga systems on these matters; if I refuse to accept all the impositions of ancient and medieval religious cults in a modern era; if, in short, I am even anti-ascetic, it is because it is my desire to infuse a spiritual essence into modern activity, to strip the spiritual path of its unessential rigours, and make it accessible to the man in the home, the office, the factory, and the farm.

CHAPTER IX

THE SCRIPTURE OF THE YOGIS

I: RENUNCIATION

HAVE Asia and Europe met but to trouble one another? Is there no deep benefit to come out of their contact?

We Westerners have been infatuated with the life of the body and have not seen much use in any other kind of life. The old East, parched by a ferocious sun, drifted into doing as little as it possibly could in the way of physical activity. It turned to think and dream of the Intangible. It seems to me that the pendulum of world growth will come to its poise midway between these two extreme points; that a new race must appear whose active limbs will be guided by spiritual dreams.

Those Orientals who foolishly despise the West because we are busy exploiting the material resources of Nature, make a great mistake. It is not because we are doing this that we are unwise. It is because we have likewise forgotten to exploit the spiritual resources of Nature. The wrong is not so much in what we are doing, as in the way we have been doing it.

The adventurous West has no need to be ashamed of itself when it steps into the presence of the reflective East. Each has something of value to the other, and neither can claim to have circumscribed the boundless Infinite with its finite compass. If the Western ideal of external progress could be married to the Eastern mystic's desire for withdrawal into the soul, we could then rightly appreciate the rich possibilities of a full life. We must learn to live in the senses and the spirit, both, without conflict. We need not allow even the business of making a livelihood to become an obsession nor the business of reverencing God to become a mania. We must be balanced.

The modern need—and especially the Orientals' need —is to swing the whole body of spiritual doctrine into direct relation with worldly life and to do this in such a way that the light and power of the spirit may become available to everyday men to help them walk wisely and alleviate their mortal distresses.

There is a very old Indian book which tries, in a remarkable manner, to satisfy both ideals. It advocates that the mystic must underlie the man of affairs, yet its pages have often been dismally misunderstood and its value thereby reduced. This ancient book can satisfy the modern need. Nearly every literate yogi in India carries with him a small edition of this inspired and profound classic, the *Bhagavad-Gita*. If this gospel of contemplation combined with action had been understood in the land of its birth as it should be understood, India would today shed the radiance of her spiritual illumination to the far corners of the world and provide a masterly pattern of a balanced material-spiritual existence for all other countries to witness.

The *Gita* summarizes various approaches to the Overself, and also describes the latter. It can be variously interpreted, and I shall reveal in selected representative lines the esoteric meaning rather than the religious. The beautiful simplicity and lofty quality of this Indian bible bring it into favourable and complementary light alongside of the New Testament.

Arjuna, a young prince who is one of the two parties —the divine teacher and his human disciple—engaged in the dialogue which runs throughout these pages, typifies in his own figure the man who seeks peace of mind amid worldly harassments, as well as the aspirant desirous of spiritual light.

However, not until he is critically placed on a battle-field, to fight against his beloved relatives whom he sees confronting him in the opposing army, does he vehemently cry out for an answer to his questions. The battlefield, obviously, represents the battlefield of life in which we are placed in all kinds of circumstances, whether we like them or not.

The disciple cries out for guidance. Only when his anguish becomes almost unbearable and his heart is deeply torn, does the teacher, who is symbolized by the figure of the god-man Krishna, appear.

Krishna not only represents the embodied spiritual teacher, but he is ultimately the Overself within man, the God within who can illuminate all dark corners and answer all questions. He finds the disciple afflicted, agitated, and with eyes full of tears. He sees him perplexed with doubts, torn between the desire to do his duty in battle and the love for his relatives who oppose him in the enemy army. The occasion is used to give lengthy instruction upon spiritual subjects and techniques. At the end of the dialogue, after hearing all the teachings, the pupil's mind becomes peaceful. He says, indeed, "My doubts are dispelled. Destroyed are my illusions."

By what magic was this mental change accomplished? Through both the guidance and grace received from his teacher and his own inner growth in striving for insight.

The difficulties one meets in modern life can be met and overcome after we gain such insight. Wisdom means the ability to negotiate all the circumstances of life adequately, correctly, and with *spiritual* success. This understanding of the power lying latent within him, becomes in time a man's anchor to windward. He can ride the storms which life brings, in the certainty that there is now something within him that they cannot shake from its position. The man of inspired life follows no iron law and clings to no rocklike plan. Sufficient for him to look within for right direction at all times and amidst all circumstances. To perceive the truth about any matter is to dispel all doubt.

The deep spiritual comfort emanating from the teachings of the *Gita* is peculiarly needed at this stage of the world's affairs.

"Of what avail is dominion to us, O Teacher?
Of what avail are pleasures and even life?
How can we be happy, after slaying our own people?
Nay, I will not fight."

The disciple is brought to the field of battle and told to fight. But he is confused with doubts. What is the use of it all, he asks? Who does not ask himself the same question in the stress and battle of our twentieth-century existence? Can one enter into the extreme competition of the business world, for instance, and still feel that he is not stifling his better instincts? Note how simply and understandingly this particular problem is answered by the teacher in the various verses that follow.

"For those who deserve no grief, thou hast grieved . . . Never did I not exist, nor thou, nor these rulers of men; and no one of us will ever hereafter cease to exist . . . Just as in this body the Self passes into childhood and youth and old age, so does he pass into another body . . . Whoever looks upon Him as the slayer, and whoever looks upon Him as the slain, both these know not aright. Unborn, eternal, unchangeable and primeval, He is not slain when the body is slain . . . Just as man casts off worn-out clothes and puts on others which are new, so the Self casts off worn-out bodies and enters others which are new . . . But even if thou thinkest of him as ever being born and ever dying, even then thou oughtest not to grieve thus. To that which is born, death is indeed certain; and to that which is dead, birth is certain. Wherefore, about the unavoidable thing, thou oughtest not to grieve . . ."

The teacher points out that wise people do not grieve over death, because there is no death. Never were you not, and never shall you not be. You are eternal and can never cease to exist. Since the disciple is perplexed with the problem of death, the teacher enlightens his mind regarding this eternal enigma. He tells him that since the inner self is unkillable, there is no such thing as death.

The body is transient and may be killed, but you are eternal. Circumstances cannot affect the real *you*. Endure them bravely, therefore, with wisdom and resignation, when they are unavoidable.

The disciple is told to fight his battle bravely, because he cannot really destroy anyone. He can kill only the bodies of other people, for, after all, these are transients. The fear of death is based not on truth, but on illusion.

Similarly, in dealing with everyday life, remember that whatever happens circumstances can only touch that part of you which is transient, which comes and goes. Keep your sense of proportion, remembering that you likewise have an eternal value, and that this phenomenal life comes and goes like a shadow. The wise may have their difficulties and troubles, since destiny brings them to all alike, but they do not grieve over them. Grief can only come if you identify yourself wholly with the lesser part, the body. Troubles, pain, and death are unavoidable and are an inevitable part of the phenomena of physical life. This is because *change* is the very nature of the physical world.

Troubles come, but they will also go. If they do not go during earthly existence, then they will have to pass with the passing of the fleshly body. So mend them if you can, but endure them bravely if you must. Throughout the events of life, you must have wisdom and you must have courage. You need the courage not only to find the truth, to strip off all your illusions and those which others propose to thrust upon you, but also to *live* the truth.

A hint of the ultimate truth that the material world is not what it seems to be, that it is illusory and shadow-like when compared with That out of which it has evolved, is thus given even at the beginning of the *Gita*. During the earlier stages of the quest, everything real is still illusory, while everything illusory still seems real. The final truth about the eternal character of the Overself is not realized until the end of the quest.

> "Of the unreal no being there is;
>   There is no non-being of the real.
>   Of both these is the truth seen by
>   The seers of the Essence."

That is the final and vital truth. We may, however, take certain illusions as convenient stepping-stones to help us to proceed towards Absolute Truth. Remember that in the highest sense this is an unreal world. The real indestructible essence is the Overself, that which secretly pervades the whole universe.

The disciple receives the teaching to fight, i.e., to act. But as one studies and advances, there naturally comes to him the question, "Why should I act when all this is nothing but a dream? One thing is as good as another. Why shouldn't I retire and let others perform the action? Life is obviously a dream, therefore I will sit still and watch the dream go by."

This attitude indicates progress on the quest and is quite an advanced one. Why should one act, when one does not want to act? Because whatever you do, you

cannot refrain from acting. You can't escape activity if
you retreat from the world, because you will still be
involved in mental action. You may sit still and yet be
held captive within the cycle of the finite, for you cannot escape from your thoughts. Your activity may change
its character and become a mental one.

The result will be that you will be no less bound to
the one than to the other. Meanwhile, the fact is that
whether you act or sit still and think, *you are still in
essence the self*. But if you know that you cannot destroy the self, why should you be afraid of physical
activity? Go out into the world, do your duty, fight if
need be, but act. Love and peace constitute your real
nature and they do not change with your changing physical activities. Therefore, be inwardly the witness of
life, as you wish to be, but do not be afraid of it. You
cannot kill anyone, because you and they are ultimately
both the one Overself.

"Thy concern is with action alone, never with results. Let not the fruit of action be thy motive, nor
let thy attachment be for inaction. Steadfast in devotion do thy works, O disciple, casting off attachment,
being the same in success and failure."

Do not lose your sense of proportion and assume that
your actions are going to make any difference to the
Witness, the Overself, which always remains unaffected.
Destiny has given you a part to play. Play your part, do
your duty, even as others have their duties. Whether you
are a maker of shoes or a stenographer in a business office,
or a general of an army, do what your place calls for at
the time. Do not make the error, however, of confusing
this counsel with the notion that you are to do it for *all*
time. That is entirely different. What is right for you
this year may be wrong for you next.

Krishna did not disdain to give his sublime teachings

to Arjuna, both on yoga and truth, in the stir and tumult of the battlefield, precisely where action was called for. Why did he not instruct his disciple in a hermitage? The "holy men" who can find holiness *only* in hermitages may rack their brains for an answer—the fact remains. Life is all-comprehensive, and has plenty of room for both action and contemplation. Neither is holier than the other.

You cannot be deluded by the illusion of life, provided you remember who and what you are. When you remember that you are the divine Self, then you can act with understanding. To act in this fashion is necessarily difficult. You must be able to plunge into the midst of activity in the market place or the stock exchange or the family home, and yet be inwardly detached from the results of your actions.

Yet wherever you are, you must keep to the sacred quest. You do your work as a matter of duty, but you are not so bound up with it, or with searching for success, that the world would come to an end if you meet with failure. Success must not be the be-all and end-all of living. To learn how to give up, how to let go of things and persons, is a lesson which all of us have to learn sooner or later. If you have learned to renounce inwardly, it may never be necessary to renounce outwardly. Try to cut loose the desire-bonds. They are inside you, and if you can cut them loose it does not matter what is happening outside.

When you understand this, you simply do what you have to do—let it be the best and the utmost that life demands of you—and then let the results take care of themselves, not because you do not care, but because you know that a cosmic power is taking care of them. The results are in the hands of the Overself and destiny. Accept this destiny with a certain resignation. Do not run away and refuse to act. Neither go to the other extreme and plunge into activity with greed and desire as the *only* motives for your action. Have the higher ones also. Act; then observe the results of your actions, retiring to the status of an impersonal witness. The earth revolves, but its axis never moves from its wonted place. Similarly, you must act and move in the external world, but your inner self must be the unseen axis—serene, reposed, and still.

The disciple then asks:

"What, O Teacher, is the description of one of steady mind, who is constant in contemplation? How does one of steady mind speak, how sit, how move?"

To put the matter most plainly, this question simply means: What is a true yogi like?

The teacher replies:

"When a man, satisfied in the Self alone by himself, completely casts off all the desires of the mind, then is he said to be one of steady mind."

Desires, wishes, and feelings, are in the end nothing but thoughts. To desire an object is either to form a mental picture or to hold an abstract conception in the mind. A passion is simply a thought, held more strongly and more intensely than other thoughts usually are. Before a desire can be formed, you must *think* of it. When it is formed, you still *think* of it. Desires, therefore, are part of your stream of thoughts. To cast off the desire you must eventually cast off the *thought* of it. It follows that the power to inhibit thoughts and live in the condition where thought is reduced to a minimum, means the power to attain at will the state of peace. Peace is the absence of thoughts and desires. Then only have you attained that state of mental equilibrium which is the state of the successful yogi who has found his inner self. Once this power is gained, you may entertain thoughts in your mind again, but they will be unable to disturb your peace.

The teacher continues:

> "He whose heart is not distressed in calamities, from whom all longing for pleasures has departed, who is free from attachment, fear and wrath, he is called a sage, a man of steady mind."

Since we have been sent here on earth, we cannot shirk the calamities of material life. We can, however, evade the conventional reaction to them. The selfsame defeat in business will merely amuse one man but completely beat another. The first may fight anew, the second commit suicide. We must understand that calamities are unavoidable because they come as the result of what we have done in former births. But we can accept them with peace and equanimity by controlling our reaction to them. In this regard, however, the teacher points out that if you wish to be able to resist the effects of pain and calamity, you must also control your reaction to their opposites. Pleasure and bad fortune, pain and good fortune are opposite ends of the same stick. Therefore, you must also learn to give up inwardly the good things of life. If you are to do this effectually, it will follow that when you are suddenly left a financial fortune, your mind will not be excited beyond control but will remain calm. Be like an actor on the stage who, although playing his part to perfection, remembers all the time who he is. You are inwardly divine. *Be* that.

> "He attains peace, into whom all desires enter as water enters the ocean, which filled from all sides, remains unaltered; but not he who desires objects."

That is the state of the true yogi. To attain peace, thoughts must flow into the mind evenly, without disturbing you. To hate is to be disturbed by the strong thought of the person you are hating. To live excitedly is also disturbing, and therefore you cannot expect peace. We have to learn to follow the middle way. Peace can be found by guarding and controlling the mind.

The teacher points out:

"What is night to all beings, therein the self-controlled one is awake. Where all beings are awake, that is the night of the sage who sees."

In this sentence, "night" means the phenomenal world around you. The sage sees through its illusion because he is spiritually awake, but the others are spiritually asleep. They are deceived by its appearance of solidity and substantiality. What is that which seems "night to all beings"? It is the transcendental being of the Overself. The sage always dwells in that life, which is divine infinitude. One who truly enters it is neither bound to be an ascetic nor a man of the world. The sage is an enigma to others, because he knows that all invisible life and all embodied life are the same to him. His is centred in the divine, and as destiny brings the panorama of life before him, he understands and accepts it, but himself remains unaltered, because he has attained the condition of perfect peace. The ascetic and the would-be yogi may try to banish all thoughts, but the sage is not trying to do anything. He understands and accepts thoughts, but he is not at their mercy, for he realizes what they really are and controls them effortlessly and spontaneously.

The disciple asks:

"If it be thought by Thee that knowledge is superior to action, O Teacher, why then dost Thou direct me to this terrible action?"

He desires to know why, if understanding the truth is so necessary, he should be asked to plunge into activity. He is still confused.

The teacher replies:

"In this world a twofold path was taught by Me at first, that of devotion to knowledge and that of devotion to action."

Since you cannot escape activity, be it physical or mental, it follows that there is a path for the man of action and another path for the man of thought.

The teacher then describes the path of action. He stresses the performance of duty and the repayment of the debt which one owes to Nature.

The real problem for the spiritual man is how to render efficient service and give himself up to his work in this feverish contemporary world, and yet remain loyal to his inner call. The blissfulness of introspection may tempt him more and more to desert externals, but excessive introspection is only commendable in those whom destiny and duty have flung out of the world into monasteries and ashrams and retreats.

Later, the teacher inculcates sacrifice, but it is a peculiar kind of sacrifice. It is a sacrifice of service. You must serve because it is right to serve, act because it is right to act, then sacrifice the result of your actions to destiny. This means that you do not act solely for reward. Do your work, perform your duty, not only for your personal need but also with the idea of service. Do not concentrate only on results and personal benefits, but also work impersonally. This is practicing a path of yoga, because it tends to curb desires and selfishness and helps to free one from bondage to the senses.

The path is peculiarly appropriate for the man working and living the twentieth-century life of action. It is my belief that ancient wisdom must unite with modern science. The mystic of today should be prepared to ride in an aeroplane; he should carry the "cave of contemplation" within his heart, whilst the press, noise, and crowd of metropolitan streets throb around him. Then you have to realize that if you have been put into the struggle and strife of modern existence in a Western city, that is just where God wishes you to be for something to be learned, some lesson which may provide you with opposition, an opposition that has to be overcome, and that through the strife and the effort of overcoming it you will learn the lesson you need.

In that path, one learns the meaning of duty and sacrifice. But what does one really sacrifice? Nothing, except the results of action, and that is done *mentally*. Do your work in the world—perform your duty, but do not make your happiness depend entirely upon personal results or benefits resulting from your actions. Act in such a manner as to set a good example to others, thus becoming a teacher of the highest order. By your setting an unselfish standard of action and thinking of the effect of your actions on others, they will imitate you, and you will teach by lifting others up.

The tribute we perforce pay to truth is usually counted in the coin of lip service alone, but the best missionaries are those who live abundantly; the best propagandists for a spiritual cause are those who give personal example and preach their precepts afterwards. The practical exemplar makes the finest tutor.

"Those deluded by the energies of Nature are attached to the functions of the energies. He who knows the All should not unsettle the unwise who know not the All."

The right attitude results only after some extended trial of these spiritual practices. It is the attitude of "agency," of instrumentality rather than doership, the sense that the Overself is doing all works in you, is acting, speaking, and working through you. When you can contact the diviner intelligence and permit it to operate freely through you, it will guide, and guide rightly; it will help wisely; it will pacify, when personal feelings become angered. It may even lead you to desert some relative good for solid good. Thus do you arrive at the highest state of Karma-Yoga. You realize that when you are acting, it is simply Nature acting and finding focus through you.

"Renouncing all actions in Me, with thy thought resting on the Self, being free from hope, free from selfishness, devoid of fever, do thou fight."

When you come to the realization that it is really Nature expressing itself through you, then you renounce your actions inwardly. You turn to the Witness-Self, letting Nature take care of the results. You then reach the final stage when you can watch your self playing its part in the work of the world, without anticipation and without expectation. No more are you concerned with the future and its burdens. That concerns Nature. You set the example and others will imitate you and be benefited. By practicing this path with faith, you can be liberated from actions and destiny. It will free you from the cycle of births and deaths. If you devotedly fulfil the earlier stages of this quest, there will come a time when the power of the spirit will bring you face to face with the secret Witness-Self. Then you will be liberated from the power of accumulated destiny. But even as soon as a substantial degree of spiritual illumination has been gained, there need be no conflict between this illumination and the majority of worldly activities. Some of the latter indeed may seem definitely unspiritual, unjust, or materialistic in the critical eyes of others, yet this is a matter which cannot be judged by appearances. A man may conceivably take part in a war, fight, and slay, and yet be living by a diviner light than the generality of mankind. The essential difference between him and the other soldiers of the same army will be one of motive. He fights impersonally, feeling neither hatred nor ill will of any kind against the enemy, understanding that life no less demands good sense than it demands good will, and knowing that he is performing a duty ordained both by his destiny and by the social structure of which he forms part in defending his country. It was in such an impersonal mood that Jesus drove the money-changers out of the temple. There was no sentimentality about human brotherhood when he performed this act.

Another man, on the contrary, who may have attained an equally substantial degree of illumination, may refuse to fight and will then be prepared to bear unflinchingly the penalties meted out by the State to such "conscientious objectors." Here again the varying destiny of the man and the symbolic relationship in which he stands to his own society may necessitate such an apparent defection from social duty. Everything depends upon the particular circumstances of the case.

The truth is that what really matters is to surrender one's ego-self to the bidding and will of the Overself, and then to carry out that bidding. If the Overself sends one into the haunts of social outcasts, one must be prepared unhesitatingly to go. And if the Overself sends one into the ranks of gilded idlers and dissipated dilettantes, one must be equally prepared to go; and if the Overself places one in the harsh atmosphere of a soulless business or noisy factory, one must follow its bidding. There will always be some lesson to be learned, or some service to be rendered, or some educative working out of destiny, wherever one is sent. Finally, if the Overself declares, "All these activities are puerile, all these persons worthless, and all time spent amongst them wasted," then also must one move unhesitatingly out of one's environment, sacrifice the world, and retire into spiritual retreat, whether it be in some secluded rural spot or a monastic home.

"But those who, carping at this, My teaching, practice it not,—know them as deluded in all knowledge, as senseless men doomed to destruction."

They destroy themselves and go down into the endless abyss. It is endless because there is no end to the cycles of birth and rebirth. It can go on indefinitely unless you follow this quest which leads out of it. Can you think of a time when your births started? In the same manner, you cannot think of an end of them. Buddha saw this awful hell of infinite embodiment and rebirth and sought a way out. It can be done only through following this quest and eliminating all false ideas, by right action, by meditation, and by indifference to results. This is the way which is taught to the disciple, the practice of which leads him to a point where he rises to freedom.

Now we come to the quest of spiritual knowledge.

The teacher says:

"I taught this imperishable yoga . . . handed down thus in succession, the King-sages learnt this. This yoga, by long lapse of time, has been lost here, O Disciple."

Why was it that this path of esoteric knowledge had to be taught to man from the beginning of time? Because the ultimate truth about life is so subtle and transcends the imagination of man to such an extent that without divine revelation, he could never have discovered it. It was first given to man as a revelation from the highest embodied being then existent on this planet. It was taught originally to the adept-kings of early China, Egypt, and other primitive African, Asiatic, and American peoples. At the time this high knowledge was imparted several thousand years ago, as mentioned in the *Bhagavad-Gita*, the knowledge had long been lost and had to be brought back. Is it to be wondered at that to-day even in India the high esoteric wisdom has again largely sunk into obscurity and desuetude?

"That same ancient Yoga has been today taught to thee by Me, seeing that thou art My devotee and friend; for, this is the Supreme Secret . . . Whenever there is a decay of spirituality, O disciple, and an ascendency of irreligion, then I manifest Myself."

A promise is here definitely made that High Beings have pledged themselves to watch over mankind, and that they will save mankind, in the only true sense of salvation, in critical moments of history. If no leader arises amongst men themselves to help them, then the gods will come down into the mortal flesh and give humanity what it must have. Such times come whenever there is a degeneration in spiritual understanding, be-cause the lamp of the divine truth must be kept alight in the world. Whenever this truth lapses from human knowledge, it must be brought back by the gods who incarnate in order to relight the lamp among the masses of mankind. The consequent awakening to things of the spirit will automatically provide the *only* condition in which all the chief economic, social, and political prob-lems can really readjust or solve themselves.

"For the protection of the good, for the destruc-tion of evil-doers, for the firm establishment of spirit-ual living, I am born in every age."

Every time that humanity sinks down to the last depth of spiritual ignorance and there is decay in true religion, then there happens the rebirth of an adept or even a god who undertakes a public mission of spiritual service. When the mystic ventures forth into action he is apt to become social dynamite, exploding wherever the letter is killing the spirit. It is easy to cite history in order to attest this truth.

Peculiarly enough, at such a time there is a reincarnation in great numbers of those who are plunged in deep spiritual ignorance or excessive desire, who are filled with hatred, envy, greed, and lust. These reincarnated beings contribute largely to the darkness of the age. At this time destiny takes a hand in their spiritual education, and they are reborn in such a period to be given their deepest lesson. They are finally destroyed physically, by great natural catastrophes, such as floods or pestilences, and especially by war. At such times, their wholesale destruction by violent death is the appropriate education which is necessary for their spiritual development. But these epochs see also "the protection of the good."

Those who have advanced some way in following a spiritual path are shielded to some extent. They are protected mentally and supported inwardly. At times this protection may extend to miraculous external help at crucial moments. Whatever happens outwardly, when these moments come they will find that a higher power is with them; its presence will be manifested to them either direct from the Overself or through another. The work of the higher power becomes more active and more effective as matters get worse. Amidst the insanity and destruction and blindness and terror of our world they may then find within themselves a sheltering haven, where others stand helpless or are swept off their feet into fear. Then, right in the midst of the greatest external disaster, they may become aware of a mysterious Presence which gives them intense calm and courage. Always a life supported by the Overself is a calm, wise, strong life, inwardly protected.

"Know this: by long prostration, by enquiry, by

service, those men of wisdom who have realized the truth will teach thee wisdom."

In India everyone prostrates himself on the ground before approaching a spiritual teacher. It is only a symbol of the fact that he seeks the higher power and that he humbly accepts what he hears as the divine Truth. Veneration and reverence for spiritually illumined men is much rarer in Western countries, to our loss. The earnest aspirant will eventually have to seek a competent teacher. When you find one who appeals to you, ask for acceptance, and then remain in touch with him until you are led into the Truth, no matter how long it takes. Krishna says that when you have the three qualifications, "humility, enquiry, and service," then the men of wisdom, who have realized the Truth, will teach you. They will give you their wisdom in various ways, some by speech and some by writing and some by silence, but ultimately by bestowing their grace. Humility means having utmost faith and confidence in the teacher, as well as in his words. Enquiry means persistent search for reality by piercing through illusions. Service means offering whatever help the teacher needs, because he gives his own knowledge freely and never asks anyone for a return. If those three qualifications are not fulfilled, it is hard to get genuine tuition. When you have found it, you need not again fall into error.

"Even shouldst thou be the most sinful of all the sinful, thou shalt verily cross all sin by the boat of wisdom."

If you can find a genuine teacher and climb the steps of this quest under his guidance, you may be the greatest sinner in the world, yet you can transcend all these sins and attain the highest liberation. Your devotion to him will be repaid a thousandfold. This is the only way that it can be accomplished.

"As kindled fire reduces fuel to ashes, O Disciple, so does wisdom-fire reduce all actions to ashes."

If you can continue with this special road to liberation, and gain a knowledge of the Truth, destiny will not harm you. No matter how sinful you are, the moment you realize the Truth you become released from the accumulated effects of your sins. What is destiny? Nothing but the collection of thought, desire, and action-tendencies which persist around you and eventually materialize, thus resulting in a material readjustment or change of your life. You destroy all these at the root by knowledge of the Truth.

"Verily, there exists here no purifier equal to wisdom. He who is perfected by yoga finds it in time in himself by himself."

This is a curious statement. When you have practiced meditation and achieved control of your mind, then you will eventually find the esoteric wisdom. You will have to wait for someone to lead you into the Absolute Truth, which will be given to you as a reward. You will be given this initiation after a lapse of time. Meditation alone will not be enough. The only truth is the knowledge of Supreme Reality.

"Therefore with the sword of wisdom cleave asunder this doubt of the Self lying in the heart and born of ignorance, and resort to meditation."

Eliminate your doubts and fears by acquiring real knowledge of the Overself. Knowledge chases ignorance as light chases darkness. Real knowledge of truth does

not mean knowledge of material phenomena. Phenomenal experience is endless.

The next path is that of renunciation. It applies only
to the man who runs away from the world to practise
meditation in solitudes or monasteries.

The disciple asks:

"Renunciation of actions, O Teacher, Thou prais-
est, and again meditation. Tell me conclusively that
which is the better of the two."

The teacher replies:

"Both lead to the highest bliss; but, of the two,
Yoga through action is esteemed more than renunciation of action."

How is that? Spiritual ecstasy is the highest state of
emotion. But it is not the highest truth. To come to the
highest truth one would then have to be initiated in
the ultimate quest. Both the path of activity and that
of renunciation from the world lead to this bliss. If you
must make a choice between the two, follow the path
which leads to activity in the world. It is more difficult,
but the results are proportionately greater.

In ancient days, in former incarnations, people who
wanted to gain a higher spiritual dimension would retreat into the mystery temples for a while and there be
taught under the most helpful conditions. Sometimes
they would spend their lives there; everything was made
easier for their spiritual progress. Today there are no
such institutions and life itself has taken their place, so
you must gain your initiations, seek your knowledge,
and develop your intuition amidst and through the very
experiences which come to you every day. There is no
use saying that you cannot learn in the midst of this
materialized environment. You learn by reflecting on

your experiences to see the lessons behind them, and
that is in a way as helpful as meditations in a monastery.
Understanding is just as important as drowning yourself
in meditation, and your experiences in the material
world present the proper opportunities to you. Both are
needed, of course. The conditions evoke certain thoughts
and feelings and you have to choose their direction.
They give you an opportunity to understand, to confront, and to overcome obstacles.

Why does the teacher advise the more difficult path?
Because of its very difficulty! It is a path that forces you
to act more directly on your own initiative. When you
live in the world of activity, there is immediate testing
of all theories by results. The man who renounces the
world may be fostering all sorts of illusions in his head.
Talk about spirituality does not make you spiritual.
Bring down to the physical plane of action whatever
you know, and *live* it. To follow a mirage made of
words is not to follow the living God who dwells in your
heart. Then also, if you remain in the world, you serve
and help humanity by setting an example. In the final
sense, however, both paths are the same. The man in
the world who is acting from the higher motives, is not
different from the man who has run away from the
world.

The sage may be a king. He may be possessed of regal
splendour. But sometimes he may be a nobody, an
obscure figure. Whatever part he has to play, he will
play it. In any situation he still remains a man of divine
realization. No one can dictate what part a man of
realization should play. For him, the contradictory has
become the complementary. You cannot say that he
must come out into the world, or that he must remain
in retreat. It is foolish for the ignorant to say that an
adept must do this or that. He may stay for years and
years in a cave, and yet he is not wasting time. If he receives the divine mandate, the true sage will surely sacri-

fice the lonely places which he loves. If the command be given from within he will descend into the crowded arenas and babbling forums of the world.

"Children, not the wise, speak of these two paths as distinct. He who is rightly devoted to even one obtains the fruits of both."

The teacher explains that the truly wise man will be a master of two worlds—the world within and the world without, and not the slave of either. He will be the child of his own epoch and not an imitation of some earlier ancestor.

"In a sage endued with wisdom and humility, in a cow, in an elephant, as also in a dog and in a dog-eater, the wise see the same [Overself]."

That is the outlook of a sage. In such a man you find wisdom and humility. He looks on all beings as ultimately expressing the same unity of life. His outlook is universal; it is without prejudice of race and caste. In India, the lowest caste is the "dog-eater" who is not even permitted to live in the villages. In the eyes of the sage, who sees the Overself in all, this outcast merits the same respect and the same kindness as that given a king.

"He knows the Overself can neither rejoice on obtaining the pleasant, nor grieve on obtaining the unpleasant,—steady-minded, undeluded, resting in the Overself."

With his mental outlook, the sage can withstand the impulses of desire and anger. This is an interesting statement because it implies that such impulses reach him. But can they reach him, and why? The common idea is that a sage, adept, or master, has no such impulses—that they have completely disappeared. The idea is not quite correct. They do come in some cases because the sage is not yet liberated from the *body*. Such registrations, however, are fleeting. They disappear a single second afterwards because the sage automatically and spontaneously refuses to identify himself with them.

Matter has lost its grip on him, and this world no longer possesses the power to enchant him completely. He may wander through the materialistic civilization of the world from Moscow to Madagascar, but he will be inwardly unaffected.

> "With the self unattached to external contacts, he finds the joy which is in the Self; with the self engaged in the contemplation of the Overself he attains the endless joy."

He is not dependent on external things alone for joy and happiness, but on the other hand, he is quite capable of appreciating them when available. He is satisfied whether sitting in a cave by himself or living among men in a modern city. Such is the state of those who have attained recognition of the Overself.

> "The sages attain Overself bliss—they whose sins have been destroyed and doubts removed, who are self-controlled and intent on the welfare of all beings."

He has no more doubts. They have been removed because he has found truth and is wedded to it. Doubts are thoughts, opinions, and theories. The sage has lifted himself above such a realm. His doubts have been removed by the light of clear knowledge. It is needless to flash a light in a room which is already illuminated. Neither is it necessary for a sage to hold theories and opinions when he is perpetually illuminated by the transcendent radiance of the Overself.

"Let the Yogi . . . remain in seclusion, alone, with the mind and body controlled, free from desire, and having no possessions."

We come to the description of the practice of full-time meditation in the path for a man who has given up the world, although the exercises can also be practised occasionally by others.

We of the young active West have to learn such relaxation from the older civilization of the Orient, although this is not to say that this path is superior to that of activity. My belief is that both can, and should, contribute complementary factors towards the balanced structure of the new and higher civilization which is the world's urgent need.

We are trying to find the higher consciousness whilst living the work-a-day life of people who dwell in large cities during this complex twentieth century—not by running away to monasteries or retreats or jungles or mountain caves—but whilst living in the world. Admittedly that is harder, definitely harder. But destiny has presented us with this existence, and we have to go through with it and make the best of it. We need not dream that one day, when we can escape from it all, we shall find a quick and easy road to spiritual freedom. The matter is not so simple. Wherever you escape to, you will take your faults with you, your mental habits will go with you, and they will remain as strongly with you in the wilderness or hermit's cave as they will in large cities. The real battle takes place in your mind. Retreats are helpful temporarily, but not as permanent lodgings. Make your own retreat just where you are, by cutting off a half-hour of your day and shutting yourself up for that period. Forget the environment where you

are; go into a brown study, into a reverie, and that is
your retreat, your escape.

For the one on the ascetic path of renunciation, however, all worldly and family ties must be given up. He
must not engage in business nor maintain a household.
He must be totally free to devote himself to finding mental equilibrium through mental effort.

He must not become anxious about possessions, nor
be troubled by desires for them, thus leaving his mind
completely free to turn inwards.

"Having in a cleanly spot established a firm seat,
neither too high nor too low, with cloth, skin, and
grass thereon."

His work now is to make the mind one-pointed, sitting motionless for many hours daily, practising concentration of thought. The practice of keeping the body
motionless is not an easy one, but it is the first struggle.
When the exercise is mastered, then he passes on to the
practice of concentration. Keeping himself erect and
motionless, he must close his eyes or look at the tip of
his nose and endeavour to restrain his mind. He must
not eat too much, nor too little. Eating too much will
make his body coarse and heavy, whereas by not eating
enough food, the resulting body hunger will disturb
the mind. Nor must he indulge in too much sleep nor
remain too wakeful. He must be moderate in all things,
treading the evenly-balanced way. His food, recreation,
and exertion must be moderate. His aim is to save his
energy for mental purposes. He must restrain his
thoughts and concentrate them in a logical chain on one
subject. Later he learns to keep them on one point. The
concentrated or one-pointed mind has been compared
to a lamp in a sheltered spot which does not flicker.
The object of these practices is to draw the mind inwards, away from the body and senses, and back upon

itself. To do this successfully entails constant practice which may take months and even years. But by constant and patient discipline of the wavering mind, it will be found one day that the thoughts can be kept quiescent and still. At this point, the mind must be kept without thoughts, utterly quiet. This is the state of meditation, where you feel that you have become bodyless, formless mind. The surest means to success on this path is constant, regular practice, together with indifference to quick results. One must not become disappointed when one does not obtain favourable results. Success usually comes quite suddenly and when one least expects it.

The teacher answers the student's complaints about yoga's difficulty:

"Doubtless the mind is hard to restrain and restless, but by practice and by indifference it may be restrained."

The wandering mind becomes tired of resisting and finally submits. However, even if you do not achieve, your reward will still mature, for,

"Having attained to the worlds of the righteous, and having dwelt there for eternal years, he who failed in concentration is reborn in a house of the pure and wealthy."

No effort is lost, and everything you have done, all you have attained during your striving, will come back to you in the next earthly birth. Furthermore, if it is possible, you will be born into a spiritual family, where it will be easier for you to attain success on this path. Such a birth is very hard to obtain, however.

"Of all yogis, he who full of faith worships Me, with his inner self abiding in Me, is deemed by Me as most devout."

The deepest worship is that of resting in the Overself. Then is one devout in the highest possible fashion. If you feel that rite and ceremony help you, use them. But ultimately you may have to give them up. For when you come to realize that the Lord of the World is forever performing the festival of the universe, and that this rite is everywhere being held, you will want no longer to be limited to some fleeting formal ceremony, but to take a place in the great temple of this world by *always* remembering and worshipping God in your heart.

This ends the first section of this wonderful and instructive dialogue, and it is fitting that it should close upon the details of the art of mental quiet. The world would be surprised if it knew how many of its famous figures, both of the past and present, have secretly made this daily withdrawal their refuge from onerous duties and heavy responsibilities, finding in their moments of meditation strength to endure their inescapable destiny, and guidance amidst perplexities, when other men grope in an unnecessary blindness. A single example out of several will suffice.

As more than twenty years have now passed since the sensational death of Field Marshal Lord Kitchener when the battleship *Hampshire* was mysteriously sunk, I am breaking no confidences when I reveal that this distinguished soldier did not disdain to seek and receive secret initiation into Oriental yoga practices during his long service in command of the British Military Forces, both in India and Egypt.

There is a little island on the River Nile near the quaint old town of Assuan which now bears his name. Here Kitchener created a delightful spiritual retreat which was reserved in his lifetime exclusively for his own use, during the period when he was virtually a dictator of both Egypt and Sudan. He planted groves of rare tropical trees specially imported from India, as well as waving, luxuriant-leaved palms, to form a perfect screen and shelter for his retreat. In the centre of the island he built a small pavilion. When the day's work was done he loved to slip into a boat and steal away to this picturesque and peaceful spot quite alone and without even a single soldier to guard him.

Here amidst a silence broken only by the musical hum of countless insects and under the superb blue sky of southern Egypt, he forgot his heavy cares and burdens and gave himself up to contemplation, to withdrawing his mind into his central interior being.

During Lord Kitchener's service in India he created a similar retreat in the foothills of the Himalaya Mountains near Simla. The environment was unforgettably lovely, and he named this place "Wildflower Hall." He was one of those few but fortunate men who have heard the deep call of the Overself and were wise enough to respond to it. One of his favourite exercises was the yoga practice which the Hindus call trataka, and which the writer has briefly described in his short reference to Kitchener on page 142 of *The Secret Path*. Kitchener used this gazing exercise as a means of fixing thought, for he went deep into himself and forgot his surroundings. He was always a lonely man and pursued an isolated course even in his profession of soldiering; here on this quiet island he could come face to face with the great Aloneness.

What strength he found herein one can measure by remembering that on his shoulders alone fell the heavy responsibility of organizing England's entire military share of the war during its early years. The British people used to complain of his solitary nature, of his lack of sociability, but they did not understand that he was like unto those who have passed inwardly through the higher initiation of the Brahmins, when the priest says to the candidate:

"He is the Loneliness that is within you. . . . You

are standing all alone before the sacred fire, and from this time on the fire that will be given to you will be Lonely, and you will be lonely with it. Are you ready to accept that loneliness?"

In plainer language this simply means that the initiate will henceforth look first towards his inner, holier self for help, light, love, and strength, and only after that towards frail mortal men. This is really the best form of self-reliance, for it brings higher spiritual powers to work through his personal life.

A divine purpose pulsates through the whole of Nature. He who learns the art of right meditation will ultimately put himself into harmony with that purpose, which will thenceforward use him as a holy instrument in his labours among the strayed sheep of mankind. The universal awareness of the one Overself as being present in all others, automatically brings him into perfect sympathy with all others, and therefore makes him yearn to bring them all into their own self-awareness. Because they are living in a physical world and in a physical body, the best way he can reach them is through physical means, which means a life of inspired activity.

CHAPTER X

THE SCRIPTURE OF THE YOGIS

II: REVELATION

THE second portion of the *Bhagavad-Gita* is illumined by the high revelation made by the Master that the Overself exists everywhere, and that the whole of human struggle is really an unconscious quest for the satisfaction its protection alone offers. This is used as a basis for its deeper and appropriate message, so suited to today, of inspired activity.

"With the mind intent on Me, practicing Yoga, and finding refuge in Me, now in full without doubt thou shalt know me, that do thou hear."

One must practise meditation not only at set times but unceasingly, remembering the benefit of aspiration.

Never forget what you wish to attain—the sacred self-remembrance. When you can hold to this remembrance continuously you have succeeded in your meditation.

Until you reach this stage you must dedicate a part of your day to trying to immerse yourself in these thoughts for the time.

From what are you taking refuge? From everything external. From everything which is not your true Self. From everything which is not pure Spirit. Not only from disappointment and suffering are you seeking refuge, but also from that which the world regards as pleasant and good.

In other words, you aspire to find that peace which abides in your innermost centre. To do so, you must become detached from your worldly experiences. Accept them but do not be swept away by them. The refuge you strive for may be found only in your heart's depths where the Spirit dwells.

To succeed in your quest you must turn your mind inwards, keeping it at rest in the heart-centre, while with the surface mind you are living the active life.

Thus shall you achieve peace, daily embodying that beautiful calmness which will render you able to accept with undisturbed equilibrium whatever life brings.

This attained, you have the teacher's assurance that "without doubt thou shalt know me." Your innermost Spirit abides in that peace, and not in emotional upheavals. These latter are states you pass through during the earlier stages of the path.

The teacher continues:

"Among thousands of men, one perchance strives for perfection; even among those who strive and are perfect, only one perchance knows me in Truth."

Very few seek the truly spiritual or strive for perfection. Enamoured by the seeming reality of worldly existence, people sink into spiritually deadening satisfactions.

There is nothing inherently wrong in seeking material well-being, because we live in a material world. But this search should not completely absorb us. It is only the surface aspect of our lives. There ought also to be the effort to understand the purpose of our incarnation, as well as the striving to attain Reality.

Observe the multitudes who seek God, Truth, in the orthodox religions and unorthodox cults of the world. How many have attained full realization of their divine objective? There are hundreds who have searched for ten, fifteen, or twenty years, yet without having found

Truth. Because Truth is so subtle, very few attain it. Once realized, all your doubts will for ever vanish.

"Deluded by these . . . things . . . all this world knows not me as distinct from them and immutable."

The world which surrounds us, itself represents the great power which blinds us. Nature, herself, is the great illusion.

"Verily this Divine illusion of Mine is hard to surmount. Whoever seek me alone, they cross over this illusion."

The reason so few people find Truth is that it is the most difficult thing in the world to penetrate the cosmic illusion with which Nature confronts us.

This universal illusion exists only in our minds. It is there we must conquer it. The first deception is the impression that this seemingly solid world is the ultimate and final state of being.

Science today recognizes that impression as illusory. It has finally learned the truth that even material objects are not the solid things they appear to be. It knows that such a thing as a table is nothing but a series of electric discharges.

Matter, as such, does not exist. For if everything is composed of force, where then is your solid matter? The scientists have analyzed the nature of matter. They have found that it vanishes into force. But they have not yet solved the nature of force.

Eventually science will be forced to the conclusion that force is a current which exists in your own mind. It could not so exist unless *you* were there to be conscious of it. The whole of this vast universe exists for you purely through your mind. As you think it, so is it to you.

So long as you think and believe matter to be real, it is so to you. But the moment you think it is not the solid thing it appears to be, you are beginning to see through the illusion.

See it as it really is, and thus conquer this illusion. The mind must be understood, and the world examined. When you understand your real nature you will also understand what the world is. To achieve this, more is required than the chanting of hymns and the saying of prayers. Religion is only a step on the way.

"The wise man, I deem, is the very Self; for, steadfast in mind, he resorts to Me alone as the unsurpassed goal."

If you make Truth your goal, you are looking for the very highest. You will find that Truth brings its own reward, because all other benefits troop after it. As Jesus said: "Seek ye first the kingdom of heaven, and all these things shall be added unto you." That is the root of the whole matter.

And the teacher comments:

"Those whose wisdom has been led away by this or that desire resort to other Gods, engaged in this or that rite, constrained by their own nature."

You have to decide definitely whether you desire the highest Truth or partial truths. These are the stages through which the seeker must necessarily pass.

In the end, you will be compelled by life's experiences to seek the one Truth. Having made this decision, you ought not to be sidetracked into searching for occult powers, or be led away into indulgence in emotional ecstasies. When you realize that you are searching solely for the Truth, you are on the path to finding it.

The teacher wants his disciple to search solely for the Truth because one who seeks for finite things cannot obtain infinite results. The finite is limited, but the one Overself cannot be measured. It is infinite and unlimited.

"The foolish regard Me as the unmanifested coming in manifestation, knowing not My higher, immutable, unsurpassed nature. I am not manifest to all, veiled (as I am) by illusion."

Some think that God is expressing Himself through this universe, which is His manifestation. But why should God restrict Himself to such an obviously limited universe? The statement, "I am not manifest to all," contains the deepest philosophy of the esoteric wisdom. Let it suffice to say that if one knew the Reality in its higher, unchangeable nature, one would know that it has no manifestation. It is the only Reality. The rest is illusion. There are no two realities, such as a material one and a spiritual. There is only one. When this is found everything worth while is found.

It is the great cosmic illusion which deceives you into thinking that this material world is real. There being but one Reality, that which is opposed to it must necessarily be illusion. To free yourself from illusion you must conquer the mind. For it is the mind which creates the illusions.

Learn to still your mind by the daily practice of meditation. Since it is thought which produces illusion, it follows that when you can empty the mind of thought and achieve mental stillness, you are able to examine the world and observe its real nature. This reality is then what your freed consciousness sees it to be, not what your thoughts inform you about it.

Therefore, use meditation as a means to an end.

The disciple asks:

"What is that Overself? What about the individual self?"

And the teacher answers him:

"The Overself is the Imperishable, the Supreme. The ego is said to be the individual self."

The mind and body working together create in you the sense of being a separate person or individuality. Yet in the silence of meditation or at unexpected moments you sometimes catch a glimpse of another being in you which normally escapes attention. You feel it to be universal and impersonal. At such divine moments you are near the cosmic consciousness. You sense it without actually knowing it.

This is the Reality of which your personal self is only a reflection. The personal self moves and thinks entirely by the power and consciousness it derives from that divine substratum.

This relationship must be well understood. You must know that the Overself is imperishable, undying. Your individuality, however, depending upon the mind and the body, must come into existence through birth, and therefore must also die.

The Overself, on the other hand, is beginningless, and therefore eternal, endless. We derive our very life from the Eternal, but the cosmic illusion makes us believe that life is perishable and limited to the body. To find eternal life we have to delve deeply into ourselves and discover that which is the *raison d'être* of our personal being.

There are two ways to accomplish this. The first is by meditation and self-analysis, and the second by self-observation. At odd times during the day, stop, detach your outlook, and watch yourself. Endeavour to sense what you really are behind this mask of the personality.

You must practise this until it becomes an established habit. "*As a man thinketh, so is he.*" If you begin to think steadily about what you really are in your innermost nature, the time will come when you find the answer to the question, "What am I?" The sole way by which it can be found is not by external vision or observation, but by entering into conscious unity with your reality.

There is no other way. To see an external vision is to see something outside yourself, even though it is inside your mind. But the divine Overself is your innermost Self. The logical place to look for it is inside yourself.

That being so, it must be deeper than the mind wherein thoughts and visions come and go and have their being. But to find the profound Overself you must enter into its actual nature. When you consciously unite with it you will know it.

"With mind and reason fixed on Me thou shalt doubtless come to Me alone."

Reason here means discrimination. By resolutely fixing your thoughts on the goal and pursuing it patiently, by refusing to desert the quest, your steady efforts will eventually succeed, although the day of reward is determined by destiny. Such are the practices by which you will find the imperishable Overself which supports us and is the life current of the entire manifested universe.

"Having attained to Me, they do not again attain birth, which is the seat of pain and is not eternal, they having reached highest perfection."

One who reaches this state need no longer experience rebirth. He is free from the bondage of matter.

Why does the teacher state that birth in this material world and body is the seat of pain? He does so because it is a fact in Nature that one who descends into material life comes under the domination of the law of opposites. This law works rhythmically in cycles. Every pleasure must be succeeded by pain. One balances the other. Therefore, as long as we live in the material world we must expect pain and suffering in some form or another, bodily or mental, at some time or other.

To free one's self from the necessity of rebirth one must transcend thought and body and find the Overself.

"(All) worlds, including the (highest) world, are subject to returning again, O disciple, but on reaching me there is no rebirth."

There are spirit worlds existing in the inner realms of being. We know the material world, the outer. There is also a denser spirit world and a finer spirit region, both of which can be called mental.

The beings existing within these three worlds are moving in a circle of reincarnation. If you want eternal peace you must free yourself from the bondage of the three worlds. You can do this only by finding the Overself.

These three worlds, vast as they are, constitute the whole of Nature's illusion. The spirit beings are not necessarily freed from illusions, but those they face are mental, whereas we face material ones.

To attain real freedom you must find the Unlimited, the Overself: "That which is unlimited by forms, by shapes, by names, by objects."

Since you have a form, you are living in the world of the finite and naturally are subject to Nature's illusion. She deceives you into seeing her as the unlimited Reality from which all forms have sprung.

The real kingdom of heaven is the Unmanifested Reality. It is not made with hands. Formless, it is eternal in the heavens. You can only know it by actual experience. When that experience comes you will dismiss all ideas. You will not be this or that. You will just "be." You will be able to say, "It is," but not to qualify it by saying, "It is good," for that denotes its opposite, bad, and brings it back in your mind to the realm of the relative.

"To thee who dost not cavil I shall now declare this, the greatest secret, knowledge combined with experience, which having known thou shalt be liberated from illusion . . . The Sovereign Science, the Sovereign Secret, the Supreme Purifier is this; immediately comprehensible, unopposed to duty, very easy to perform, imperishable. Persons having no faith in this doctrine, O Disciple, without reaching Me, remain verily in the path of the mortal world. By Me all this world is pervaded, My form unmanifested. All beings dwell in Me; and I do not dwell in them."

By "Me" is meant the Overself: the one Reality from which have sprung all objects, all creatures in this world, and which pervades everything.

This must be understood in the right sense. It means that all things move and act by reason of borrowing their life current from the Overself. But God's real form is not manifested because it is inexpressible and transcends all imaginable forms and manifestations.

"All beings dwell in Me" means that all beings draw their life current at second-hand from the Overself; all beings and creatures exist in the mind, and mind exists in the Spirit; therefore the latter does not dwell *directly* in them.

This "mind" is simply a collection of thoughts which come and go. Since they are impermanent, they are unreal and have their existence in the unreal. Their existence is illusory, similar to that of a dream. When you wake up from your limited ideas of the universe you will see the Reality, the One Truth. You cannot limit the Unlimited and say, for instance, that It is dwelling in a table. All that exists is only your idea. Beyond it is the One Reality.

"Sustaining all things, but not dwelling in them is My Self, the cause of beings."

Your thoughts and ideas, which for you constitute the universe, draw their existence from the reality which you are. But their existence is an illusory one. They are sustained by the Overself, but the Overself does not directly dwell in them for it does not recognize forms and limitations. It knows only its own self-reality, although it is the cause of everything.

What you know of the universe is only your idea of it. Take an example: A corpse sitting in a chair has the same physical organs as yourself. Why, then, does he not see the things in the room? Obviously because the mind is lacking. Therefore, we see that it is the mind behind the senses which really perceives the universe, and not the physical organs, the eyes. But the mind which perceives is made up of the sum total of your ideas. Therefore, it may truly be said that it is only your idea which represents the universe.

The life current does not depend upon thoughts for its existence. The exact reverse is the fact.

The truth of the one Reality, of the unity of Spirit, is something which you can realize only after you have had some experience in advanced meditation. At that stage you can begin to grasp the fact that everything exists in mind, and that all ideas ultimately exist within the Overself, the only thing that truly IS.

"The sages, O Disciple, partaking of the nature of the Gods, worship Me with mind turned to no other, knowing Me as the imperishable source of all beings."

These sages, who are the highest souls, worship the Overself with a single-pointed mind. They do not practise duality, but worship and live in the One who is the Source of all things.

The ordinary man sees the world which seems solid and real, and he is satisfied with the apparent substantiality of its appearance. The scientist says he must find out what it really is, and goes a step further by investigating. But the seeker of Truth must go all the way to the ultimate Source to learn its essential nature. This can be done by a sharp, concentrated mind only. Having found it he will realize and know that it is the one fountain from which everything flows.

"Those men who, meditating on Me as non-separate, worship Me all around, to them who are ever devout I secure gain and safety."

When you understand that the reality of the universe is not separate from yourself, that it is the very depths of yourself, you are beginning to know Truth. Knowing this universal soul, you will realize that it runs in you and throughout all matter.

Deep enquiry is necessary to attain this realization. Having done so, you know the real purpose of life. Gaining it is the only permanent thing in life. Everything else is illusory and will eventually leave you; even if destiny does not take it away, death will.

But when you have found Truth you have safety and security in something which cannot be taken from you. Nothing else in life is safe, for what appears to be so, exists but for the time being. Whether you place your faith in material possessions in the form of money, for instance, or in any other form of apparent security, you will find that the loss and gain in material life are dictated by destiny.

Destiny will give and take, regardless of all your pre-cautions. Observe the state of the world today. People lose fortunes overnight. There is no actual safety, only the illusion of it.

Real safety exists only in the Overself, in Reality, and in Truth. There only can you find in your conscious-ness a sense of security of which nothing can rob you. Nothing can harm the real You. Find your permanence in the Overself. This is the only path of life worth fol-lowing.

Follow this path and you will find the undying life and the ever-satisfying reward. It is the one way which ancient and modern teachers have pointed out to hu-manity throughout the centuries. If we seek aright we shall find it, because it is within us and not remote. There lies our guarantee that someday we shall find it.

"The same I am to all beings; to Me there is none hateful or dear; but whoso worship Me with devo-tion, they are in Me, and I also am in them."

When you have realized the deepest Truth and found your life in the Overself, you will regard all people with-out exception as sharing that life with you. You will not consider anyone as being outside; therefore you will not be able to hate or enter into conflict with them.

That is because you recognize your own self in them. It then follows that you show perfect understanding and sympathy towards them and all other beings.

In this verse the teacher makes a wonderful promise. And it will be seen that it is essentially the same promise that Jesus made:

"If one of even very evil life worships Me, resort-ing to none else, he must indeed be deemed right-eous, for he is rightly resolved."

Your present state is unimportant. You may be the worst of sinners, but if you begin to seek for the highest Truth you are qualifying for the bestowal of grace.

This eternal peace is for everyone. No matter who or what you are, you too may attain it. If you sincerely change and seek the highest Reality it will take care of you, whether you are saint or sinner, wise or ignorant.

"Finding refuge in Me, they also who, O Disciple, may be of a sinful birth . . . even they attain to the Supreme Goal."

The teacher continues:

"Fix thy mind on Me, be devoted to Me, sacrifice to Me, bow down to Me. Thus steadied, with Me as thy Supreme Goal, thou shalt reach Myself, the Self."

By making the quest of the highest Truth the object of your thoughts you must reach it, for it is your own Self. Look inside without ceasing. Then when you begin to find it in your heart you will also see it in the external world, since there is only one Reality and it is universal.

In the next chapter the teacher enumerates several of the qualities of character which are helpful on this quest. He points out that the most essential thing is devotion; then intelligence, which embodies the ability to discriminate between things as they appear to be and as they really are.

Next you must have wisdom, a sense of right proportion. Weigh things well and learn how to give up the fleeting for the eternal. You also need patience, for you are searching for something which is very, very subtle, so subtle that "few there be that find it." Your patience must be marvellous, but withal you can be con-

fident and hopeful, for you are seeking the Real and
not the illusory. Never give up your quest for Truth.
Learn to value it above everything.

Self-restraint is the next requirement. Bring your body
and thoughts under some degree of self-control. You will
have to fight yourself because you have built up habits
throughout your incarnations which have shaped your
personality. You must learn to resist them and to declare: "These habits are not myself, they are of the
mind and body."

You must have calmness. Try to be calm in life, especially in the midst of activity, the time when you most
need it. Practicing calmness, you will find that it brings
you other virtues. The most important reason for practicing it, however, is that the Overself with which you
are seeking conscious union lives within you in a state
of intense stillness and peace. When you are calm you
are becoming more sensitive to the state of the Overself, thus rendering union with it more and more possible.

Then the teacher mentions pleasure and pain, the two
opposites. You cannot avoid experiencing these, but
when you do, you should query: "*Who* is it that is experiencing this pleasure, or that pain?" Do not seek these
two conditions, but do not be afraid of them either.
Yet do not run away from pleasure, because you must
learn from both pleasure and pain, but do not identify
yourself with them.

Gradually, very gradually at first, you will begin to
develop a sixth sense, a sense of a mystic Presence whenever you mentally inquire of yourself, "Who is experiencing these things?"

Learn to cultivate endurance and indifference to fame
and shame. No one can hurt you, no one can injure you.
They may ruin your reputation, but that belongs to
the personal self and you are not it. When such a thing
happens, it should be utilized as an opportunity for you

consciously to disassociate yourself from the personal self.

In the same manner, when you receive praise or flattery you should cultivate indifference to it and not let it affect you. It is addressed only to the personal self which is not You. Truth will eventually conquer falsehood. You can afford to wait. Those who attempt to hurt you are hurting themselves. They will eventually realize this, for they will have to expiate their wrong doing.

The teacher is questioned by the disciple:

"Thou Thyself knowest Thyself as the Self, O Supreme Teacher, O Source of beings ... Thou shouldst indeed tell without reserve of Thy divine Glories, by which Glories Thou remainest pervading all these worlds."

The teacher replies:

"Now will I tell thee of My heavenly Glories, in their prominence, O best of the disciples; there is no limit to My extent. I am the Self, O Disciple, seated in the heart of all beings; I am the beginning and the middle, as also the end of all beings."

Whenever you see life in any creature, know that you are seeing the universal Reality. Whether it be a mosquito or God in heaven, the one real Life is there. He who knows the Overself as it is in Reality, knows its power and glory. It is infinitely above what the mind of man can imagine.

The teacher then gives a description of the unlimited forms, and of the myriad of solar systems of which the Overself is the Secret Mover. Cosmic birth and cosmic death are facts in Nature. Universes manifest, live, and die. The Overself remains the One. If it manifested in a universe and that universe ended, that would result in part of It going out. But such is not the case. These manifestations appear *within* the Overself.

"Of the alphabet the letter 'A' am I."

The letter "A" symbolizes that the universe is beginningless. Since nothing comes from nothing, it follows that the letter "A" arises out of something which is without beginning. "A" is the symbol of the eternal in most Oriental languages.

Here follows a curious statement:

"I am the gambling of the fraudulent . . . I am the goodness of the good."

You can understand that the Overself is the "goodness of the good." But it is difficult to realize that it is also the gambling of the fraudulent.

However, consider further. Why does a man gamble? Is it not because he wants money to buy pleasure that he believes will result in happiness? If so, he is not gambling for money but for happiness. Gambler, mystic, crook, and saint—all are looking for the one and the same thing, though all have different ideas of what constitutes it. The gambler confuses it with a certain thing called money, while the saint thinks it is something called God.

The Overself is the happiness which the gambler is seeking, only he seeks it in money or pleasure. One day he will seek rightly—inside himself. The very existence of the divine Self within him drives the gambler to look unconsciously for It. One day the man will awaken and realize what he is really searching for.

The drunkard may believe that the whiskey bottle will bring him happiness. But he also is unknowingly seeking the bliss of the Overself. The ultimate thing for which all life searches is happiness, and it may be found only in the Overself. To find the Overself, you must turn inwards to the stillness—the inner stillness where thought does not intrude. In that great silence you will face the Inner Self. Then the end of the quest will be in sight, and ultimately happiness will be reached.

"But of what avail to thee is this vast thing being known, O Disciple? I stand sustaining this whole world by one part (of myself)."

In effect, He asks, why enumerate the endless catalogue of phenomenal things wherein He may be found? He states that though He sustains the entire universe and its incredibly vast phenomena He does so by only a part of Himself. The Overself remains undiminished because it is infinite.

In that Infinite is our real nature. The finite world is only our stepping stone to it.

In the next chapter a certain initiation is given the pupil by his teacher. The spiritual sight is temporarily opened and he is enabled to verify high truths by his own personal experience.

He *sees* the reality behind matter as in a divine vision, which, however, is not the same thing as actually knowing it. The Overself cannot be seen in any vision. You have to *be* it in order to know it.

The vision is of God, the Supreme Creator, in which He is seen as infinite Light. And truly God is light. Only as light may He be known.

Light is the first state of matter. In the final analysis, the scientists will find that matter is nothing but the condensation of light. All objects exist and are built up out of this root of light which is God.

It is a terrifying revelation for the disciple to discover by this spiritual vision that the teacher's statement is real; that there is only the Overself present in all things.

He implores forgiveness for doubting the teacher, saying:

"I am delighted, having seen what was unseen before; and (yet) my mind is confounded with fear."

Remember that the *Bhagavad-Gita* deals with the problem of a disciple, a spiritual aspirant who is faced with the world and the problems of life in the world; who cannot see in the normal way that there is a divine activity in the world. He has then to believe by faith or intuition.

Having seen the exalted truth by means of the spiritual vision, however, he finds the revelation too stupendous. He is shown not only the so-called good, but also the so-called evil. He sees the then-living in their future state of death. The beginning is disclosed; also the middle and the end of things.

When the Overself vision has vanished the teacher says:

"Be not afraid nor bewildered on seeing such a terrible form of Mine as this; free from fear and cheerful at heart, do thou again see this My former form."

He tells the disciple that the vision he has received is a very rare one; that it is bestowed only on a few.

"Those who, fixing their thought on Me, contemplate Me, always devout, with supreme faith, those in my opinion are the best Yogins."

Devotion is excellent. However, it is not the highest path. Devotion of thought can be given, but concentration of all thoughts upon the Absolute is more difficult.

"But those who worship Me, renouncing all actions in Me, regarding Me Supreme, meditating on Me with exclusive devotion; for them whose thought is fixed on Me, I become ere long, O disciple, the deliverer out of the ocean of the mortal illusion."

Observe that you must renounce all actions. Whatever you do, hand your life over to the Highest. Do your duty, then surrender the results of your actions as a devotional sacrifice on the altar of the Overself. This does not involve shutting yourself up in a monastery. On the contrary, you must live and act in the world but be unmoved by the results.

If you follow this path with intense devotion you will ultimately be led to the highest path as a reward for your sacrifices.

When you are once initiated on this highest path it will take you but a comparatively short time to attain the Overself. Before long you will be delivered.

This path of Truth is the ultimate one. The disciple asks, in effect:

"What if a man is unable to travel this highest path?"

The teacher replies by telling him that if he cannot concentrate throughout the day he should make the great gamble of faith; live his life by intense faith, do everything in the spirit of service.

Regard yourself as an instrument through which the Divine expresses itself. Do what you can each day, obeying the highest promptings of your highest Self.

"If thou art unable to do even this, then refuged in devotion to Me, do thou abandon the fruits of all actions, self-controlled."

If you surrender the fruits of all action, working in the world, doing the best you can each day, mentally abandoning the desire for reward, you will certainly gain peace, if not the highest Truth.

To achieve Truth the sole way is by the path of self-knowledge followed by the sage, of whom the teacher again presents a picture to his disciple:

"He who neither rejoices, nor hates, nor grieves, renouncing good and evil; he who is full of devotion is dear to Me. He who is the same to foe and friend, and also in honour and dishonour; who is the same in cold and heat, in pleasure and pain; who is free from attachment; to whom censure and praise are equal; who is silent, content with anything; homeless, steadyminded, full of devotion; that man is dear to Me."

Such is the condition resulting from the manifestation of the Overself in man. The Overself consciousness is present in all beings, though not all are aware of its presence. It gives the man who has discovered it a perfect sympathy with all. His freedom from attachment results from this discovery, and he does not look to external life alone for happiness.

CHAPTER XI

III: REALIZATION

THE general subject of the discourses in this final section of the *Bhagavad-Gita* is the realization of the supreme being of man.

"This, the body, O disciple, is called the field; him who knows it, they who know of them call 'the knower of the field.' "

The term "field" is here used symbolically, as representing the body and the whole of the material or physical world. The body is a very representative part of the world, containing as it does so many of the elements which you find in the rest of the material world.

"And do thou also know Me as 'the knower of the field' in all the 'fields,' O disciple. The knowledge of 'the fields,' and 'the knower of the field' is deemed by Me as the knowledge (of the truth)."

The knowledge stressed here is that of the Knower who dwells in all bodies. It is the Witness-Self. The teacher explains that the Truth, the whole and complete Truth, is the knowledge of both the inner self and the external universe, the latter including the mental and spirit worlds, because they are not the One Reality. In other words, whoever finds the inner self has found only half the Truth, and not the whole Truth. The inner self is the ray, but it is not the Sun. It is a part, and possesses the same qualities as the whole, but still differs in degree. The whole Truth is found only when you find the Overself.

Mystics and yogis have written and described their ecstasies, but that is not enough, for it is not the whole Truth. They have reached the gate through which they must pass to the Overself.

What you have to do is not only to penetrate into your inner self, by withdrawing in meditation from the world, but also to examine the world once again by the light in yourself. The material world was forsaken because it was a dream which you cast aside in order to turn inwards, but coming back to it with the lamp of inner understanding in your hand, you then discover that this world is also divine and real.

It is as much a part of the supreme unity as the inner self, only it appears in a different way. When you discover this, there is henceforth no sense of duality, no divorce between spirit and matter. There is only one Reality in Truth, which cannot be divided into two. The mystic who has penetrated to the inner self but has not gone beyond that stage, sets up this divorce between spirit and matter, and regards the external world as evil. Profounder examination and understanding would have shown him that it is just as much divine as the wonderful inner realm which he has now found within himself. There is no real separation between the two. There is only the One.

Most people who achieve that state of withdrawal turn aside from the external world. They think it should be avoided as evil. This prevents them from having the whole Truth. Nothing must be left out if we are to attain the ultimate Truth. The whole Truth must be embraced, because Truth is the Reality. The Reality is the

One, and the One involves the entire universe, and not just the part of it which dwells inside yourself. Religious mysticism can lead you to a very high stage, but it is not enough. When you are able to come back and examine the external world and not be afraid of it, you will find that it exists as part of the one Reality. You see through the illusion and you know what it is.

Thus when you see it in truth, you will have no reason to run away from it. You can live in the world or in the jungle—it makes no difference. The mystic who lives in the jungle is still surrounded by the world. When he comes out of his trance, he is forced to observe this world again before him, so why flee from it? When this understanding comes to you, you can live as normally as others do, but you will find the inspiration to a higher inner life.

The goal is the Truth which embraces everything, including the world. If you achieve knowledge and come back and learn to live in the material world by this higher light, then you create no further destiny and live as unaffected as lotus leaves in the water. You are free, because after all your bondage is not an external thing. It is not because you are living in a great city that you are bound. Bondage to destiny is in the *mind*. You may bury yourself in jungle or monastery and still be bound, because your mind is binding you. Observe the constant reiteration in the *Gita* on the need for inspired action, and for indifference to the results of action. The results of your actions are not your worries. Do your best and leave the rest to destiny or the higher power.

"Humility, modesty, innocence, patience, uprightness, service of the teacher, purity, stead-fastness, self-control."

Some of the virtues which will aid the seeker to come

into this understanding of the Overself are now listed. Remember, however, that no virtue in itself will ever give you understanding. The most it can do is to prepare you. Most essentially you need meditation, or mindstilling and reflective inquiry. This is a double process that you must carry on at all times during the day. Virtues are helpful to get the right mental state. It is hindered, however, by certain qualities of character which prevent you from obtaining that stillness of mind and that concentrative purpose which you need.

The first quality is that of humility. This condition places you in the mental attitude of a child who wants to learn. Without humility, you cannot advance on the quest, because that means you do not grasp that there is something beyond your present outlook. It is necessary that you feel humility and realize that there is a higher being towards which you aspire, and that in comparison with it you are as nothing.

After humility, comes the virtue of "non-injury." You must adopt the attitude of helpfulness and compassion which tends to dissolve the strength of the personal ego. If you begin to practice non-injury, you are beginning to manifest that which will have to be manifested when you come into the realization of the unity of life. Even before attainment, it helps to reflect that you are one with the universal Self.

The virtue of patience is hard to acquire, and some tire when they do not get quick results. They would not tire if they engaged in a pursuit of worldly success which required several years of effort before it could be accomplished. Why then, should they expect to engage on the highest and most important of pursuits, the realization of Overself, without similar patience?

You must be confident that one day the great reward and grand results must come, and that they will come at the right time. The precise time is dictated by destiny. Patience means that one must never desert this quest, even when conditions seem hopeless. You will find that because you stick to the path, help will come to you.

The next virtue is uprightness. That means that if you are looking for Truth, you must live a truthful life, both mentally and materially. Stick to the ideal of uprightness, no matter what temptations come to you. If you want to find Truth, live Truth.

"Service of the teacher" is said to be the next step. Its meaning is that you recognize that the teacher stands for something more than just one man to you. In serving him, you are also serving humanity, because he is serving many others. You take a short cut to serving mankind through helping him. Win his grace by devoted service and your own development will be more rapid.

Then steadfastness. You have to go through a stage of discipline in order to bring the body and mind to heal. Take smoking, merely as an example. If you can control and regulate your addiction to it, it is just an incidental which may help you gain that mental control which is needed to investigate truth. When you can get your mind under control, then it does not matter whether you smoke or not.

"Absence of attachment to objects of the senses. . . . Unflinching devotion to Me . . . resort to solitary places. . . . Constancy in self knowledge, perception of the end of knowing the truth."

If you are enslaved by external objects, it is difficult for you to direct the mind into that calm state which it needs in order to find Truth. The Truth is subtle, and the mind must not be pulled this way and that. It must be brought to a point and held steady. Then only can it look for Truth, and not be coloured by its desires. That is why absence of attachment is asked, that the mind can be kept free to find the Truth. Not that there is anything wrong in the material objects themselves. Once you have found the Truth, you can return to them. For a time only you have to cut these things off. Only the free mind can find the truth.

"Constancy in self-knowledge, perception of the end of the knowledge of truth." The knowledge of the self leads to the knowledge of truth. First you have to know yourself, and then you will be led on to the knowledge of the universal self. To know yourself you must practice meditation and self-observation, then ultimately you will come to the consciousness of your inner being. When you have found this light, you must try to understand, by its aid, the universe in which you live. That is knowledge of the One, because everything that is not the one Reality is simply an idea. No matter how wonderful it may seem to us, it is still only an idea and ignorance.

Ignorance means that you confuse the unreal with the real, and that you take sense-impressions, thoughts, opinions, or visions to be the one permanent Reality which is unchanging. There being only one Reality, everything else is ignorance. Knowledge of the Reality is known immediately once and for all. Things which are taught in lectures and in books, belong to the sphere of ignorance. The Reality you will know as one tremendous rebirth, and after that there is nothing more to be known in this sphere. All else is comparative ignorance. Whether spiritualism or occultism, it is still ignorance because it is still in the sphere of the mind-plane. The teacher wants the disciple to seek the highest knowledge. When he knows that, he becomes immortal. Everything else is mortal and therefore illusory. Everything else has a beginning and an end, but the highest Truth has no beginning and no end. When you do find it, you discover that it was always there. It was there in you, and outside of you, and it was you.

"That (the Overself) exists enveloping all . . . un-attached, yet supporting all; devoid of qualities. . . . Without and within (all) being; the unmoving as also the moving."

The Overself is motionless. Where can it go? It has nowhere to go, because it fills all space. It is also the moving, because all living creatures are in motion by virtue of borrowed vitality from the Overself. It is also exceedingly subtle, because you cannot hear it, see it, or touch it. It cannot be sensed by any of the five senses; even the intellect cannot grasp it or draw a mental picture of it.

"Near and far away is That."

Nothing can be nearer than your self. Yet it is far away, because, strangely enough, nothing seems so hard to find. It seems easier to go to Australia than to find your Overself. The Overself is both near and far away.

"Undivided, yet remaining divided as it were in beings; supporter of beings too, is That, the Knowable; devouring, yet generating."

This is not a description of the inner self which you find in meditation. The teacher here is describing the ultimate Self. It is undivided because it is One, yet, strangely, it *seems* divided because every being and creature and plant has a fragment of that life. But this division of life is only an appearance which does not exist in actuality. It is devouring, because there is death everywhere. But when creatures die, what happens to them? We see the form die and change and turn into dust, but what has become of their life? It has returned to the Overself.

"The Light even of lights, That is said to be beyond
darkness. Knowledge, the Knowable, the Goal of
knowledge."

The Overself is called "The Light even of lights,"
because, as I stated before, the primal Light is the root
of the universe. It is the root of matter and of life; it is
our first manifestation of God. It fills all space, and
since space is unbounded, it fills all possible forms. Even
that has a finite life in the sense that it appears and disappears. It comes into being with the creation of universes and disappears with the dissolution of universes.
It emanates from the one Universal Self. The latter, in
the highest sense, is the one God, and all other gods derive their life from That.

In the foregoing passages, the disciple is taught that
the whole process of evolution and involution, creation
and dissolution, is endless.

"He who thus knows Spirit and Matter together
with (their) qualities, he is not born again."

Thus, when you know the truth, you have freed your-
self from illusion of the personal ego and are liberated.
You are not born again because nothing can hold you.
You have no strong desires which impel you to rebirth.

"Yet others, not knowing thus, worship, having
heard from others; they, too, cross beyond death,
adhering to what they heard."

It may be that you have not known the truth by
personal experience. Yet, if you listen to those who do
know it, they will act as a raft which will carry you
across the river of illusion and thus you will be led to
your own knowledge of truth. The teacher hints that
more important than taking part in rites, ceremonies,

and prayers is the hearing of truth from competent guides.

"He sees, who sees all actions performed by Nature alone and the Self not acting."

After all, the Overself is the Absolute. What has it to do? What can it do? How can it act? That which seems to be carrying on in the world is simply Nature. The Overself does not really act. It seems to act, but it is simply Nature that is acting. Nature is the cosmic mind. It creates all these processes and forms around us. The Overself itself has nothing to act for. It is full and self-sufficient in itself. We must not lose sight of the ultimate truth that the whole of this world is nothing but a mental appearance, because the Overself has nothing to act for on its own behalf. It is itself self-sufficient.

"When a man realizes the whole variety of beings as resting in the One, and as an evolution from that (One) alone, then he becomes the Overself."

When you are no longer deceived by the multitude of appearances, when you know it all as a manifestation, then you have pierced the illusion. You become Truth and are liberated. To see that, you must not be satisfied with the everyday viewpoint, but you must search for and find the real. The first great illusion is the cosmic illusion with which Nature presents us. These solid material forms are not so solid and material as they seem. They are ultimately ideas of solidity and materiality existing in your mind. You will find later that these ideas are created by cosmic mind. You must remember always that amid the seeming movement of evolution, the one Self never changes and never loses its nature. However evil a man apparently becomes, that which is divine in him is never touched.

"They who, having resorted to this knowledge, have attained to unity with Me, are neither born in the creation, nor disturbed in the dissolution."

The world moves through tremendous aeons of time going through the cosmic processes of creation and dissolution. In the same manner that individuals are born and die, so do whole systems of universes go through an actual existence of birth and death. But one who has attained supreme knowledge is free of all that. World systems cannot claim him. He is free from the wheel of world evolutions, because they belong to the finite sphere. He has become inwardly infinite. As long as you think only in finite terms, so long must you be born again and again. You must learn to cultivate fourth-dimensional intuition or awareness. By trying, we develop the very faculties which will help us attain realization. The teacher describes the state of those who have come into this knowledge:

"He to whom pain and pleasure are alike, who dwells in the Self, to whom a clod of earth and stone and gold are alike, to whom the dear and the undear are alike, who is a man of wisdom, to whom censure and praise are same."

If you live in the Overself, you are detached. If you see this world as it really is, you cannot be deceived by it. Whether the world presents you with painful or pleasant sensations, you know them to be transient. Detachment should be achieved secretly, in the heart. You will place the exact value on money which it needs, but you will not be unduly attached to it. You know that underneath the outer form there is always the divine Self. Whether it be a raging tiger or a beautiful deer, both have divinity within them. You accept them both as expressions of the Overself, hating neither. You re-

main detached and indifferent, because you do not depend on externals for your happiness. Within that depth
which you find in yourself, you contact the peace of the
eternal.

People may say what they wish in criticism. They
are talking of your personal ego. You will feel too detached from your personal ego to worry. Again, if they
flatter your personality, it is the same, because you have
learnt not to identify yourself with the personality.
Criticisms will mean nothing to you, neither will praise.
You may even prefer criticism to praise. The essential
thing is to take an impersonal view of yourself.

"The same in honour and disgrace, the same towards
friends and enemies, abandoning all undertakings,—
he is said to have crossed beyond Nature."

It is Nature which is responsible for causing humanity to act as it does. When a man has conquered Nature
and crossed beyond it by transcending the mind, then
he is so detached that whether the world honours him
or shames him, he does not lose his peace. Whatever the
world gives him cannot rob him of the knowledge of his
self. His enemies are as divine as his friends, and he
welcomes them with equanimity and detachment. That
does not mean that he need be foolish, for he will not
give his enemies the same opportunities he gives his
friends. But he understands them and feels no hatred.

"Those who strive, endued with Yoga, perceive
Him dwelling in the self; though striving, those of
unrefined self, devoid of wisdom, perceive Him not."

Until you have brought the mind to heel and purified it of all those prejudices and desires which affect
its balance, you can never see the Truth, you can never
find the Overself. It is so subtle that you must approach

it with undivided mind. If anything is pulling your mind this way or that, you cannot find the Truth. To refine the self means to train the mind so that it can enter into this highly concentrated and balanced state which moves directly towards the goal. To refine the self means to free yourself from illusions, to eliminate the false ideas. Mental illusions are the greatest ones. When you have got rid of them, then you can perceive more clearly. Illusion and ignorance dwell in the mind and must go. This, therefore, is the reason why the teacher says that the ascetic who merely practices self-mortification and does not free the mind from illusion, does not find the Truth.

"I am seated in the hearts of all. . . ."

That is a true statement, because when you find the Overself, its actual abode is in your heart. It is in the heart that we find the atom which is for us a gate whereby we know the cosmic Self.

"From Me are memory, knowledge, as well as their loss."

All the mental functions operate only by virtue of the life and light which have been borrowed from the Overself. The mind functions from this borrowed life, taken directly from the divine atom in the heart; otherwise the brain could not work and there would be neither memory nor knowledge. Ultimately, the mental process obtains its functioning power from the divine life.

"It is I who am to be known by all the scriptures, I am indeed the author of the scriptures as well as the knower of the scriptures."

Why are all these scriptures written? Primarily not to build churches and mosques, but to guide us to the entrance to the higher path of living. Those great revelations contain an esoteric content also. They were written, in many instances, by the light of the Overself.

"Thus, this most Secret Science has been taught by Me, O sinless one; on knowing this, (a man) becomes wise, O Disciple, and all his duties are accomplished."

The secret science is the esoteric wisdom, that which distinguishes illusion from reality. The knowledge of metaphysics may be open to all to learn, but the secret path has been kept for a few. Had it been given to the many, it would have unsettled their minds. It has been given only to those who have been ready, and till today has remained a secret. Humanity has changed mentally, however, and that which mankind could not grasp before, they are more ready to grasp now.

In following the Secret Path a man becomes wise. You may possess encyclopaedic knowledge; you may be the leading professor in a university, and not have true wisdom. But when you have become aware of the Overself in your innermost consciousness, then your highest duties are accomplished. You have fulfilled the law of your incarnation.

"Ostentation, arrogance and self-conceit, anger as also insolence, and ignorance, belong to one who is born, O Disciple, for a demoniac lot."

The different kinds of humanity are described by the teacher. He divides them into two orders, the higher and the lower. Gripped by the darkest illusion, the lower types of humanity have none of the divine light which guides the higher, possess inert or violent qualities of character, and are more arrogant than their more spiritual brethren, who are always modest and humble. Depending on the material things entirely as they do, they become braggarts. They are governed by violent passion. They are ignorant as well, because they think that the present life is the only one, and this world the only real world.

"The divine nature is deemed for liberation, the demoniac for bondage."

Bondage is the lot to which the lower class of persons is doomed. They will come back for hundreds of births because they are born to suffer. They may have pleasure, but they will have much more pain, because continued re-embodiment itself is ultimately a form of suffering.

"Holding this view, these ruined souls of small intellect, of fierce deeds, rise as the enemies of the world for its destruction."

The term "small intellect" is used with the meaning of small understanding. They take appearances as reality, hence they can be said to be limited in outlook, to have small minds. They are ruined souls, because they are not fulfilling the purpose of incarnation and are making no attempt to do so. There can, therefore, be no real success in life for them. They may have apparent success for a time, but their enterprises will generally end in ruin because that is to be a part of their spiritual education. Nevertheless, they are still used for the purpose of destiny, which works through both creation and dissolution. Destiny uses them as instruments to fulfill destructive purposes.

"Filled with insatiable desires, full of hypocrisy, pride and arrogance, holding unwholesome views through delusion, they work with unholy resolve."

This expresses the natural outlook of the materialists. They are deluded, for what they imagine to be real is nothing but a vanishing dream.

"Bewildered by many a fancy, entangled in the snare of delusion, addicted to the gratification of lust, they fall into a foul hell."

This describes their inevitable end. That which they seek ultimately betrays them. For they must learn. In the spirit-world or after-death state, they will be tied to the stake and compelled to worship vainly that which they sought so ardently in this life. Thus do they get their education. It is only for a time, however, for there is no everlasting hell.

"The food which is stale, tasteless, putrid and rotten, refuse and impure, is dear to the ignorant."

The teacher discourses on certain material facts of existence which are conducive to the higher spiritual life. He grades the types of food into bad, good, and best.

Such bad food appeals only to the lowest types of humanity. The food we eat builds up the body, and it is a truism that our bodies are nothing other than what we eat. It is also a fact that there is a subtle element, a magnetism, in food which rises and affects the mind. Thus, people who eat coarse and gross food tend to have coarse and gross minds. That is why, whenever possible and when it can be done without too much inconvenience, a non-flesh diet is generally preferred by students of yoga. Nature has supplied us with sufficient food from the vegetable kingdom to maintain our bodies in good health. This is a question which does not matter very much for the masses, but when you are on the path of yoga your mind is subtler, tending towards a higher vibration. In that case, it is helpful but not essential that you eat food which will help this purpose. When you give up meat, you have less to overcome in pacifying the mind. Once you find the truth, however, it does

not matter whether you eat meat or not, although you
will probably wish to continue on a vegetarian diet for
other reasons.

"That worship which is practised with the object
of gaining good reception, honour and worship, and
with hypocrisy, is said to be of this world, to be half-
ignorant, unstable and uncertain."

What is this but making religion a bargain counter
with God on the other side of the counter? Those who
worship because it is right to worship and not because
they are seeking material rewards, represent the higher
type.

"That austerity which is practised out of a foolish
notion, with self-torture . . . is declared to be ignorant."

Those who practice asceticism in this manner represent the lowest grade of humanity. I have seen such a
man in India, rolling his body along the ground, mile
after mile, in the hope that he is pleasing God, Who
will reward him eventually with some material boon.
Such a man is a fool.

"The gift that is given at a wrong place or time,
to unworthy persons, without respect or with insult,
that is declared to be (dictated by) ignorance."

Even such a subject as the giving of gifts must demand our attention. It must be done with intelligence.
Do not make a spiritual or intellectual gift to a person
who is not ready. If you give instruction to someone
who is not ripe for this quest of truth, you are being
foolish. Remember the admonition of Jesus, "Cast not
thy pearls before swine." There must be the right time

and the right place and the right person; that is the perfect gift. When you give to the unworthy, you are betraying ignorance and are acting foolishly. The highest type of person gives when he knows that it is a duty to give, and not because he is seeking a return. This covers the entire field of gifts, material, intellectual, verbal, and spiritual.

"Sages understand renouncement to be the renunciation of interested works; the abandonment of the fruits of all works . . ."

The renunciation of results simply means doing your duty and then remaining unaffected by what happens afterwards, whether success or failure, reward or disappointment. You have done your duty and that is enough; after that, accept whatever destiny offers. Such renunciation is an inner giving-up. It is the only real renunciation and the only one that matters.

"Practice of worship, gift, and austerity should not be given up; it is quite necessary; (they) are the purifiers of the wise."

Religion has its place. It is necessary, for it purifies the masses and lifts them from a gross materialism to something a little finer. You need not abandon it in order to find the truth. It acts as a purifier, provided that you perform your religious practices without seeking for any rewards. Don't ask God to give you anything in return for your worship. Do it out of reverence to a higher Power. Do not, for instance, give your local temple a large amount of money, simply because you want God to give you a son for a child. In India parents value male children above female. So the priests are loaded with gifts in the superstitious hope that a male child may be born.

The external forms and customs of a religion were instituted to create habits of internal mental and spiritual states corresponding to the forms. The true aim of those who set the great pendulum of rule and rite swinging was to instil and perpetuate these *states* in men; not to perpetuate the rules among men for all eternity. For when a rite loses its power over men, then it loses the purpose for which it was instituted.

When one obtains wisdom, one has no longer any doubts. Then the teacher makes the statement:

> "Verily, it is not possible for an embodied being to abandon actions completely; he who abandons the fruits of actions is verily said to be an abandoner."

It is impossible for anyone who is in the body to give up activity. Even in the jungle, one is still acting with one's mind. From the highest standpoint of view, mental activity is a subtler form of material activity. Since you cannot get away from it, perform it rightly and wisely but with inward renunciation.

Then the teacher analyzes and grades the different types of action. He explains that if action is foolishly and blindly undertaken without thought about its consequences, that is the lowest and most ignorant type. Going a grade higher, he says, in effect, that if you act because you want certain pleasures or benefits, even though they bring you trouble through your efforts to get them, this is a grade higher. The teacher defines the highest type of action as that which is free from attachment and is, therefore, a form of spiritual activity. To understand Nature is to understand the forces which are driving man to action.

> "Resorting to a sequestered spot, eating moderately, speech and body and mind subdued, always engaged in meditation and concentration, endued with dispassion."

The mind must be restrained and brought to its own place in the heart. Self-enquiry is an intellectual exercise in the beginning, but one that leads ultimately to the abolishing of intellect's tyranny. You must learn to say no to your thoughts, to refuse continuance of the very process of thinking itself, to reject the endless upheavals of intellect and find peace.

The Overself is so subtle that one cannot reach it by the ordinary intellect, which is always dealing with concrete things, with pictures and forms. That intellect is too coarse, it cannot grasp the abstract. It has to be grasped by something finer than the mind which we use in ordinary everyday life. What is that finer mind? It is something which you will find through meditation. A delicate sensitivity develops in time when the mind is withdrawn from its out-going tendencies, and instead of incessantly paying attention to the outside world, you practice turning the mind in upon itself. That develops the spiritual sensitivity.

"Becoming the Overself, or serene self, he neither grieves nor desires, treating all beings alike; he attains supreme devotion to Me."

The sage cannot help treating all alike, for he sees everything in the Overself. He does not differentiate *at heart* between those he likes and those he dislikes. Such division has now become meaningless to him.

"By Devotion he knows Me in truth, what and who I am; then knowing Me in truth, he forthwith enters into Me."

It is not enough to say that we believe in God; we must know Him *in consciousness*. That is what we have to find, this highest knowledge. You know that the entire world, whether material, mental or spiritual, is nothing but a play of mind. Its appearance is the result of the interworking of our own mind and of the cosmic mind. Do not forget that mind is still an illusion. You may have wonderful experiences in this mind world, but they are not real in the true sense. To know God, you must become like God, and this is a state of consciousness which you cannot ever lose once you attain it.

"Doing continually all actions whatsoever, taking refuge in Me,—by My Grace he reaches the eternal undecaying Abode."

Henceforth, you are free and nothing can bind you. No one can dictate as to what your actions shall be. You do what the Christ-Self dictates, not what the world dictates. Your life ought not to be an apology for itself, but an assertion; not a continual request for favours, but a bequest of them. But you can do this only when you have found yourself.

"Fixing thy heart in Me, thou shalt, by My Grace, cross over all difficulties; but if from egotism thou wilt not hear (Me), thou shalt perish."

The final message of grace comes at the end of the book. It is true that without grace there is no entry. You may strive and weep, but unless the grace falls on you, you cannot enter into the gate of Heaven. It is there to draw you inwards deeper and deeper into yourself, and your work is to relax and to let it bear you, draw you within. That means that you have very little to do, in the beginner's sense, but what you do must be done rightly and intelligently. You must understand what is being done. Remember that this stage is like sinking internally. Don't try to cling to something on the way, whether vision or experience. We have so many conceptions about yoga, which are all right where they belong, but they don't belong to *this* path. Do not cling to them. Keep your mind flexible. How and when grace shall come depends partly upon your personal destiny and partly upon God or the human instrument (teacher) He uses. The final advice which the teacher gives the disciple is not to worry. He tells him to free himself of all his ego-burden and give it up:

> "Mentally resigning all deeds to Me, regarding Me as the Supreme, resorting to mental concentration, do thou ever fix thy heart in Me."

The message behind these words is identical with that of Jesus when he said: "Come unto Me, all ye that labour and are heavily laden, and I will give you rest." If you do this and devote yourself to the highest, the grace will come. It may not come at the moment you wish, but eventually the reward will come, for the Overself wants your joining with it fully as much as you do. Then you will conquer all difficulties, one by one. The gist of the lesson is to fix your heart on the highest and on nothing else.

In this manner the illumined man moves through the street of life. The scenes change and portray now sorrow, now pleasure, but he remains the calm witness through it all. The vicissitudes of fortune may overwhelm another man but leave him unperturbed, for he draws deep strength from the soul.

> "Abandoning all righteous deeds (duties), seek Me as thy sole Refuge; I will liberate thee from all sins; do thou not grieve."

Here is a definite promise of the grace. If you will seek for Him in your heart and in your mental concentrations; if you are resolute, if you will devote yourself to the quest day after day, year after year, the hour will surely come when grace will be bestowed on you. In most cases, this grace is received through a teacher.

"Thus has wisdom, more secret than all that is secret, been declared to thee by Me; reflect thou over it all and act as thou pleasest."

You can see by this verse that the genuine teacher never interferes with the free will of the disciple. If we make a wrong judgment, then the suffering resulting as a consequence will educate us. The true teacher does not try to impose his will on his disciple, but gives him the freedom to act without hindrance.

"Hear thou again My word supreme, the most secret of all; because thou art My firm friend, therefore will I tell thee what is good."

This is the highest teaching which the teacher can give the disciple, because it is the Truth, and there is nothing higher. The teacher senses the devotion and confidence which the disciple brings to him, then the pupil gradually becomes dear to him and the Truth is imparted to him.

"This (which has been taught) to thee is never to be taught to one who is devoid of austerities nor to one who is not devoted, nor to one who does not do service, nor to one who speaks ill of Me."

The teaching which he has given is not to be broadcast to the world. There are certain people who should not have it,—those who are complete and utter materialists and yield to every desire are not ready for it. In any case, they could not grasp it, for they want something that will please their desires. The mind cannot grasp such subtle teaching until it has been purified to some extent. People who are not seeking for truth should not be given this teaching. Neither should it be given to one who has not expressed the desire to hear the teaching. We choke our best thoughts by offering them where they are not desired. It is better to let them live by keeping them to ourselves and reserving them only for the ready. Those who do not wish to get learning from the teacher should be left alone. This teaching must never be forced. Those who do not see any use in spiritual life and perhaps speak ill of it, should not be taught the doctrine. Otherwise time will be wasted and contempt is brought upon it. Anyway, the truth is imperishable because it is written, not in the pages of ephemeral books, but in the deepest heart of man. Therefore, the gods wait with unflickering patience for their mortal kindred to come into its recognition, for they know that no act of man can wipe out this ageless unseen scripture. The gods wait and watch whilst men quail and women weep, for it is the universal fiat that none may enter Truth's abode save by his own free will.

On the other hand, read the other phase of this:

"He who with supreme devotion to Me will teach this Supreme Secret to My devotees, shall doubtless come to Me."

If you find people devoted to the truth, who are seeking for it, and ripe to understand it, then you may teach it to them, for it is your duty. If you do that, you will be rewarded, for:

"Nor is there any among men who does dearer service to Me than he; nor shall there be another on earth dearer to Me than he."

It is the greatest gift you can give anyone. If you give this bread of spiritual truth to those who hunger, what greater service can you render them? In that fashion, you are fulfilling and helping to fulfil the purpose of material incarnation. When conditions are ripe, then reveal the truth, thereby earning for yourself a good destiny.

"Has it been heard by thee, O disciple, with an attentive mind? Has the delusion of ignorance been destroyed, O Seeker for truth?"

The truth given in these verses is not an obvious one. It is so subtle that unless you concentrate, you may miss it. The disciple replies:

"Destroyed is delusion, and I have gained recognition through Thy Grace, O Teacher. I am firm, with doubts gone. I will do Thy word."

The *Bhagavad-Gita* is one of the few scriptures in the world which definitely and purposely explain the principles and practices of the gospel of inspired action.

Now the disciple has a basis for life, for it is based on reality. He stands firm, for he feels no more doubt. When you are reborn into supreme Truth, all possibility of doubt disappears. The reason for this is that doubt arises in the intellect and can come only to the man who is living in the intellect. But for the one who enters into transcendent Reality, there can be no more doubts. This is the final beatitude which awaits man; that he shall at last arrive at the possession of himself; all else are but ports of call and not the final harbour.

Finally, the teacher utters a blessing:

"Wherever there is a Divine Teacher, wherever there is a human disciple, there prosperity, peace and other blessings will be established."

How can you know when you have found the goal? Do you experience a sudden illumination? You cannot really get sudden illumination. What you can get is a sudden cessation of ignorance; a sudden falling away of egoism; a sudden dropping off of all false ideas and errors. When they fall away, then you are conscious of what was always within you. The divine Light is always there; it is there even at this very moment. It is not something new which you have got to gain or attain. It is something which you, as mind, are obscuring yourself. It is for you to stand out of your own light.

The final lesson is that Divinity is everywhere. Everywhere God can be found, and God is good.

CHAPTER XII

ERRORS OF THE SPIRITUAL SEEKER

THERE is a very widespread misconception in America, a misconception that is much more prevalent here than in any other country of which I know, and that is that if you attain spirituality, if you realize your divine self, you will then automatically demonstrate prosperity, perfect health, and everlasting good fortune. This, probably the gravest error that could arise in the mind of the seeker after Truth, is believed by millions of American people. It is a doctrine which carries all the glitter but little of the weight of gold. Let us try to understand the implication of this claim.

If prosperity is to be made the criterion of one's spirituality, then Jesus was a failure, a spiritual failure. He had no prosperity at all. He carried no purse, possessed no capital. Buddha gave up all he had, so he would also have been a spiritual failure. Jesus never said that if men followed him, they would become wealthy; so why should such claims be made by the professed followers of Jesus today?

If perfect health is to be made a criterion of spirituality, then we must admit that some of the greatest saints in Christian history were not saints at all. In the Orient we have the examples of various sages like Ramakrishna and the Maharishee who did not enjoy perfect health, but who are regarded as the highest of sages.

There is a way known to yogis to attain perfect

health; you can make the body as resistant to all diseases as steel; you can make it as strong as any human body can be; you can prolong its life span far beyond normal. There is a way, but to find and practice that way requires that you sacrifice everything else, because the discipline necessary to attain that condition demands all your time and all your energy and the severest régime of asceticism. It demands complete monastic withdrawal from the world. The price is as high as the prize. It is an impractical way for us, so let us rule it out.

So we have to decide whether these things mean anything at all or whether they mean nothing. Men, you will say, have performed marvels of spiritual healing either upon themselves or upon others. That is true; but it is the result of an occult, not a spiritual power, and all occult powers are powers of the mind, not of the Overself—latent or, little known, perhaps, but still powers of the mind, and of that part of it which I call the overmind. There is no such thing as spiritual healing in the sense of direct spiritual healing, but indirectly, yes.

For an adept or for a man who has attained the consciousness of the Eternal, to use an occult power is to step down into the world of form, time, and illusion. From the standpoint of a man who has realized Truth, all occult powers are of the illusory self and worth having only after this realization has been obtained. Whether he possesses these powers or not depends upon the line of evolution along which he has gone in former lives. If he has worked for occult powers, he will get them now, if he has not sought for them, they will not come to him. But he will still have one power, the power of the Overself, and that is the root of all power.

So you must understand that the consciousness of the Spirit may be obtained, and yet one may have no healing power other than the one primal power of healing souls and hearts and minds. But do not expect that every man who has entered into the Spirit will therefore attain perfect health, or will be able to give others perfect health. He may or may not; that is entirely a matter of destiny, that particular self-earned destiny which has come to him as the result of his evolution.

Until you have finished your quest, you can have nothing but opinion, theory, fancy, because the quest finishes suddenly. It is not a gradual dawning of more and more truth. The quest is a sudden rebirth into the kingdom of heaven, and once it comes, it comes like a flash of lightning.

From the standpoint of a man living in Truth, the body is an ephemeral thing. He knows that the body will die as surely as it was born, that he has had, maybe, hundreds of bodies, and he looks upon it as he looks upon the rest of this material universe, as nothing more than an idea passing through consciousness—just a mental picture to be born and to die.

From the standpoint of truth, which is the standpoint of reality, the entire universe is nothing but a dream. All life is almost a phantom, a mental picture, something that flows through consciousness and is gone. How then can a man who lives in that eternal consciousness so overvalue the body that he can regard a perfect state of physical health as the only perfect demonstration of spirituality? He will have enough common sense to know that good health is necessary and desirable, but he will not allow that knowledge to delude him into thinking that the ephemeral body can dictate to the eternal Spirit. The Spirit has only one power, and that is the source of all other power. Mental powers come ultimately out of the Spirit power, but they come only to those who seek them, not necessarily to those who do not seek them.

Can everlasting good fortune be a criterion? Can one enter into tune with the Infinite and thereafter experience nothing but good fortune? Is it possible that all the gifts of the gods will fall into your lap; that you will never know what misfortune is; that everything in the garden of life will be beautiful and lovely until you die? That, I am sorry to say, is another illusion. This ephemeral world here is definitely a world of mixed suffering and sweetness because it is a transient world— a world which has a beginning and an ending. Therefore, you cannot find perfect happiness in it, although you can find it in yourself. Nothing can remain perfect forever; no good fortune can remain permanent.

There are people who have founded cults here in America, with adherents numbered by the millions. The founder of one cult that I have in mind, and perhaps the most famous in the United States, died after an illness of two years. Throughout her life she taught that consciousness of the Spirit infallibly brought perfect health. But she could not bring it to herself. Realizing that the tangible results did not square with the theory, her illness was kept secret. The worth of any spiritual cult is not to be measured by its amplitude.

A lecturer who was addressing thousands of people a day in a certain city I was visiting, told his listeners that if they would tune in to the Infinite, they could eliminate all of their bad destiny immediately, and henceforth everything would be beautiful in life, no illness, poverty, or lack of any kind. Not long after, he stopped his classes and lectures, disappeared for a whole winter, but later came back lecturing more beautifully than ever. He could only give lectures! He had had a nervous breakdown, which had to be kept secret, too. He was telling people that to tune in to the true Spirit would give them a perfectly harmonious and healthy life, but he could not eliminate the destiny of his nervous breakdown.

I will tell you what in these teachings is false, and what there is of truth in them. If you happen to have been a member of one sect or another for twenty years and have formed a set of stiff notions, such as that there exists a brotherhood of adepts in Tibet, or that there is a continuation of earthly existence in the after-death state; if you firmly believe these things, all right; but if you believe them to the extent that you cannot disbelieve them, it is all wrong. You must hold such beliefs loosely; and if the Truth would come and say, "That is not true," you should be so delicately poised that you can let those beliefs go, even though you have held them for twenty years. If you are not so delicately poised it means that you have become dogmatic without even being certain of the actual reality of your beliefs.

People come to me with talk of occultism and put questions that are really requests to endorse their cults. Well, there is a good deal in the teachings of these latter that is certainly correct and much that is incorrect, but I do not like the way in which they have complicated simple truths: they have made the finding of the kingdom of heaven more difficult than the scaling of Mount Everest, which is the loftiest height I have ever seen.

Credulous people take to these studies and become subject to hallucinations which they glorify as truth. Because I am sorry for those who have lost themselves in a forest of foolish doctrines, I have written this chapter in an effort to assist them out of it.

You must beware first of all of becoming captive in dogmas implanted in your mind by others. You must beware of persons who dupe themselves and deceive others by unscientific speculations which cannot prove themselves, which are wrapped in unnecessary mystery. You must refuse to give uncritical credence to them.

Jesus gave demonstrations of his character and power, saying: "By their fruits ye shall know them." Scientists use the same rule; if they cannot demonstrate their theories, they discard them. The acid test of all spiritual theories is in the laboratory of daily living. That is where you must test the claims of these cults to ascertain their value.

§

The omission of the factor of fate in so many of these cults is due to ignorance. That is where Asia has something to teach you. To put your heads in the sand like an ostrich and refuse to see the existence of an element of predestination in most of the major events of your personal life does not cross out its existence. It is still there.

Man lives a twofold life—an outer material life and an inner emotional-mental life. His outward deeds and actions are simply the result of his inner thoughts and feelings. They may take centuries to materialize, often not till a later birth, but ultimately they do. The world which you do not see, the unseen world of thought and feeling, is the real world of causes; the world which you see around you is the world of effects.

Because man tends to express his inner self by his outer actions, it may safely be said that his outer life corresponds to his inner life. The world as a whole in itself is nothing else but the expression of Divine Ideation, the very thought of God expressed. Man, in his own little way, is also a creator and is creating his own world—the world of his own experiences—the expression through which he lives. That chain of causal connection between man's inner thought, his inner feeling, and his outward experience, is unseen. But it is there, and it is there by a subtle force, the law of destiny.

Destiny is something entirely self-created, self-earned, whether it is for good or for evil. If man does not know that whatever he gives out in life to the world is ultimately thrown back to him by destiny, that does not excuse him. Nature never excuses ignorance. Man is the builder of his own life, the creator of his own fate, both outward and inward. Destiny is not a blind force; it is one expression of that greater cosmic Intelligence which rules the universe. It has a purpose to fulfil, and that purpose, so far as man is concerned, is an educative one. Destiny is like a balance; if you depress one side of the scale you find the other side goes up in proportion. Destiny restores the balance in man's life because she wishes him to understand himself, his powers, and possibilities as well as the fact that he is here to fulfil the higher purpose of his incarnation.

Destiny is quite impersonal and universal. It has no sense of retribution. There is no motive of punishment in that great force. As a man creates his own destiny by his thoughts and feelings and actions, he gets back unerringly from life sooner or later what he himself gives to life. There is no escape.

You are here to learn—to learn who and what you are. That is the purpose of your incarnation, and the experiences of life are the lessons which will ultimately teach you. Mostly you learn blindly and unconsciously, but still you are learning.

It is unfortunate that most men learn more from sufferings than from pleasures. Unfortunate, because they seldom learn enough with a single sorrow. It has to be repeated, perhaps getting worse with each repetition, until the lesson is etched into the heart, burned into the mind.

Until you arrive at the real self you are distorted and warped; you cannot think truthfully and you cannot act truthfully. Go back and look at your past; you will see how, even in this birth, you have created much of the experience through which you have gone. Many of those very warpings were present in former lives; they reappear in succeeding lives and they bring with them the destiny which is attached to them.

The destiny which you have earned in former lives you are working out now in this life. From that kind there is not much hope of escape, but there is every hope that it can be modified or altered.

There is a second kind of destiny: the fate which has been stored up for you in previous embodiments and which will be allotted to you in some future earth-life. That represents the greatest mass of destiny which is attached to any individual, because naturally he can work out only a little in a single life. That does not affect you now, but it will affect your next earth-life.

I shall try to explain this in another way. If you shoot at an object in a jungle, believing it to be a tiger, and, after the trigger has been pulled and the bullet sped on its way, you see that the object is a man, a friend of yours, you cannot recall the bullet and lodge it in the gun again. The bullet must take its course. The body in which we are born in this particular incarnation, together with the circumstances and environments attached to it, is the bullet which was shot out from your past, *and the past cannot call it back again.* It must speed its course.

All future shots, however, belonging to the lives that are to come, can be recalled, can be stopped at their very source. That is, it is possible to stop creating any fresh destiny as well as to wipe out the possibility of all future incarnations, because they have not yet begun.

So long as your body is here, its destiny is attached to it. But you can alter your reaction to it. You can react to the misfortune of losing all that you love and possess by taking it calmly. You can say: "Another cycle of my life is finished, and I must begin a new cycle; I will therefore readapt myself to the new cycle without fear. I will do everything that common sense counsels to mend matters and meet results." Or, in a state of deep depression, believing that you are finished, that life has no further hope for you, you can commit suicide. Both attitudes are the expression of your own choice, but the happening which you face is one and the same for the two moods.

The best way to escape is to get to the region where

these forces do not work—to become fate-free. You can do that only by returning to your divine centre and staying there. If you do that whilst you are in the flesh then that vast store of destiny which was awaiting you in future embodiments becomes dissolved and disappears. Why? Because it is the destiny of the personal ego, and when you have eliminated the tyranny of the latter you have eliminated the tyranny of the destiny attached to it; you are free, and with death that vast mass of accumulated stored-up destiny disappears completely. That is what Buddha meant when he said that you enter into Nirvana to escape the terrifying cycle of unending rebirths.

If you wish to avoid the misfortunes, the unpleasant experiences of life, you must learn to *nullify* the so-called evil destiny. If you live in the material world, then you must go through world experiences. But you can conquer your destiny *inwardly*. You can give up both pleasure and pain so that they do not touch you within your innermost being. You can stand aside from the processes of life inwardly, and although these experiences come to you, you can see them for what they are and realize them at their true value.

To find yourself is to find perfect mental equilibrium. Even if the greatest sufferings come to you, they cannot disturb your peace. Neither can the greatest pleasures disturb you. You remain rooted in your divine centre, which is the only place where peace can be found. There is no running away from yourself, except to run *within*.

This is what happens to the adept. All the immense storehouse of destiny which has come down to him from the past and up to this particular incarnation in which he now lives, is wiped out; but not that which belongs to the present body. He must endure it, and he does. But he will endure his destiny with a different attitude than would the average man. Sorrow does not mean sorrow to him; good fortune does not mean good fortune to him; he is detached. He looks upon both pleasure and pain with calm eyes. No matter what his personal self is passing through, he enjoys perpetually the consciousness of eternal life, so he is happy within. He does not particularly seek good fortune. He will welcome it if it comes, and enjoy it; he is not incapable of enjoying it. But if pain and sorrow were allotted to the body, he would not object. He does all that common sense would dictate to modify and alter, but that which cannot be modified or altered, he accepts resignedly.

The adept refuses to be swept hither and thither by destiny, and neither the greatest pleasures nor the greatest misfortunes can break his wonderful calmness. You, too, must try to reproduce the same attitude by living as close to the divine as you can get.

You do not eliminate present destiny when you enter the eternal; but what you eliminate is the destiny which has been stored up through countless lives; not that of the earth-life you are now living.

But remember always that it was within your power to modify and to alter your destiny. Life is not a cast-iron thing, because fate is only *one* of the forces that is playing upon us. There is also the force of free will, and the stimuli resulting are a mixture of both. Your own free will once created your present destiny, so you can create something even now.

Destiny sends the circumstances of your life; the major events are brought you by destiny, such as birth, death, marriage, the meeting with the spiritual teacher, —all those come to you by its mysterious operation. Troubles also come, but it is in your power to make them better or worse. And so you should never fall into that fatal lethargy into which so many in the Orient fall, when they sit down helpless and hopeless and say, whatever the misfortune: "It is God's will; we can do nothing. We must sit down and bear it to the bitter end."

Thus they repudiate their own innate divine power. This has been their degradation. It explains why they have fallen into such a state of servitude, as so many of them are today. If India is a subject nation today, and has been the prey of alien invaders for hundreds of years, it is partly India's own fault. The abuse and misuse of the truth of destiny is the cause of many troubles. You can not become weak through knowing truth; but you do become weak by ignorance. Be strong!

In the face of adverse fate we have to learn two things: when to accept it and when to resist it. There are times when it is wise to resign yourself to overwhelming circumstances, learning their bitter lesson, but there are other times when it is wiser to fight them with the courage of a lion. You must find out for yourself which is the right time. Such wisdom comes only in its perfection to the adept. Why? Because he has learned to stand aside from the purely personal.

There are times when misfortunes are cups of blessing, and they should be accepted; there are also times when good gifts are cups of poison, and they should be rejected. Only by becoming absolutely impersonal can we judge between them. The "I," the ego, is your enemy; it can become your friend. It is your enemy so long as it monopolizes your attention; it becomes your friend when it stands aside and says: "Not my will, but Thy will be done." If you look for that which is behind your personal self, your personal life, your mind, your body, for that which is true reality and spirit, there you will find peace. No one can rob you of it; no one can take it away from you. You will have found life eternal.

§

The chief beneficial contribution of those aforementioned cults which presume to teach us much that Jesus and Buddha quite forgot to mention, is their encouragement of courageous moods rather than cowardly ones; their constant reiteration that optimistic, positive, constructive, and cheerful thoughts are more valuable to man than pessimistic, negative, destructive, and hopeless ones; and their frequent reminder that it is good to hear what the silent minutes of mental quiet have to say to us.

Apart from that, some of the movements of today which set out professedly to spiritualize materialism have merely succeeded in materializing spirituality.

This happens especially when they degenerate into systems for turning thoughts into things, mental images into physical realities, and airy nothings into solid somethings—by believing in them!

The magical transformation of poverty into prosperity, of sickness into good health, almost overnight, is frequently claimed by the theorists of these systems but seldom demonstrated by the followers. The matter is somewhat complicated by the fact that there is some truth mixed with their fable, some wisdom with their nonsense, and some virtue with their vain assertions.

The root of the matter, however, is that they cater to the satisfaction of man's personal desires, whilst assuring him that they lead him into the kingdom of heaven at the same time. Thus they seem to provide him with a method of making the best of both worlds. The thing can be done, of course, but not in their way. There is a vital difference of approach and result between the two ways. That difference centres in the attitude adopted towards the personal ego.

This misconception must be cleared away unless you wish to delude yourself. People want so much to cling to the personal self even when trying to enter into the highest realm, the realm of spiritual truth, which can be attained only by the surrender of the personal self. It will never be possible to find the Spirit unless you are willing to let go of the personality. If you find spiritual life, and then believe you have demonstrated material gain as a consequence, you are simply deluding your-self, and sooner or later life will disillusion you severely; it is not the truth. It is better to seek for truth, whether the truth is painful or pleasurable. Let us love truth and accept it, and not try to dictate that truth shall always be pleasurable. Let us accept truth for its own sake, whether it brings us bad problems or good health. If you seek truth only for the benefits it is going to bring you, then you are not going to find it, because you are seeking the benefits, and not the truth itself. Truth is so like a proud and exclusive lady that she will never give herself to you unless you seek her for her own sake.

We hear sometimes of successful results obtained amidst many failures. We hear always of the successes, we do not always hear of the failures, which greatly outnumber the others. The successes are real but they are few, and they can be accounted for by the powers of the higher part of the mind, the so-called subconscious. They are achieved by the powers of the over-mind.

Unless these persons understand that they are dealing with the latent but little known powers of the human mind, and not with the powers of the divine Self, they are just blind leaders of the blind. And dealing with such mental powers demands care not to fall into black magic and hypnotism. Many of these cults are unconsciously practicing black magic. It is easy to use hypnotism, to influence other persons, but there is always a price, a penalty, to be paid.

When you have access, through some mood of strong concentration or of self-absorption, to the planetary overmind, and share its powers temporarily, in that moment of sharing you may perform miracles; miracles which may be material, or they may be mental, but they will never be higher than mental; they will never be spiritual.

Similarly, with reference to so-called demonstrations of prosperity. That is done in a similar way by concentration of the mind upon money. If you can concentrate hard enough and long enough, and if you do it with self-absorption into the overmind, at times you will get money. You will get it because you are demonstrating a mental power. But if you attempt to do these things out of your own wisdom, you are running certain risks, and the risks are not always to be desired. You may get what you seek by mental concentration but you may get other things along with it which you did not seek. You may get the demonstration of perfect health, and die the next day. I do not say that you will, but I do say, if you wish to deal with powers that you do not understand, try to understand them before you try to use them. And do not deceive yourself into thinking that you are using spiritual powers. They are purely mental, not spiritual.

If you can picture the overmind as a great ocean with myriads of inlets, each representing an individual human mind, you are on the way to understanding the source of occult phenomena and the principle of telepathy. We hear a great deal of occult powers. And people think that the development of these powers is either a necessary complement of the quest or desirable in itself. Occult powers have nothing to do with our quest. In seeking the Overself we must not stop en route. All occult powers belong to the plane of mind. They are phenomena within the region of the planetary overmind. If you obtain access to regions of the overmind, you obtain access to occult powers.

But the overmind is not the Overself. It is a plane lower. If you are going to remain within the region of the overmind, you will never reach the Overself. What do you want? Do you want the kingdom of heaven? Then you must go on. You must leave the overmind behind you, and with it all the occult powers. Learn to enter into that narrow gate where everything is left behind—material possessions and mental possessions.

If you cling to occult powers, you will never pass through the gate which leads to the kingdom of heaven. These powers are no concern of ours in our quest of the Overself. Some people spend their time and energy on the pursuit of these powers, but very few people succeed in acquiring them. If they do succeed, however, they will halt in their spiritual quest. And they will be halted until they relinquish their pursuit of occult phenomena. It is easy to understand how so many cults arise following leaders who have stopped still at various points along the way in their search for the truth.

Healing is perfectly possible, yes. The power of the overmind is such that it can save you from the jaws of death, where doctors have given up in despair. I have seen this power successfully exercised, and more than once. But the secret is that it worked through a human channel who did not deliberately and egoistically set out to heal, consequently the healing was right and permanent.

Mental healing can justify itself only when it creates a higher outlook in the patient, when it gives him the understanding that he is not his body, but something non-material.

Jesus promised that all things would be added unto you if you seek the kingdom of heaven. So you see there is a higher way of getting demonstrations, a higher way which requires that you seek the kingdom of heaven. And if you want to find the kingdom, you must give up your own personal ego, and if you give up your own personal ego you give up desire for material things. You will have certain material needs, but then you have entrusted them to your Father in heaven and He will take care of them. But if you think you are wiser than your Father and you attempt through mental concentration to dictate to the Father, then He leaves you alone to find things out by means of your own experience.

You have the way of Jesus, or you have the way of these cults; they are two different ways. And although the cults use the name of Jesus and pretend that they are following him, it is not the same. The ways are different. Material demonstrations are possible through both ways, but certain through none. God has the last word, not we. But the first is the way of surrender of the personal self-will, and therefore always brings inner peace and inner fortitude to endure our troubles, whether or not it succeeds in attracting good fortune or health. The second is the way of *using* the personal ego to satisfy personal desires, and always brings mental restlessness and mental uncertainty with which to face our troubles. The first way is divine and *right;* the second is egoistic and *wrong.*

So far as these claims are based on the principle that concentrated thought tends to become creative on the objective plane, they are correct. Nevertheless, such teaching is not true for the thinking of ninety-five per cent of the people who study it, simply because their thoughts are not sufficiently powerful to become quickly creative. This doctrine is true only of the adept, whose thoughts are filled with the creative power of cosmic mind. Hence, only those followers of these cults who have practised yoga to an advanced degree and drawn upon this universal power, can begin to materialize their thoughts.

If an adept possesses magical powers it is because he has concentrated upon them and sought for them, not only in this birth but in previous incarnations as well. This was his line of development, so when he finally attained adeptship, these powers were available because he had sought them, and the fullness of Truth brought them as a reward. If he had sought only Truth, then he would not have these powers, but he would be no less an adept, because his consciousness would be real and eternal, and to him the physical world, however omnipresent it might seem, would not constitute reality, but rather would have the value of a dream.

The adept who has occult powers looks upon these powers as dream powers. To him they do not matter very much, because in order to practise them he has to step down from his highest consciousness. It is for him a form of self-sacrifice to use healing or occult powers, because they do not belong to the plane of eternal spirit; they belong to the plane of mind, which is lower.

Vanity is the first of the snares which lie waiting for the person with half-developed occult powers. The supernatural is merely the natural misunderstood. Each finite mind is but a whirlpool, a vortex, in the infinite overmind. It has no distinct and separate existence in reality, in substance, but it is like a trough of a wave in the ocean, different in form only. It has never at any time been separate from overmind.

Do not, therefore, make the common mistake of expecting occult marvels from an adept, or you will be disappointed. He will use these occult powers when he thinks fit, but not otherwise. There is one thing we must remember, and that is that the man who has found the divine Spirit has found the source of all power, even occult powers. Magical powers are themselves lesser expressions of the higher powers of the Overself, because ultimately there is only one power, and one force in the whole universe, as there is only one mind. As this force comes down and condenses, it divides itself into inferior forces, and these again into feebler expressions and into the various forces and energies which we know.

An adept may not, for example, have developed the healing power. He may have worked for the power of the Overself, which is the greatest power in the world. With that power he can accomplish the greatest miracles, much greater than those performed by any occultist. The greatest miracle an adept can perform is aiding others to a change of consciousness, because that assists their awakening from illusion to truth. Nevertheless, such is the power of the Overself, being at the base of all things, that it can and does at times perform the most striking miracles, through the agency of the over-mind, of course. Those who have appeared in this world, and who have performed marvels and miracles, have not generally been adepts in the best sense. They have not found eternal life. If these people wish to become true adepts, if they wish to become as Jesus was, then there is only one step for them to take, and that is to re-nounce their powers, and then set forth on the highest path. Such powers become a stumbling block when they begin to seek for something higher. They are mental powers, and to find the plane of spirit the seekers must transcend the plane of mind. Such men, if they have transcended the mind and renounced the powers, will later find that these powers are returned to them. The Overself then uses them to perform miraculous feats so that there is no longer an egoistic motive. The powers will be used only as an expression of the will of the Overself, not of the personal self, which makes all the difference in the world.

There is a great mystery connected with spiritual consciousness, a mystery which Western people will find very hard to understand and which lies in the sur-render of the ego, or as Jesus called it "the giving up of your own life." When you surrender your ego and attain the truth, you no longer act but are acted upon; you no longer speak, but are spoken through. It means that the Overself has found a focus and an outlet in this material world which it did not have before. That is the miracle. The Overself is everywhere, it is ever-present. It is at the base of all things; it permeates all space.

The outside observer saw miracles performed by

Jesus, so he thought that Jesus deliberately willed that a certain thing happen. Jesus willed nothing, but he let himself be willed through. The Overself, which is the one Spirit present in others as in Jesus, knowing perfectly what must be done, what must be served, willed at those moments that these miracles should be done, and did them.

Follow the way that Jesus taught us, which is to surrender the ego. Your Father knows what you need. He put you into this world. If you know it, surely He should. Follow this quest without qualm, for you have nothing to fear. You have committed your life in its entirety to God. You have done this not by an act of faith alone, but also by conscious communion. The burden which most mortals carry upon their minds and within their hearts, has fallen away from you. Henceforth you live as an inspired man or woman, listening for the dictate of the Christ within.

When you have found the kingdom, then only may you have health, fortune, love, occult powers, if it is your destiny to have them. Without the slightest effort you can pick them up. Only then is it right for you to have them. They will be perfectly safe in your possession, because you will keep them in their place. They will play a subordinate and secondary part in your life, when you have finished your quest. But until then, do not seek them by supernormal means. It is wiser not to do so.

Trust in the Overself. Surrender yourself to it and you will find relief. You will have lost your burdened self, and whatever comes, even death, you will accept. For to know your Overself is the hidden reason for your existence. Out of suffering even, beautiful things will be shown you. Something of the Eternal Spirit will come to you.

CHAPTER XIII

THE GOSPEL ACCORDING TO ST. JOHN

IT WILL be my interesting task to deal with the esoteric significance of various representative passages of the Gospel according to St. John.
The first verse deals with the matters most profound.

"In the beginning was the Word, and the Word was with God, and the Word was God. The same was in the beginning with God."

The "Word" represents the very first motion of the Creative Power. The term "God" does not here stand for the Absolute, the Great Void which is the Ultimate of all things, but for the individualized Creator of a universe.

Properly to understand this verse we must also understand something of the process of creation and realize that in the beginning there was nothing but the great Void, the true Absolute wherein all was still, empty, lifeless, and silent, and where there was eternal darkness. It was the quiescent Ultimate Root out of which all transient creations and all perishable individuals emerge.

The infinite, eternal Overself does not know the vagaries of mind, nor the changes of appearance, hence it always IS. It has neither expressed itself in matter nor improved itself by evolution. All such concepts are human notions which disappear when the Absolute and the ultimate Truth is known. The ultimate Self is *not* a creator, it is the One which forever remains the One without a second.

In that undifferentiated, motionless, and silent Void in which was neither condition, thought, nor individuality, and which the Orientals symbolize by the conception of infinite space, in That there somehow appeared a mysterious point of Light, the primary birth, God!

God must be viewed in two ways, either as the personal God or the unoriginated impersonal God. As the personal God, He is the Creator of the universe, and you cannot separate Him from His creation. As the impersonal God, He is nothing but the Infinite Reality. There are many personal Gods, because there are many universes, but there is only one absolute God.

The Creator has the same value for the sage that the world has. All these Gods exist so far as the worlds exist. Consider God as the life of the world, but where did God come from? He came out of the absolute Self. No matter how exalted He is, He had to emerge from That. Then He emanated the universe and so forth. That God has a form and has a name. But in the one Absolute there is no name and no form, nothing to be seen.

Here let me interpolate that God, however exalted, is still individual. For while from the human standpoint there is but one God, from the standpoint of the Absolute there are as many Gods as there are universes, each of which has come forth from its particular Creator— or God—and has its own separate being. But all individual Gods and beings have emerged from the unconditioned ultimate Absolute Darkness.

After it first appears, the point of Light spreads out and develops. The Creator of the universe is born as a body of Light. With this appearance, and not before, begins the possibility of all other creation and evolution. For the Absolute itself has nothing to create, being utterly self-sufficient, seeking nothing, and having no purpose within the limits of creation.

But God as circumscribed being within the Absolute, vast though He be, has a purpose. He appears. He is individualized. It is the Creator of the universe to whom St. John refers as God in the first verse of his Gospel, and not the True Absolute out of which He has emerged.

With a well-defined purpose the Creator begins His creation of the universe out of the Light-substance which is His being and body, spinning it out as a spider spins out its web from itself.

God projects His idea of the universe first.

"The Word," any word, represents a thought and idea, or a picture; even a mental picture is the expression of an idea.

So the text means that in the beginning the *idea* of creation was with God. Without this divine idea there could be no creation, because everything has first to be mentally made. Therefore John writes:

> "The same was in the beginning with God. Without Him was not anything made that was made."

Because God made the world out of His own Light-substance and being, this statement is accurate. Science verifies it, having now discovered that matter can be converted into its primal entity, which is radiant energy, nothing less than light. This proves that light is the ultimate state of matter. God said: "Let there be light." After that there came the world.

The Light is seen by mystics when they say they see God, which is all you can ever see of God, who is both the soul and the first state of matter.

Further, the cosmic ideation expressed by St. John as "the Word" is not only in the beginning, but also in the end, and even in the middle. It must be, for this idea is the real and enduring prototype of the universe of which the material one is but the shadow and reflection.

All that you know of this universe is your idea of it, not what it appears to be in matter. Proof of this has been offered by such intellectual metaphysicians and philosophers as Kant, Schopenhauer, and Bishop Berkeley; also by Sir James Jeans in the closing chapter of his book, *The Mysterious Universe*.

Science is being forced to declare that this is a mental universe. Matter is dissolving before the eyes of the enquirer who peers behind its appearance eventually to find it existing within man's consciousness.

What is it that can exist within man's consciousness? What but those ideas which are kindred to the mind, which is capable of grasping only that which is of its own nature?

The divine idea of the universe, then, is the more enduring reality behind it. To enter into the world of the spirit is to enter the world of primary processes. All that we perceive is but a materialization of creative cosmic mind. The material appearance is the reflection and nothing but a mass of electrons which, in turn, are but electricity, energy.

There is nothing substantial there, only a mental sensation of substantiality and solidity.

Now you cannot have motion or movement without sound. Hence the silence of the Absolute was broken by the *sound* of God creating. Whether you hear it or not, it is there. There are unheard sounds in the universe as well as heard ones.

Sound is the accompaniment which the creative play of God brings forth, and sound is a force. It is not a force which works alone. It appears simultaneously with the appearance of divine ideation. Thus the creative *power* of God, and His creative *thought*, "the Word" to which St. John refers, are twins.

In Him was life; and the life was the light of men. The divine energy is both the creative sustaining power throughout the universe and the primal life current of all creatures. It has been rayed into us, thus rendering mental and physical activity possible. It is the life of the body, of the mind, and of consciousness. Without it, everything from universe to atom collapses and disappears again into the primal darkness of the Boundless Being.

This current flows through the human nervous system as a veritable light-flow, imperceptible to the naked eye because of the high rate of vibration.

Just as our very existence on this planet is dependent upon the nourishment we get out of it; just as this planet's nourishing power is dependent in its turn on the energy which it received from the sun; so is our entire material and mental life supported ultimately by the divine Light, and it alone.

Moses told his people this same truth of the Overself's existence as the secret source of the life current in man's physical body, when he said:

"The Lord thy God is thy life and the length of thy days."

The Apostle Paul put the identical thought in the following words:

"Know ye not that ye are the temple of the living God?"

The Overself is here and now and always. It is everywhere and nowhere. It is the ever-present Reality. You must hold to that as the key thought. If you keep on thinking only in the human and intellectual way, you limit your progress. To develop your intuition is to transcend intellect. You will have to know yourself

finally through your intuition and not alone through
your intellect. At this very moment in your inner mind,
if you wish, there is That which is the ever-present witness and which is the One. That means it is present in
all the multitudes of separate selves, but itself is only
one. It exists always in a state of perfect harmony,
undisturbed. It is like the deep body of the ocean. The
waves and the foam and the froth make a tremendous
noise on the surface, but deep down all is still.

"And the light shineth in the darkness; and the
darkness comprehended it not."

Universally, this speaks of the Infinite Consciousness
which transcends all mortal thinking, all mental experience. Thoughts cannot grasp it; hence it is for ever
wrapped in darkness. This unconditioned Ultimate cannot come into awareness of anything conditioned and
finite, not even of the Light which is the Creator. It
knows nothing, as other than itself, and of it we can only
say, It *is*.

It recognizes the presence of no other existence, no
other reality. But on the human plane, this verse means
that the body goes about walking, working, eating,
talking, and feeling utterly self-sufficient. It lives as part
of the personal ego and thinks, "I do this, I do that, I
do it by my own power." But it could do nothing, not
even exist, unless the primal life current from God func-
tioned in the heart-atom within itself.

Animated by this borrowed current of life, the body
falsely believes it is working by its own life. It does
not understand that the Light which causes it to exist
is not its own but is derived from a selfless Source.

That was the true Light which "lighteth every man
that cometh into the world." This amounts to the same
thing. The Light-substance which is God forms the
Overself-atom in each man's heart; it "lighteth every

man" to the extent that his spiritual growth renders him capable of receiving it.

"John bare witness of him, and cried, saying, 'This was he of whom I spake. . . . He that cometh after me is preferred before me: for he was before me.' "

John announces the coming of Jesus. He is not alone. The ancient oracles of Rome, the Sibylline oracles, had predicted this coming, whereafter they fell into ominous silence.

In other words, John the Baptist received a degree of illumination which rendered him capable of recognizing that an avatar, an incarnation, had appeared; John had to find him.

"For the law was given by Moses, but grace and truth by Jesus Christ."

The law Moses brought to the Jews was entirely adequate and suitable for its time and for the Jews to whom it was given, but people evolve—or else suffer by missing the purpose of evolution. Therefore, to a more evolved people, Jesus taught forgiveness in place of the old vengeful law of "an eye for an eye."

Hence John says that Jesus came to give grace and truth. None other than an avatar or adept may do this.

Jesus does not claim that the miracles he performs provide proof that he comes from God. Miracles are not enough.

"Except a man be born again he cannot enter the kingdom of heaven."

Obviously to be born again means an inner rebirth, an inner change. You must first die to ignorance and illusion before you can be spiritually reborn. This process of dying takes a long time, sometimes many incarnations. But gradually, with the help of the teacher, you overcome both illusions and ignorance with their errors of thought and feeling, and liberated from their limitations you are suddenly reborn into the kingdom.

You cannot achieve this alone. You must have a competent guide. It necessarily takes many lifetimes, but when the greater part of these obstructions are removed the rebirth will come suddenly.

This experience will never be duplicated. When you are born again you remain born. It is permanent, bringing forth your inner being, so that you function for all time in Reality and Truth.

Few have attained to this rebirth, but all must do so who would enter into the kingdom of God.

Therefore, when the dull-minded Pharisee, Nicodemus, asked whether a man who is old could enter a second time into his mother's womb and be born, Jesus answered:

"Verily, verily I say unto thee, Except a man be born of water and of the Spirit, he cannot enter into the kingdom of God . . . That which is born of flesh is flesh; and that which is born of the Spirit is Spirit."

You cannot mark this rebirth with any finite measure because when it happens you discover to your amazement that the mysterious element of Spirit and of Divine Reality into which you consciously merge has always been with you and in you.

Proceeding with characteristic patience to instruct the unintuitional Nicodemus, Jesus continues:

"For God sent not His Son into the world to condemn the world; but that the world through Him might be saved."

There is neither condemnation nor punishment in destiny. This is a human idea. Destiny is an impersonal force. The coming of Jesus or any avatar brings with it a double-edged sword of Truth which helps and awakens the receptive, and punishes those who reject it.

The destiny which flung Jesus among the Jews gave them the opportunity to accept him or to reject him at their peril. Such rejection must automatically bring punishment, which you should in no way attribute to God, whose desire is to save.

Likewise, a Messiah does not come to punish, but to save. He comes to redeem us from untruth, ignorance, and illusion, and to restore us to our original spiritual condition.

Jesus explains that by their rejection of him, the Jews automatically condemn themselves to punishment. He says:

> "He that believeth on him [God's Son] is not condemned: but he that believeth not is condemned already."

Continuing, Jesus declares:

> "Everyone that doeth evil hateth the light, neither cometh to the light . . . But he that doeth truth cometh to the light . . ."

This is true. This is the Law. We see it illustrated by the manner in which people automatically gravitate around those ideals and conditions best suited to them. A message of truth will attract those possessing true ideals, while untruth in any form will always draw to it those whose ideals are similarly untrue.

None can accept the Light but those who have made themselves worthy of it. Greedy, world-worshipping, selfish, and therefore evil, people have not prepared themselves for it, and automatically shut themselves off from it.

In the fourth chapter of St. John you come to the incident of the Samarian woman at the well. Jesus tells her:

"God is Spirit, and they that worship Him, must worship Him in spirit and truth."

Jesus moved among people who, contrary to this, practised idol worship and adhered to dead dogmas, formalized truths bereft of their inner spirit. This was a semimaterialistic worship.

Jesus states that God must be worshipped differently, "in spirit and in truth," without rite or ceremony. He made it clear that no human priest could be a substitute for the direct communication of man's soul with Divine Spirit.

In the subsequent chapter you read that the Jews persecuted Jesus and sought to slay him because he broke the Sabbath by healing a man, and also because he said that God was his Father.

Jesus justifies himself on both counts:

"My Father worketh hitherto and I work."
"The Son can do nothing of himself but what he seeth the Father do."

Inflexibly formalized and hidebound in their customs, the Jews cannot understand that for this Holy One all days are sacred, all suitable for the work of ever-present Spirit to be performed. They seek to limit the Illimitable to their own standards and rules.

". . . the Son can do nothing of himself but what he seeth the Father do."

Who is the Father but the Overself? And surely each one of us represents a son, even though we may not recognize our divine relationship.

Jesus points out that the son can do nothing of himself. This is because we each live only by the power of the central life current of the Overself which is in the heart. Without it, we collapse and die.

Jesus knows that the Father ultimately does everything through the son, and he lets the Father work fully and freely through him, knowing that of himself he can do nothing.

You have to realize that the fragment of the life current manifesting through you as the personal self is minute and atomic in comparison with Itself. In the personal self we express but one spark of a mighty flame, but Jesus shone and burned with the entire flame.

Ignorant men imagine they are self-sufficient. The adepts are wiser. They know that all they can do is done by God through them. Because they freely permit Him to use them, they are perfect instruments and channels for His Truth and Power, while unawakened men are merely instruments and channels for their own personal power.

Because the adept stands aside and allows the Overself to function through him, he is in that sense equal to God, since he is cooperating with God. All of you who wish to find the Overself, who wish to become Overself-conscious, must learn to stand aside in the personal self and become non-obstructive mediums through which It may express.

The spiritual path is simple in essence. Its achievement entails allowing the profound depths of yourself to come to the surface and manifest.

To do this successfully the practice of mental stillness, meditation, is essential. While you are constantly active mentally and physically these depths cannot arise and manifest, but by quieting your mind and your body, you provide the right opportunity for the Spirit within to manifest. After training has made you able to do this sufficiently, you can again be active without interfering with Its manifestation.

Jesus declares:

> "I can of mine own self do nothing. . . . I seek not mine own will, but the will of the Father. . . ."

The greatest men are the humblest. The smallest are the most arrogant. Real sages are always modest, claiming no superiority, and they always put you at your ease. This is because they have silenced the personal self and become as channels, allowing That which is behind to manifest.

Jesus' hearers could not understand him. They continued persecutions. He says to them:

> "I know you, that ye have not the love of God in you. . . . I am come in my Father's name and ye receive me not: if another shall come in his own name, him ye will receive."

Jesus represents the Overself, but their grossness can not recognize this—

These people condemned themelves by their unbelief and lack of intuition. Only by intuition, and never by appearance, may you recognize a prophet.

Jesus also reiterates:

> "I came down from heaven not to do mine own will, but the will of Him that sent me . . . And this is the Father's will which hath sent me, that everyone which seeth the son and believeth on him may have everlasting life."

Such, then, is the Father's will and the reason for Jesus' coming. Those who see and believe in him may receive the grace he longs to bestow upon all, but which can only reach those who accept him in their hearts with faith and devotion.

For though the Overself sends a Messiah into incarnation to help mankind, we must cooperate with him in order to benefit. He asks nothing but the gift of our faith and devotion.

Jesus knows only his own can come to him. He says:

"All that the Father giveth me shall come to me; and him that cometh to me I will in no wise cast out."

This is very plain. Those fortunate enough to be incarnated in his time and land can contact him, and by inward recognition answer his call.

These people have begun the search for the Father and, however dimly, have come into some communion with him. Jesus knows that their Spiritual Self is drawing them to him. Others will come and persecute him, but his son will come and stay.

Then he says:

". . . he that believeth on me hath everlasting life."

Those believers who accept him and follow the path he shows can receive his grace. They will eventually come to have the inner awareness of the presence of that eternal Reality which is the everlasting life of Jesus. Then they will know It for their true being.

You will notice in this book that Jesus repeatedly points out that he is an instrument. Even the greatest Messiah is this, a channel, powerless if he has to depend upon his own intellect or mind. Accordingly Jesus asserts:

"My doctrine is not mine, but His that sent me."

He tells his listeners, in effect: This truth is not mine, it is given me by the Power which illumines me. You,

too, have that Power within you and may become Its
instrument. He claims nothing for himself.

Jesus has come to look for the few who are his own,
knowing that only they are competent to receive his
message.

To them he says things which the masses cannot
understand, giving them plain, direct truth instead of
speaking in the symbols and parables he uses to instruct
the multitude.

These few who stand in special relationship to him
are destined to meet the brunt of the persecution dealt
out to the first Christians. Because of this, they are initiated into the mysteries of the kingdom of heaven. They
partake of the strength of its Light and receive power
which enables them to undergo the persecution.

". . . But he that entereth in by the door is the
shepherd of the sheep . . . To him the porter openeth
and the sheep heareth his voice; and he calleth his own
sheep by name and leadeth them out . . . And when
he putteth forth his own sheep, he goeth before them
and the sheep follow him, for they know his voice."

Jesus knew before he incarnated that there were those
who through prior evolution had reached the point
where the touch of the Master would awaken them to
spiritual consciousness.

Those few are to be the bearers of that which he will
give mankind. They are incarnated within his lifetime
so that he shall find them. They are not merely his followers, but constitute his disciples.

Jesus knows when he goes to preach in the streets
that among the multitude there will be four or five who
belong to him. Not to him personally, but to the power
working through him.

He finds his own! Those destined, by their quest for
God and truth in former incarnations, to be found of

the master. Those who are ready to receive from him the reward of illumination. *The* illumination—he calleth his own sheep by name and leadeth them out.

Jesus goes on to say:

"And a stranger they will not follow, but will flee from him: for they know not the voice of strangers."

Trained to know the voice of the shepherd, the sheep will follow no other. Meeting him, his own know they have found the truth for which they seek. Sensing the power which expresses itself through him, they will harken only to his voice.

Predestined from birth to be disciples of their master, any other who attempted to draw them away would be a thief and a robber, to whose sheepfold they do not belong. No teacher who has attained truth will seek to take those who do not belong to him. Any so doing have not attained and are but blind leaders of the blind.

Jesus and his disciples reincarnated at the same period as one group. Lost in matter, identified with the body, the disciples spent years finding their way back to the teacher. But eventually, fulfilling destiny, they came to him.

"Then Jesus said unto them again; verily, verily, I say unto you, I am the door of the sheep . . . All that ever came before me are thieves and robbers; but the sheep did not hear them."

Here the master indicates that no other guide, no orthodox priest or teacher, can be the destined leader of his own. All such are thieves and robbers.

"I am the door: by me if any man enter in, he shall be saved and shall go in and out and find pasture."

Not only for his disciples, but for all his hearers willing to place complete faith in him, Jesus is the door;

the outlet through which the Overself can touch their conscious minds.

The Overself is everywhere, but before you can become aware of it, there must be a channel through which it can connect you, a door by which you may pass to it. That channel must be in the flesh. A human being in whom the Overself is the moving power. No teacher in the invisible world will do.

So Jesus says:

". . . if any man enter in, he shall be saved."

What is salvation? Surely it consists of finding that spiritual truth which will lift you out of ignorance and materiality; out of the belief that you are only intellect and physical. Ignorance constitutes the cause of your heavy load of fate, which you have earned during former lives on this earth. It hangs over you like a shadow, stored up, waiting for recognition now or in some future birth.

That fate demands expression, readjustment on this earth, causing you to reincarnate here again and again.

Hence salvation has a double meaning: to free yourself from your fate and the resulting rebirths into a physical body; and to be lifted up from the state of spiritual ignorance in which you exist.

"By me if any man enter in he shall be saved."

This means that if you will find your master and faithfully follow him and the path he indicates to you, you will free yourself from your fate and be lifted up out of spiritual ignorance.

"I am come that they might have life and that they might have it more abundantly."

This does not mean physical existence. Jesus came to give you eternal life in the Overself, without beginning or end.

But there is a deeper meaning: I have told you that God is Light. That Light is the primal substance of this universe. In finding your inner self you find that primal Light current. Until that is done, you are only living partially, living in the body and the intellect.

When Jesus states that he came to bring more abundant life, he means that he has come to bring you back to the source of it, the life current which flows through the universe and through mankind,—that which enables your body and mind to function, as the heat of the fire in the poker enables it to become red hot.

"I am the good shepherd and know my sheep and am known of mine."

This means that when the master meets the disciple he will know him for his own. The disciple may also know it, but not so clearly as the master at first, though he will be conscious of something which perturbs him or rejoices him. In the ensuing period, his intuition will become clearer and clearer and he will finally know that he has found the master.

". . . I lay down my life for the sheep."

In fulfillment of the mission for which he came, in which was involved the fate of the world, as well as his work of enlightening his disciples by making himself their channel of the more abundant life, Jesus had to relinquish his physical life. He had to be crucified.

This had to be. Not only was the act symbolical, but it was associated with the fate of the particular people with whom he incarnated; also the fate of mankind in whose countries Christianity was to appear.

"And other sheep I have, which are not of this fold: them also I must bring, and they shall hear my voice; and there shall be one fold and one shepherd."

Those who at some future time were to receive the life current of Jesus through his disciples, were those "other sheep." They were not present in his lifetime. They would come down to earth at a later period. Through his disciples and their later followers, he would give them his inner life current, which can only be achieved in the waking state and in the material world.

Spiritual development, so far as our planet is concerned, must be attained here. It must be found in the waking state, otherwise you could have achieved it in the spirit worlds without incarnating.

"No man taketh it [his life] from me, but I lay it down of myself."

All has been preordained. The people are merely instruments in the hands of the higher destiny.

Further, Jesus says:

"I have power to lay it down and I have power to take it again."

He has the power to materialize his physical body, to conquer death, and to triumph over material life. He demonstrates this power by the resurrection of his body after three days.

Then Jesus says:

". . . This commandment have I received of my Father."

Destiny preordained his mission. He obeyed the command of his Father, God, the Overself, or those Great Beings through whom the Overself works.

Thus the parable of the shepherd. When you understand its esoteric significance you realize that what happened in the beginning of Christianity was utterly preordained. It was the visible enactment here of a drama which had already been played out in the higher worlds. To crystallize it and make it what it must be, it had to show forth in the material world.

"I told you and ye believed not; the works that I do in my Father's name, they bear witness of me."

Jesus had a public mission to perform. Because of this he had to mingle with the public, on the highways and in the market places. In so doing he met every type of humanity—believers, unbelievers and the bewildered.

They asked Jesus to still their doubts: "If thou be the Christ, tell us plainly." To them Christ meant the Messiah and Deliverer sent from God.

"But ye believe not, because ye are not of my sheep as I said unto you."

There you have the reason. His disciples, his sheep, believed him, even if at first they had doubted. But the others had no inner link with him. They could not believe.

"My sheep hear my voice and I know them and they follow me . . . And I give unto them eternal life and they shall never perish, neither shall any man pluck them out of my hand."

They are his. He holds them in his hand, his consciousness, his heart, and mind. Steadily he holds them and no man may take them away. Eventually the higher consciousness will overwhelm them and they will receive the life eternal which he has come to give them.

"My Father, which gave them to me, is greater than all; and no man is able to pluck them out of my Father's hand."

Observe they are now in the Father's hand, yet previously he says they are in his. But he explains:

"I and my Father are one."

When you achieve the Overself state of unity, the ego—the personal self—becomes merged into oneness with the Overself. There is no conflict of wills. The ego surrenders. Thy will be done.

The personal self is not blotted out. It remains as long as you have your body. But it becomes a channel through which the Overself functions, an agent for the Overself, and hence one with it.

Jesus represents the Overself, the Father, and allowed it to function through him. In essence they are the same, but there is an ultimate difference in appearance. It is not for himself he holds his sheep. It is for the Father.

You will never discover your spiritual self by seeing it in visions. Such visions you may have, but the only way you will discover that self, is by becoming and being it.

Such visions denote duality, something outside yourself. Not necessarily outside the body, but inside of the mind and you.

All visions seen by the mind are psychic visions seen within it. The mind is not yourself. Therefore, they are outside of you. All psychic, even superpsychic visions are in the mind. Hence not in your self.

The self is the see-er and cannot be that which is seen. Spirit, the self, is you. You may only know and realize it by becoming it, by merging consciously into the Overself. Then you may truly say, "I and my Father are one."

Understanding the relationship between spirit, mind, and body, you will comprehend why Jesus says that both he and the Overself are holding the sheep. He has unified himself with the Overself.

But to materialistic people who picture God as a gigantic human being sitting aloft, his claim of being one with God seems to be blasphemy.

"Judge not according to appearance, but judge righteous judgment."

Thus Jesus rebukes the Jews for their utter blindness to the things of the heart and mind that really matter; for their adherence to the letter "which killeth," and neglect of the Spirit; for the fuss they made over external trivialities.

He reminds them of his departure:

"Yet a little while am I with you, and I go unto Him that sent me."

His presence is a divine opportunity, for it is not every day that a Messiah, an avatar or an adept appears among men.

Again he reminds them:

"Ye shall seek me, and shall not find me: and where I am, thither ye cannot come."

The coming of a teacher who is used by the Overself is like the giving of an ultimatum. Take the teaching or leave it! Take it and be blessed; leave it and be punished!

Tremendous forces are centred in the teacher and use him. Whatever you give him you receive back a thousandfold. Not because he personally wills it but because those forces centred in him give back a thousandfold the good or evil which you send him.

On the other hand, if you give him non-belief and rejection, you not only shut out the truth, but you plunge yourself into greater ignorance than ever before. Should you hurt or injure him, you will bring terrible physical suffering upon yourself, because by spontaneous reaction you have to get back from him infinitely more than you gave him, and in the same coin.

Jesus assures the people that he has no personal interest in punishing them. He leaves such punishment to the Higher Power.

"Ye judge after the flesh; I judge no man."

He reminds them that the opportunity for salvation has come and will go:

"I said therefore unto you, that ye shall die in your sins: for if ye believe not that I am he, ye shall die in your sins."

In rejecting him they sin, and instead of salvation through him, they will naturally remain and die in ignorance. If they accept his Light, they will have been saved from the related continuous cycles of birth and death.

This is what Jesus means when he warns the people that not to believe in him involves dying in their sins. It is not a matter of orthodox belief in his physical body, but having belief in that which he stands for, That which is working through him and accepting him as the channel of Its outpouring.

The mere belief that Jesus once physically existed is not enough. He cannot die for your sins unless he is amongst you. You must have a living master. Jesus points out that the presence of a living master is a blessing to be taken hold of. He says:

"Yet a little while is the light with you. Walk while ye have the light, lest darkness come upon you."

Take every advantage of the master's presence. When he is no longer here, you must grope your own way in the darkness.

To the few whose spiritual eyes are open and who accept him, Jesus says:

> "If ye continue in my word, then are ye my disciples indeed. . . . And ye shall know the truth and the truth shall make you free."

"Continue in my word," means to follow and practice his teaching. If you pursue this course with faith, doing the best you can, the master will do the rest, leading you into the truth which ultimately frees you for ever of ignorance, illusions, and unhappiness; the truth which is Reality brings neither happiness nor unhappiness, but a condition of unbroken peace.

Jesus expresses that modesty and humility which are not only essential in the first steps on the path, but which are also a factor in the last:

> "If I honour myself, my honour is nothing: it is my Father that honoureth me."

You see, then, the necessity for humility. You must relinquish all self-sufficiency and become as a receptive little child, so that the great Power can enter in and work through you freely.

Until you do this It stays away, letting you carry on by the personal so-called wisdom until you realize by your suffering that it is not enough.

People seem to think the adept is an adept only if he possesses magical powers, such as healing of the sick or turning water into wine. Jesus performed miracles that he might reach the people.

Miracles, however, are not performed by the power of the Overself, but by that of the mind. Their doing involves the use of a lower faculty and not the faculty of the Divine Self. This the adept knows, for he expresses truth, and truth is a non-mental state.

On the path you begin by finding the outer master. To find the teacher in the flesh is a great achievement. This done, he sets you the task of finding him as the inner teacher. To do that you have to understand that he is not the body which you see, but the soul inside it. At first you see his outer form. Later in your mind's eye you picture his mental image. Then you succeed in realizing him as a soul presence in your heart.

This is a most desirable stage to reach. See the teacher, no matter where you are, and even if he be thousands of miles away, see him as though he were visibly present.

There is a yet higher stage. Gradually you learn to dismiss the picture and feel only the presence. Finally the great day comes when your teacher says: "I have done my work. I withdraw that you may find your own self."

Then you forget his presence, and even him. You find yourself, you are your own light. The teacher's work for you is completed.

Jesus says:

"Believe me that I am in the Father and the Father in me."

Here is a paradox. Not only is the Divine Overself-atom present within your heart, but you exist within the Overself as the Universal Self.

Spirit all-permeating, filling infinite space, is yet present as a microscopic point within your heart. The Father is in you and you are in the Father.

You have, however, to find the Father's Spirit within you. Until you do, you cannot find the Spirit in the universe.

There are two stages in this search. The first, which you might call mysticism, is the discovery of the Father in you; the discovery of your Soul, the Divine Atom within your heart. This is achieved through meditation, through yoga, aspiration, and prayer.

Some time may then elapse. If you keep up the quest, God will reward you by bringing you to the Ultimate Path into which your teacher will initiate you.

This is the second stage. This will bring you to the discovery of the universal, everywhere-present Spirit, and there you complete the cycle. You find the two halves of truth. That which is within and that which is without you.

To those who have thus attained Jesus says:

"Even the Spirit of Truth; whom the world cannot receive, because it seeth him not, neither knoweth him: but ye know him; for he dwelleth with you and shall be in you."

Intangible, invisible, unfelt, the Infinite Overself is not received by the world because the world cannot see it, and as Jesus says: "Neither knoweth him." Nevertheless, though you may be the rankest materialist of this world, yet you cannot get away from the Overself. You are in it and it is in you. Therefore Jesus says: ". . . but ye know him; for he dwelleth with you."

In addressing his disciples Jesus tells them:

"Peace I leave with you, my peace I give unto you."

That peace is his grace. He gives it only to his disciples because no one else is capable of receiving it. In the disciples this gift of grace manifests, as it always does at first, by burning aspiration for spiritual realization. When the teacher fans the spark of spiritual yearning in the seeker's heart, the latter begins to search more desperately than ever before.

His aspiration intensely speeded up by the teacher's bestowal of grace, the seeker may pass through a period of unhappiness, turmoil, and unsatisfied spiritual longing.

This thirsting and burning for spiritual realization is the result of the contact made in the heart with the teacher. It may be so poignant that fits of weeping may come and continue for long periods.

Through it all the seeker knows a strange inner peace. The more he experiences the weeping periods the more grace is being bestowed upon him. The tears are the expression of an unconscious recognition of the distance between the present stage and that ultimate one which is sought and which is the true home. Though it may last several weeks, or months, or even years, varying with individuals, this stage will pass.

With the coming of the second stage, the turmoil dies down and the Master's peace appears increasingly in the heart. Therefore, Jesus says:

"... my peace I give unto you."

This very peace, however, may begin as the most heartrending spiritual agony.

"Abide in me, and I in you. ... I am the vine and ye are the branches. If my words abide in you, ye shall ask what ye will and it shall be done unto you."

These words of Jesus mean that from the moment you find your destined teacher you must hand over your inner life completely. Not to him, but to the Higher Power working through him. In him you have a bridge whereby you may reach the Overself. You must use it, trusting always to that higher power and intelligence.

You have only to think of your teacher to achieve realization of power. Jesus defined it thus: ". . . my words abide in you . . ." This means that his truth abides in you.

The teacher's truth will begin to live in you. By his grace you will draw from him the conditions you need. Periodically at first, then after a while you may ask what you will and it shall be done unto you.

Gradually you will begin to develop some of the conscious creative power the teacher possesses. But this is a double-edged sword, for if you are truly in touch with that power you will no longer be able to ask for the things you formerly desired, your every desire will be: Not my will, but Thine be done . . .

The personal meant nothing to Jesus. Whether people loved, hated, praised, or blamed him, mattered little to him:

"Remember the word that I said unto you. . . . He that hateth me hateth my Father also."

Jesus speaks of the ultimate teaching when he says:

"These things have I spoken unto you in proverbs; but the time cometh when I shall no more speak unto you in proverbs, but I shall show you plainly of the Father."

This points to the great initiation. Those who are faithful to truth and who diligently practice turning inwards in meditation are put upon the ultimate path where they will be shown plainly of the Father, by the teacher bringing them face to face with their divine Self, and with their Universal Self. They will receive from him the highest esoteric truth. The teacher will no longer instruct in parables or proverbs, the instruction of appearances. Neither will he deal with methods of technique, but his teaching will deal with ultimate Truth, with the Ultimate Itself.

Finally Jesus tells his disciples:

"These things have I spoken unto you, That in me ye might have peace."

This indicates that so long as they hold inwardly to the Father's power in the teacher, through faith and inner recognition of it, they will know the peace of Spirit. They will have a stability and peace they never before possessed.

CHAPTER XIV

THE MYSTERY OF JESUS

THE adept who dwells in his aloneness is always safe, but the adept who ventures forth into public notice is always in danger. He is in danger of being misunderstood. One wandering Galilean adept suffered misunderstanding to such an extent that those he sought to save, slew him. Let us try to get a better understanding of Jesus Christ.

Nearly two thousand years have elapsed since his departure, and we have many accounts and interpretations of his life. Yet today our understanding of him has lessened rather than increased. If you read the current writings about him and his sayings you get distortions and misrepresentations and above all, misunderstandings.

You should realize in reading a book like the New Testament that all parts are not equal in inspiration and value. Because of the time which has elapsed since they were compiled, we find in these Scriptures interpolations, additions, mistranslations, and even misrepresentations.

In view of these facts, you will understand that every word embodied in a Scripture is not necessarily sacred, and you should, therefore, use your intuition and your critical faculty to sift what really matters from what does not.

When you consider that it was some centuries later than Jesus' death that certain books were collected by a self-elected council and compiled as the New Testament; that other books were arbitrarily rejected by this council, it is little wonder that misunderstandings exist today.

There was great controversy as to which books and sayings were authentic. Some men in that council held out for reincarnation being included in the doctrine of Christianity. They would not have done this had they not been justified by some thoughts and sayings of Jesus. However, they were in the minority, and so the doctrine of reincarnation was rejected. Today it has disappeared completely from the Christian religion. Suppose that minority had been triumphant! Reincarnation would then have been included in the doctrine of Christianity today.

Examine the books of the New Testament. You will find very little about the personality of Jesus. When you consider the importance which was assigned to him and to his place in the history of religion of that time, it is strange that so little has been written about his personality. This should indicate to you how little was really known about him; that his fame was quite local and limited to a small sphere; that it spread only after his death.

Men doubt whether Jesus ever existed; they point to the paucity of historical proofs as convincing testimony to the fictitious nature of the story of his life. I can reply only that the paucity indicates how obscure he was and that no great movement stirs the world, as Christianity has done, without having the inspiration and impetus of a great person behind it. Nothing comes from nothing. Something stirs from something. The Christian religion came originally from Jesus "the Christed"! I hold strongly that Jesus existed, that he was a living man and a divine one, that he told high truth mercilessly and paid the price for this courage upon the bloodied cross.

The grossest misconceptions exist in the West about

those beings, whether historical or known, whom we call variously, masters, adepts, teachers, sages, and even Messiahs. It is said in the East that only an adept can understand an adept, and that is true. The reason for this is that we have no standard by which to judge. The only ones we know are those who have perished, who belong to vanished history. We do not know of any in our midst, and so we have no real criterion. Some people think that an adept is someone who has hidden himself away in a cave, a jungle, or a monastery, and who lives in a perpetual trance. Others think he is a man who is able to perform the most amazing miracles, who can by a mere touch turn water into wine, lead into gold, or heal the sick. Others believe, as in the East, that he is sort of a glorified fortune teller. All of these are mere opinions; they are not knowledge.

It is the same with people who profess to prove that Jesus never lived. They talk vainly because the entire matter is beyond their limited range of experience. They can offer expressions of theory but not certitude.

Modern historians, who take nothing on trust, have focussed the beams of their electric torch upon this remote period of myth and gloom—but in vain.

We are told that ideas rule the world. But ideas must have a focus, they must appear vividly demonstrated in the life and person of *one man*, who becomes their progenitor among his fellows. The trite simile of the sun's rays wasting their power, but becoming highly effective when concentrated in a burning-lens is apposite here.

The Overself Spirit streams all around us, but we are unaware of its existence until we meet it suddenly in one man's life or in one book's page, just as we are unable to perceive the rays of light which pass invisibly through space until they meet an object.

The usual picture of Jesus Christ is purely fantastic, being based upon what people would like Jesus to be, and not on what he really was. It is so with every other great sage. I have had the good fortune to come in contact with some of these sages and have observed how misunderstood they were by several who came in contact with them. Fairy tales and fables are being built up around them during their own lifetime, so what will happen when they have gone? If people who contact sages form misconceptions in the present, how much more will this be true after they have vanished for three or four hundred years?

Let us first recognize that Jesus came of obscure parentage. That suffices to account for the little that is known of his early infancy and childhood. The current and conventional picture of him is of a man who was ordained by God to fulfil a special mission; who, in fact, occupied a peculiar relationship to God, such as no man ever held before or since, and such as no man can hold again. That is why he is called the Son of God.

It is believed that his mother, Mary, conceived him while yet a virgin. Such a belief is not unknown elsewhere. It has occurred in other lands in ancient times. The Egyptians believed more than one of their ancient deities, such as Osiris, had been born under similar circumstances. In India births of a similar nature have been recorded. In other parts of the world you will also find the same account of a divine man born of a virgin and having for father either God or the Sun.

All this should make you very cautious about accepting this story. It has appeared in other parts of the world before and after the time of Jesus. You should realize that there is something of a universal rather than a merely local significance in it. And when you comprehend that mythological and religious traditions are fraught with esoteric, symbolical, superstitious stories of this type, you must then be doubly careful to investigate such so-called historical tales if you want the truth.

Physiologically, the virgin birth is impossible. Yet we are told it is possible as a miracle from God. This raises the question as to who or what God is, and when you begin to understand that you realize that this is not the way in which God works. God works through laws, established universal laws. Otherwise the universe could not properly exist; it would be queer and erratic.

Something unusual was connected with the personality of Jesus, and the one way his biographers could give expression to it was to repeat fantastic and marvellous tales in order to emphasize it. It does not follow that these tales are completely untrue and inaccurate. They are pointers indicating that there was something remarkable about the nature of this man. A number of the happenings in the Scripture stories of Christ are allegories, and have to be interpreted in this light; a number of the sayings attributed to the Messiah are interpolations; while a number of the real words of the Master were misunderstood by their recorders and hence wrongly set down.

I am sorry to disillusion you, but when you know the esoteric significance of the story of the virgin birth, you know on spiritual grounds why, quite apart from common sense, Jesus could not have been conceived in that miraculous way. However, that does not matter. The essential thing is, who and what was Jesus, and what did he really do?

Like some other great beings who have come down to teach our world, he did not belong to our planet. If you gaze up into the sky at night you will see that there are other planets besides ours, and since ours is inhabited there is no reason why others should not also be inhabited. Why should our earth alone be inhabited? Why should only we have that glorious privilege? The other planets are also inhabited and those planets which are nearer to the sun—the physical sun—have beings which are more evolved than ours. Those planets which are most distant from the sun have less evolved beings, and the sun, to all intents and purposes, can be taken as the heart of the Supreme Creator.

The intelligences on some planets—I call them that because they are not human in our sense, yet are individuals—are far ahead of ours in the understanding of life and of what you would call spirituality. Such beings naturally possess greater power and understanding and it is possible for them, because they have this power, to commune at times with other parts of the universe and to observe the precise spiritual condition of those parts. They may feel a great compassion for those on what might be regarded as backward planets. If they do, they may offer themselves to the Overself to be used as instruments to be sent to help such less evolved parts of the universe.

Some of these beings from the higher planets have taken pity upon mankind and have come voluntarily to this earth to help humanity. In order to do what man could not do for himself, they came. It was the Overself which sent them, using them to bring help to man. The wonderful telepathic communication throughout the universe is such that in the one cosmic Mind there is no distance and no separation. Hence, the need and the lack which was felt here produced a supply from infinitely distant planets from which these great teachers came. It was an echo answering a vibration. The Overself brought them here in the most beautiful manner, by making them aware of our lack, arousing their pity so that they were willing to come.

Such beings, therefore, have incarnated from higher planets onto ours. They did this before Jesus was ever born. Buddha and Osiris were Messiahs. That is the real meaning of the virgin birth. It indicates that there is something unusual about the birth of this particular person, something superhuman. They are not ordinary humans. They have come from planets where supermen dwell. To emphasize and symbolize this fact, stories are circulated of their divine origin. "Virgin birth" is a helpful doctrine by which simple minds can grasp the higher origin of such spiritual beings. But we who have matured must find the plain facts. The twentieth century is no time for symbolic statements when intelligence can grasp realities.

Jesus came down from such a planet and incarnated here. That is, his spirit incarnated in a human body on this planet Earth. He voluntarily did this because he wished to help our humanity.

Jesus did not belong to our earth. He came from a star where men live an infinitely higher life, a life that is nearer to the beauty, dignity, truth, and the reality of the Overself.

But you must remember that for such beings to come here is for them a form of self-sacrifice. It means they have to step down into a lower vibration in every way, physically, mentally, and spiritually; and that can only mean intense suffering. Jesus was crucified even before he was placed on the cross. He was crucified mentally and spiritually. He knew that his physical crucifixion would have to come, but that to him was the lesser. Even before Jesus incarnated, the greater Beings who watch and control the spiritual evolution and the material destiny of humanity upon this planet, as well as the governorship of the earth, showed him a picture of what he would have to do here, what he would have to experience, and what his end would be.

These mysterious spiritual Beings are four in number. They are the real executives who carry out the laws which God has laid down for certain departments of this planet. Their work is to see that as a whole it evolves through all its various experiences towards the goal which has been set for it. Apart from this, they have charge of the life and mass-fate of mankind. Jesus accepted the task shown by these four mighty archangels.

In profound vision he saw the essential work which was required of him, and the dark fate which would be his.

Little can be said of these Intelligences. They suffer by devoting themselves to the welfare of the lesser species—man. They have descended from higher realms to benefit mankind. The supreme spiritual wisdom is under their guardianship and protection, and all earnest seekers receive inspiration on their quest from the general help imparted us.

Jesus had offered himself for the self-sacrificing task of planting peace in the hearts of men. He was really an instrument in the hands of the Sacred Four.

He knew the task which he had undertaken, but he had to pay the penalty of fleshly embodiment and pass through the loss of divine memory which such incarnations bring to the mind. But this loss was temporary, of course, in his case.

What he was in his infancy and early childhood does not concern us, because that does not represent the Jesus who came to give a message. That was only the beginning. *Jesus had to find himself* in the same way that you have to find yourself.

No God, no Deity, can incarnate in the flesh and take on a human body as a baby without having to suffer the limitations of a baby; without having to learn to operate his consciousness gradually through infancy and into maturity as all human beings have to. The laws of nature are inexorable. The only way in which he can avoid that is to take the full-grown body of an adult, and this can only be done under rare circumstances where a body has been specially prepared by some highly advanced soul.

Christs have to grow; they are not born ready-made. They are simply the Perfect Flowers of mankind. Even the ordinary human being has to spend roughly the first twenty years of his life preparing for his mature existence. Is it any wonder, then, that Christ did not an-

nounce himself until he was thirty years old? He had
to prepare the spiritual man and so took longer at it.

A man like Jesus, who came for a special mission, one
which involved helping mankind, and particularly the
masses, could not have done other than he did. He had
to know what human life was like. He had to know
what it was to be a child and to be a youth if he was
to help ordinary people. He had to understand what
kind of a life the masses lived. He had to be born among
them.

So he came in the natural way and went through the
privations of human consciousness, through all that limitation of what he really was, suffering himself to be
born in the ordinary human manner, to grow up in the
ordinary human way, and gradually and slowly to
awaken to his inner light.

He awakened a little more quickly than others. So
much so that by the time of puberty he had begun to
think, to reflect, to seek, and to understand something
of the spiritual significance of life. Jesus, the boy, un-
tutored, could confound the academic teachers of the
Jewish temple. But he had not found himself.

It was not until the age of thirteen and a half that
he realized that he must set out consciously to find himself and regain his higher consciousness. People think
that he seems to have disappeared completely between
the ages of twelve and thirty, when he suddenly reap-
peared ~~again~~ and made himself felt in the particular land
where he was born. Under intuitive guidance he left
his parents' home and went to Egypt. He worked and
studied there under strikingly different conditions. He
was a student in the schools, imbibing ancient lore. He
was a young workman who earned his living part of the
time by the hard labour of his hands.

The world knows little of these youthful years. The
books which give the fragments the world has of the
history of Jesus were not written down during his life-

time. Therefore they were not contemporary historical records written at the same time as the events they
recorded. Long after Jesus' death the authors wrote
down what they believed to be his history.

Once I stood under the tree where the young Jesus
had been carried while his mother rested on the flight
into Egypt. And I mused on the miracle of time. The
republic of Rome and the kingdom of Chaldea have flut-
tered through history like vanished butterflies; the empire of Babylon and the civilization of Sumeria have
become but desiccated dust. A century from now the
world's greatest conflict will mean no more than the
history book's description of the Napoleonic wars means
to us today.

Egypt, its neighbour, had a far older culture than
Palestine. The Jews had linked one land with the other.
An entire chapter and a half of the Book of Proverbs in
the Old Testament have been copied word for word
from the text of the Egyptian sage, Amenemope.

Go into any Jewish synagogue today and you will
see symbols, geometrical and otherwise, which you could
have seen in any Egyptian temple of the past. It is a
striking thought, yet a true one, that the religion which
Moses gave to the Jews was a side-branch growing from
the religion of Osiris, which in turn came to Africa
from Atlantis. Attend, if you can, a Masonic lodge meeting and you will find the same spiritual heirlooms.

The first Christian monastery was established in
Egypt.

It was inevitable that Jesus had to face the Sphinx.
He went to Egypt because in those days that nation
still had the tradition of spiritual culture and secret
learning on a vast scale and of great antiquity, and this
he could not find in his own land. But Egypt had fallen
on evil days compared with the grandeur of her past.
There was a little left of the lost grandeur to furnish
food for his soul.

He studied and practised the exercises which he was taught. He travelled in various provinces. Part of the time he worked in the humblest of capacities at menial and manual work. He left handwork at the age of eighteen and embarked upon purely intellectual study. The pathetic remnants of the Egyptian mystery schools and temples opened their doors to the young foreigner.

On the Mediterranean coast, he found a group of mystics, philosophers, students, and teachers gathered in the quest of Truth in the city of Alexandria. One mystics' community which he joined in Alexandria practised meditation twice a day, at dawn and at eventide. As the sun rose they prayed for sunshine that their minds might be filled with spiritual light. As the sun set they prayed that their minds might withdraw into their own profound depths in concentration on the Truth.

In those days the city was not only the centre of much cosmopolitan learning but also a port on a great trade route. Ships carrying cargoes of grains and spices were constantly coming and going. Those ships kept up communication with Rome and Greece and other parts of Mediterranean Europe. At intervals convoys of ships would arrive at the point nearest to Alexandria on the south side of the Isthmus of Suez. The vessels were either Arabian or Indian, more especially South Indian. At that time there was quite a trade in spices and silks from India, which were carried across the Isthmus to Alexandria after being disembarked.

Portraits figuring Indian types of men and women have been unearthed at Memphis. The Egyptians used to trade with Musiris, the modern Cranganore, the seaport of South India. Moses referred to cinnamon and cassia being used in worship. These are products peculiar to the Malabar coast where later Jesus and St. Thomas landed. The Mother Goddess was worshipped originally in the form of a cow in Egypt. The cow has ever been sacred to the Dravidians of India. The sacred bull of Egypt has its analogue in Siva's bull. The social institutions of the Nayars, a prominent Dravidian branch, were duplicated by those depicted in Egyptian literature as existing there originally. Palm leaves and iron writing pens were common to both Egypt and South India. Ancestor worship of Egypt is paralleled by ancestor worship of the Malabar Dravidians.

These ships sometimes brought passengers. Occasionally some Indian traders would arrive who had learned something of their scriptures by listening to the Brahmins, the caste of spiritual teachers of India. The Brahmins never came themselves, for they were forbidden to travel. But the traders, through listening to the priests at the local temples and to their family guides, would thus learn something of the spiritual aspects of their own religion, and in contact with the philosophers of Alexandria they would exchange experiences.

In this way Jesus became acquainted with an Indian trader, a merchant, and eventually his mind became so aroused by what he heard that he freely and gladly embarked for India in the company of his friend and landed on the southwest coast of that country. Thus began the next important, if not the most important, phase of his life.

It was not for nothing that the first Christian missionary to land in India, landed likewise on the southwest coast. And he did not land in the eighteenth or nineteenth century, as most of us believe, but within the same century as Jesus' death. That was St. Thomas. He was martyred and crucified. He had been an Armenian merchant.

Jesus studied keenly, travelling slowly in India. He made his way across the south and then struck eastward to Benares. After an instructive sojourn in that city he went to the mountain wilderness of the Himalayas, where he lived for a while in a cave. He was not alone, but with a teacher and other disciples. This cave was in a secluded recess of the range and it was there that he finished his apprenticeship to spiritual truth. All around were crags, chasms, precipices, valleys, forests, and snowy pinnacles.

He did not go to Kashmir, as some medieval Indian legends assert; nor did he go into Tibet, as modern European occultists declare. He lived on the southern side of the Himalayas.

The years passed eventually; and after he had completed his training in yoga and had been initiated into the highest esoteric doctrine, he then cast aside all his learning. All that the Brahmins had taught him, all that the master had taught him, was put aside, and he went off alone. Then and then only did he find himself.

At that time he was in his twenty-eighth year. In finding himself, he had forgotten the Indian and the Egyptian teachings which he had sought. Only after he had forgotten all these was he able to find himself. Then when he did so he remembered his mission of service and awakening for which he had come.

Remembering his sacred mission, he left India and returned to his own country to give his message to those who were ready to receive it. The great teachers come but to help and to bless all. They make no reservations for a privileged few. Their love and knowledge flow out to all. They give the same essential teaching of devotion to the divine to everyone alike. Christ taught everyone who sought his help. He gave his pearls to the poor and illiterate equally as to those of higher station.

Before he began his public mission he had to pass through the test which all his like have to undergo; Satan, voice of conventional society, offered to make Jesus a king. But God, voice of lonely places, destined Jesus for something higher—a wandering revelator, teaching unpalatable and unwanted truths.

From the moment he entered into the market places in the villages of the so-called Holy Land he began his mission. Thus Jesus broke his long silence and returned to converse with men. The mysterious magic which had been kindling within him during the years without utterance, dwelt henceforth in each of his words and proved to man's heart the divine truth of every phrase and every sentence. As is the custom in the East, which has always reverenced true mystics as deeply as we reverence cinema stars, the news slowly spread by word of mouth about the existence of this God-realized person. Devotees and pilgrims began to flock to him to ask for his blessing or his help, and some were permitted to become disciples. Though his teaching was destined to spread over many countries and most continents, still it was not a universal mission. There will never be a Christian world, because Christianity was not intended for the whole world, but it was intended for the West. The Carpenter of Nazareth came apparently to convert a small Palestinian sect; he succeeded in converting the whole Western world.

However, Jesus knew where his doctrine would spread, and he knew that it would not spread until after his death. Jesus stood in a particular geographical relation to his age and to the coming ages too. When Krishna spoke, his message flowed eastward from India, to Java, Sumatra, Cambodia, and even southward to Ceylon. When Buddha spoke, his message flowed still farther eastward, to China and Japan, northward to Tibet and southward to Ceylon. But in neither case did the message flow westward. Moses spoke, but his message was not carried in any direction, for the Jews kept it to themselves. For them in their arrogant pride, the rest of mankind were not of the chosen race.

Jesus did not desire to work for a certain people, merely because he was co-operating with the law of destiny. Inwardly he had no consciousness of being a Hebrew. But the words of Jesus were heard all over the West. Jesus did not limit himself to any one people, or

to any one country, in his sympathies. He did not want
to save particularly Greece or Rome. He knew that
there would be only comparatively few during his own
lifetime who would accept his words of truth. He sought
those few. They were waiting ardently for him. For a
true sage is very hard to find, because he does not ad-
vertise himself, and he never labels himself as such. He
never says who and what he is, except when the gods
give him a special mission in the world, as in the case
of Jesus. It was quite all right for Jesus to proclaim
publicly, "I and my Father are one." But unless such a
public mission has to be performed, the sage will say
nothing and will leave men to discover him. All those
who bore a message did not convert and did not want
to convert. But to find the few, Jesus had to speak to
the many. And so he appeared amongst the multitudes.

We need not only a teacher but also an inspirer. We
need, in Emerson's phrase, "Someone to make us do the
best that is in us." Let the man appear and we shall follow him. Let him bring not merely the aeons-old message of God, but divine fire to scatter among us.

From the very beginning Jesus knew what his end
would be. He knew they would crucify him, or rather
that destiny had ordained such an event. However, such
is the power of divine love, he had to find his own,
those few who were to be the bearers of his spirit and
his work after he was gone.

In finding himself, what did Jesus find? He found
the Overself. He found his innermost being. And because there is only one Overself, only one Universal
Spirit, he found within himself that same condition
which you also might find within yourself. There are
not two Overselves, *only one*.

It is a universal existence, not a personal one, something which cannot be split up and separated into two
different persons. It is not a mental state nor a physical
state, but Something without limitation, shape or form.

When, at the age of twenty-eight, Jesus found and knew himself as THAT, he found his mission in life. Because, not until you find yourself, or at least not until you have begun partially to find and to know your Real Self, can you find your real work in life. Until then you are merely groping.

The sense of identity with the universal self replaces the ego. Therefore the man who understands who and what he is, cannot help but desire the welfare of all creatures, and he will not be satisfied with the mere desire, he will *do* something about it every day of his life. This is the final test of realization, this service of the world, whether it be secret or public, and this is why Jesus moved and taught ceaselessly among those who *he knew* would one day reward him with the cross. But every nail driven into it was driven also into their own dark destiny.

What was his work? In the succeeding three years before his so-called death, Jesus was able to do that for which he came. This was not what most Christians think. He did not come to found a new organization or to establish a new church. He came to plant an invisible seed in the hearts of men, a seed that would grow to maximum stature; but like all other trees and plants, the growth was destined to flourish for a while and then finally decay. Jesus founded no religious organization, no church. He advised his followers to pray in private, not in churches. He appointed no clergy, no priests. The whole superstructure of human organization was begun by others.

That which Jesus brought to the world is now going through the process of decay. Men like Lenin and Hitler are thrown up by their age, because they are merely instruments of destiny, whereas a Messiah like Jesus throws up his age. He gave what he came to give. It was something intangible, invisible. Something he planted in the hearts of men, which we can only call

Spirit. He brought a new gift of Spirit onto this planet. All that you see of Christianity is the fragmentary manifestation of that Spirit struggling to express this Word.

The world believed, as ever, in force. It was always ready to bend or break a man when it sought to subject him to its will. Hence it looked—if it looked for one at all—for a saviour who would arise and compel it toward salvation in spite of itself. The world was disappointed. Jesus never interfered with the free will of another person. He stimulated souls towards truth; he gave an impetus towards self-discovery; he showed men what the spiritual life was really like, but he never compelled man to adopt it.

What Jesus did, therefore, was something which was not to be measured by outward achievement, in his own time or in later times, because it was something which lives inside the hearts of men for ever. It is profound and priceless.

The New Testament carries something of the flavour of this divine man. The pages of the four Gospels are inspired; they glow like lamps. Although he has disdained to give the world any systematic framed philosophy, Jesus has given it something better—his own inner attainment of that which transcends all philosophy. Those terse paragraphs are lustrous with illumination. He says the last word and leaves us nothing to say. Jesus' fine thoughts are caught and pinned to crisp and compressed sentences, which are not readily forgotten. It is not necessary to thread these thoughts upon a string of logic, because they are each superbly self-sufficient, undeniable, divinely authoritative.

§

The idea of an approaching advent of a Messiah has caused the usual crop of false teachers and fanatical prophets to appear. For the latter, consciously or unconsciously, create futile sidetracks down which the sincere-minded seekers waste their energies and lose their aspirations.

There are several self-proclaimed "Messiahs" in the public eye at the moment, and there must be many minor ones who command little notice. The resulting effect of all their work is but to mystify the thoughtful and to mislead the thoughtless. But when the truth is known, all those deluded and deluding ones vanish into unimportance and concern us no longer. The stupidities which misguide mankind and the sophisms which delude it will not last for ever.

These men have nothing to say to us, although they open their mouths. What can they say that could compare with the master's sparkling statement, "The kingdom of heaven is within you." This truth which he gave to wondering hearers is a mind-opener. Its lucidity is lightning-bright. For we have mostly lost our heads and make the path we tread, the rites we observe, the dogmas we cherish, of greater importance than the salvation we would attain.

The only man I can worship as a Messiah is he who has the Power. From him one can acquire a new momentum. He alone is worthy to receive my highest oblation. Teaching does not touch me, but he who can give me a new orientation in character, or turn my will away from worldly foolishness or open the windows of my mind that the higher consciousness may shine in— him I will worship.

The coming of Jesus was a benediction to the world. He instructed and inspired men, he taught them the deepest secret of life and urged them to take to the divine path. He exemplified in his own everyday existence a holiness that casts our common life in the shade.

As I look back into the past pictures of history and see his figure file past me, bearing the high dignity of the apostolic mark upon his brow, I receive renewed comfort and assurance. We are not left quite alone; God still sends companions for our stumbling feet, and apostles of the Infinite for our groping minds.

INDEX

A

A, the letter, 220
Absolute, the, 73, 233, 269
Action, different kinds of, 242
Adept, the, 258, 259, 265, 266, 267, 279, 289, 291, 297; misconceptions regarding, 299
Adept Kings, the, 190, 191
Africa, the gods of, 20, 160; the heir to Atlantis, 306
Alexandria, 307, 308
Amenepope, Egyptian Sage, 306
Amen Ra, the sacred books of, 47
American peoples, the, 190, 223; cults of, 253
Ancestor-worship, 308
Aphrodite, 16
Archangels, the four mighty, 303
Arjuna (Bhagavad Gita), 176
Asceticism considered, 153-158; the middle course in, 163; ascetic disciplines, 163; in relation to the sex impulse, 165-174
Ashramas of India, 156
Asia, 160, 255
Astral bodies, 64
Atlantis, 306
Atom, the first seen in this generation, 31

B

Babylon, the empire of, 306
Babylonian tablets, the, 28
Beatitudes, the seven, 75-109
Bell Telephone Laboratories, the, 29
Benares, 308

Berkeley, Bishop, 272
Bhagavad Gita, the scripture of the Yogis, an exposition and interpretation of, 175-249; the gospel of inspired action, 248
Bible, the, 28
Black magic, 262
Body, the, wrongly identified with the "I," 139-143; a sacred habitation, 170; transient and mortal, 179; control of, 218; an ephemeral thing, 252; the destiny attaching to, 257
Brahma, 28
Brahmin initiation, 203
Brahmins, the, 308
Brain, the, 55
Breath control, 122
Broadway, solitude in, 163
Brother Lawrence, 103, 104
Browning, Robert, 49
Bucke, 33
Buddha, 25, 73, 108, 145, 190, 250, 258, 260
Bull, the sacred, 308

C

Cambodia, 310
Carlyle, Thomas, 20
Carpenter of Nazareth, the, 310
Celibacy, a monastic fetish, 169, 171; not essential to holy life, 172, 173
Ceylon, 310
Chaldea, 306
Chastity as an ideal, 165; benefits of true, 170; an acceptable destiny for some, 173
Cheapside, 163

317